Social Learning in Environmental Management

Towards a Sustainable Future

Edited by
Meg Keen
Valerie A. Brown
and
Rob Dyball

EARTHSCAN

London • Sterling, VA

9701293

To our children, Ben and Julien, Matthew, Robina and
AJ and Jack, Claudia and Hazel, who inspire us to
learn and to pursue a more sustainable future.

First published by Earthscan in the UK and USA in 2005

Copyright © Meg Keen, Valerie A. Brown, Rob Dyball, 2005

ISBN: 1-84407-183-9 paperback
      1-84407-182-0 hardback

Typesetting by JS Typesetting Ltd, Porthcawl, Mid Glamorgan
Printed and bound in the UK by Cromwell Press, Trowbridge
Cover design by Yvonne Booth

For a full list of publications please contact:

Earthscan
8–12 Camden High Street
London, NW1 0JH, UK
Tel: +44 (0)20 7387 8558
Fax: +44 (0)20 7387 8998
Email: earthinfo@earthscan.co.uk
Web: **www.earthscan.co.uk**

22883 Quicksilver Drive, Sterling, VA 20166-2012, USA

Earthscan is an imprint of James and James (Science Publishers) Ltd and publishes in
association with the International Institute for Environment and Development

A catalogue record for this book is available from the British Library

Library of Congress Cataloging-in-Publication Data
Social learning in environmental management : building a sustainable future / edited
by Meg Keen, Valerie Brown, and Rob Dyball.
      p. cm.
   Includes bibliographical references and index.
   ISBN 1-84407-182-0 – ISBN 1-84407-183-9 (pbk.)
   1. Environmental management. 2. Sustainable development. 3. Environmental
management–Case studies. I. Keen, Meg. II. Brown, Valerie A. III. Dyball, Rob.
   GE300.S59 2005
   333.7–dc22
                                        2005003303

Printed on elemental chlorine-free paper

Contents

Section 3 Learning Partnerships with Government

Section 4 Personal and Professional Learning

Section 5 Learning for the Future

List of Figures, Tables and Boxes

Figures

Tables

Boxes

List of Contributors

Jennifer Andrew
Director, Resource Policy and Management Pty Ltd, Kingston, ACT; Associate Fellow, Applied Ecology Research Group, University of Canberra

Jennifer's research and consultancy interests are in rural social issues and rural community learning. She has contributed to community-based education and research, and has delivered presentations and workshops throughout Australia, the US, Canada, South America and southern Africa. Her background and experience include environmental policy, social research and community-based education. Jennifer has consolidated this background through undertaking many consultancy projects focusing on understandings associated with the social aspects of natural resource management. These include issues associated with power and control, and ethical and cultural aspects of different settings.

Richard Baker
Science Faculty Associate Dean of Teaching and Learning, Reader in Geography, School of Resources, Environment and Society, The Australian National University (ANU)

Richard Baker is a Reader in the School of Resources, Environment and Society and Convenor of the Geography Programme. He was awarded ANU's 1996 and 2002 Vice-chancellor's awards for teaching excellence. He was a finalist in the 2002 Australian teaching awards and his first-year course won an Australian teaching award in 2003. His research experience encompasses community participation in environmental management and planning, environmental education, the social impact of tourism, resource management in Southeast Asia and the management of cultural heritage sites.

Sara Beavis
Research Fellow, Centre for Resource and Environmental Studies, ANU

Sara Beavis's teaching activities include providing educational support to rural (including isolated) communities, public education and lecturing for the School of Resources, Environment and Society. She researches the temporal and spatial aspects of anthropogenic disturbances to landscapes and impacts on catchment hydrology; the measurement of land degradation processes (erosion, salinity and acid sulphate soils) affecting land productivity and water quality; and the hydrological and policy implications of farm dam development. Sara is also the Convenor of the Graduate Programme in Environment at ANU and works closely with National Institute for Environment (NIE) staff in that role.

Valerie A. Brown

Visiting Fellow and Director, Local Sustainability Programme, Centre for Resource and Environmental Studies and School of Resources, Environment and Society (jointly), ANU

Valerie A. Brown has moved from the position of Foundation Professor of Environmental Health at the University of Western Sydney to that of Visiting Fellow at ANU, where she is continuing her research programme on the conditions for collective decisions and action among individuals, community, specialists and organizations. Valerie's previous research publications explore the themes of managing conflict in environmental management and the local management of global issues. She is now investigating collective approaches to a sustainable future, with case studies of integral research, whole-of-community engagement, transdisciplinarity, whole-of-organization change and holistic thinking. Issues for social learning arising from her work include the management of social change required to move from fragmented and analytic to transformative and collective responses to breaches of global ecological integrity.

Chris Bryant

Emeritus Professor, The National Centre for the Public Awareness of Science (CPAS), ANU

Chris Bryant is an Emeritus Professor at ANU and a Visiting Fellow at CPAS, ANU. He was its first Director. A graduate in zoology and biochemistry from London University, his research on the host–parasite relationship is described in more than 100 scientific papers and several books. In 1963 he moved to ANU, taking up a lectureship in the Zoology Department, eventually being appointed to the Chair of Zoology and subsequently to the position of Dean of Science. He retired early at the end of 1994 to concentrate on science communication and the centre, where he continues to work. He is a Fellow of the Institute of Biology (UK), the Australian Institute of Biology and the Australian Society for Parasitology. In 2000, he was made a Member of the Order of Australia (AM) for services to science communication, research and education.

Victoria Critchley

Masters Student, School of Forestry and Environmental Studies, Yale University, New Haven

Victoria is in the final year of a two-year Masters of Environmental Science Research programme in the US. Despite residing on the East Coast, her project is focused on the collaboration between indigenous communities and environmental organizations to conserve wildlife habitat in the Canadian Northern Rockies. This research stems from a long-held interest in indigenous management of natural resources and experiences of community partnering while employed as a local council Sustainability Program Coordinator. Victoria was responsible for working towards changing the council's corporate culture to encourage a fundamental shift towards sustainability and a long-term investment in social and environmental capital. While this was a strategic role, it also involved coordinating educational and natural resource initiatives at the community level.

Peter Deane
Postgraduate Student, School of Resources, Environment and Society, ANU

Peter Deane is interested in what it is to 'know' (broadly, ontology/epistemology) and if this is of use in opening up spaces for multiplying potential socioecological futures, practically and theoretically. He has been grappling with this interest to such an extent that he decided to write a thesis on the topic. Taking a plunge, Peter flung critical realism, eco-feminism and critical contextual empiricism onto paper, mixed it with a set of publications from within a segment of the forestry discipline, and now hopes the resultant creation is neither too acrid in criticizing the capacity of the research community involved to produce complex accounts of the world, nor too sweet in offering up options for the future. Not unsurprisingly, this was (and remains still) an uncomfortable and humbling place to go wandering, perpetually engaging the struggle to craft self with society in a meaningful manner.

Rob Dyball
Lecturer, Human Ecology Programme, School of Resources, Environment and Society and PhD Candidate, Centre for Resource and Environmental Studies, ANU

Robert Dyball teaches in the Human Ecology Programme within the School of Resources, Environment and Society. Human ecology at ANU takes an integrative and explicitly transdisciplinary approach to human cultures, their needs and desires, and their consequent interactions with their ecosystems. Robert's research focuses on the dynamics of change in human–ecological systems over the very long term, and seeks to develop a rigorous procedure for integrating key concepts and understandings of processes drawn from various disciplines into a coherent framework.

Rory Eames
Postgraduate Student, School of Resources, Environment and Society, ANU

Rory is a PhD scholar in the School of Resources, Environment and Society at ANU. His PhD research examines the role of community and community-based environmental groups in managing catchment and regional scale environmental degradation issues such as non-point source water pollution.

Rory is also a member of the management committee of the Nature and Society Forum, a community-based environmental and human health and sustainability organization based in Canberra.

Mike Gore
Adjunct Professor, CPAS, ANU

Mike Gore trained at Leeds University (UK) in electrical engineering and joined the academic staff of ANU where he taught physics for the next 25 years. In 1980, his great love of teaching – both students and the general public – was the spur that led him to establish, under the auspices of ANU, Australia's first interactive science centre, Questacon. In 1982, he was Canberran of the Year and was awarded a Churchill Fellowship that enabled him to visit and study overseas science centres in North America and Western Europe. In 1986 he was made a Member of the Order of Australia (AM) for his services to science education. In 1987, he left academia and became the foundation Director of Questacon – The National Science and Technology Centre. In 1992, Dr Gore and Questacon were jointly awarded the ABC's prestigious Eureka Prize for 'the public promotion of science'. Mike retired as Director of Questacon at the end of 1999 and returned to ANU where he is now based in CPAS. He is an Adjunct Professor in Science Communication at ANU. Since retirement, he has continued to receive international awards for his services to science.

John Harris
Vice-president, Australian National Biocentre (ANB); former Senior Lecturer in Ecology and Environmental Education, University of Canberra.

John is Vice-president of the ANB, which has a vision of 'healthy people on a healthy planet'. John chairs the ANB working party developing a feasibility study to build an Australian Centre for Sustainability in Canberra. He is writing a book based on interviews with over 50 graduates of environmental science after they left the University of Canberra in the cohorts of the 1970s, 1980s and 1990s. He has written research publications on marine fish and invertebrate populations, cave-dwelling bats and cave ecosystems, bird distribution in the urban environment, environmental weeds, the environmental impacts of urbanization in Papua New Guinea and the teaching of environmental education. He has been responsible for designing and teaching a nationally inaugural undergraduate Applied Science course in ecology and environmental management, and an innovative field-based postgraduate curriculum for community-based environmental education.

Ray Ison
Professor of Systems, and Director, Open Systems Research Group, Systems Department, The Open University, UK

Ray Ison joined The Open University as Professor of Systems in January 1994, where he led a process of organizational change resulting in the formation of the Centre for Complexity and Change. He was foundation Director of the Postgraduate Programme in Environmental Decision Making, as well as being actively involved in the production of new Systems Practice and environmental courses. During 2001–2004 he coordinated a major European project entitled Social Learning for the Integrated Management and Sustainable Use of Water at Catchment Scale (SLIM), which involved researchers from Sweden, France, Italy, the Netherlands and the UK. He is also coordinating an Engineering and Physical Sciences Research Council (EPSRC)-funded project to develop a research network concerning Systems Practice for Managing Complexity. His research has been involved in developing and evaluating systemic, participatory and process-based environmental decision making, natural resource management, organizational change, and research and development (R&D) methodologies. Examples discussed in his publications include second-order R&D; systemic inquiry; soft systems methodology; systemic action research; communities of practice and participatory institutional appraisal.

Stefan Kaufman

Postgraduate Student, School of Resources, Environment and Society, ANU

Stefan's research interest is in the theory and practice of creating and sustaining intentional change in human ecological systems. The focus of his current PhD research is on the significance of differences in the ontological, epistemological and methodological approaches for intentional change used in 'social learning' and 'social marketing'. He has previously worked in environmental management roles with ANUgreen, ANU's corporate environmental management plan, and as a research and development officer for student programmes in the university's NIE.

Meg Keen

Senior Lecturer, Environmental Management and Development Graduate Studies Programme, Asia Pacific School for Economics and Government, ANU

Meg Keen teaches in the Environmental Management and Development Graduate Studies Programme at ANU on topics concerning integrated environmental assessment, research methods and participatory resource management. Her research focuses on institutional and organizational dimensions of natural resource management in Australia and the South Pacific. Meg's previous publications concern local environmental management, environmental communication planning in Australian rural industries, and environmental governance and sustainable livelihoods in the South Pacific. Her current research projects focus on integrating sustainability assessments into local planning, applying concepts of organizational learning to the practices of development agencies, and enhancing environmental governance in the South Pacific.

Judy Lambert
Director, Community Solutions Pty Ltd, Sydney, Australia

Judy Lambert is a director of Community Solutions, a consultancy firm specializing in bringing interested parties together to help build sustainable communities. Her most recent work includes values mapping projects to assist in integrated natural resource management; assisting non-governmental organizations to better engage in the corporate sustainability debate; working with local government sustainability officers and university researchers to enhance local government sustainability; and a major project to improve remnant woodland conservation in rural landscapes. Judy has tertiary training in disciplines as diverse as paramedical, social and environmental sciences and business administration, underpinning a changing career as research scientist, environmental advocate, ministerial adviser, small business consultant and elected local government representative. Her own social learning has benefited from each of these professional experiences, in which she has focused on bringing together those with different knowledges to contribute to the greater good.

Sango Mahanty
Visiting Fellow, Asia Pacific School for Economics and Government, ANU

Sango Mahanty is currently a Visiting Fellow with the Environmental Management and Development Programme and also teaches within the programme. Her current research interests include participatory resource management, with a focus on using monitoring and evaluation as a learning process. She is also working on sustainability appraisal in local government and protected area management, with a particular focus on the Asia–Pacific region and marine and coastal resource management.

Nicki Mazur
Research Scientist, Bureau of Rural Sciences, Canberra, Australia

Nicki Mazur is a scientist in the Social Sciences Programme in the Bureau of Rural Sciences in Canberra, Australia. She is responsible for undertaking complex social science research and evaluation on the social science aspects of sustainability and productivity of Australian industries. Currently, she is leading a project, which assesses public and stakeholder responses to marine and coastal aquaculture. She is also part of a team that is examining attitudes to environmental philanthropy. She has provided design and implementation advice for a consultation process relating to greenhouse and agriculture policy, and more recently for the Draft National Animal Welfare Strategy. Before joining the Social Sciences Programme, Nicki completed a range of research and evaluation projects in the university, private and local government sectors on environmental and natural resource management, including reviews of zoo conservation policies and wildlife policy and management programmes in Australia. Her work on zoos, *After the Ark?*, was published by Melbourne University Press in 2001.

Tom Measham
CSIRO Sustainable Ecosystems, Canberra, Australia

Tom Measham is a human geographer who researches social dimensions of natural resource management for the Resource Futures Programme of CSIRO Sustainable Ecosystems. His interests are focused on understanding community aspirations for places, evaluating capacity building and understanding behavioural change. His research has involved working with members of rural and outback communities of Australia, including farmers and indigenous peoples, as well as working with scientists and policy-makers to assist integration of different approaches to natural resource management.

Jennifer Pitcher
Director, Child Care Quality Assurance, Australian Government Department of Family and Community Services

Jennifer Pitcher commenced her career as a social worker and moved on to lecturing in graduate and undergraduate social studies courses. Jennifer is currently Director, Child Care Quality Assurance, with the Australian Government Department of Family and Community Services. Prior to her current position, she worked in the Community Partnerships team of the Australian Greenhouse Office. In this capacity, she initiated and managed the leading-edge community greenhouse action project, Cool Communities. Jennifer's background is in the social sciences, and she was Senior Social Policy Analyst with the Christchurch City Council in New Zealand, which is recognized internationally as a leader in participatory democracy and social justice issues. In this role, she was recognized as a national expert in New Zealand on social policy, partnerships and community consultation. She won a study tour award to the US to study private sector involvement in social issues and facilitated the nationally acclaimed review of Christchurch Early Childhood Education Services. Jennifer is particularly interested in the interconnection between behavioural psychology, community development and environmental action.

Ian Robottom
Associate Professor, Faculty of Education, Deakin University

Ian Robottom is an Associate Professor in the Faculty of Education, Deakin University. He has a first degree in biological sciences and graduate degrees in science (BSc, first class honours), science education (BEd), curriculum innovation (MEd) and environmental education as educational reform (PhD). His current research interests lie in community-based participatory research as a methodology in linking curriculum development and professional development, especially in the areas of environmental education, science education and teacher education. He has attracted external research funds from the Australian Research Council, NH&MRC, AusAID, Commonwealth Departments of Education, Environment and Primary Industries, and overseas funding agencies. His recent research has been in the area of community-based environmental education, with major projects in Australia, South Africa, Vietnam and Scotland. He has published widely in the fields of environmental education and research. He was editor of the *Australian Journal of Environmental Education* for nine years and is on the editorial board of several other international journals.

Jennifer Scott
Lecturer, Environmental Risk Management, School of Environment and Agriculture, University of Western Sydney

Jennifer Scott has many years of experience in a range of environmentally related research projects and consultancies. Her areas of research have focused on environmental management tools, impact assessment methods and development dilemmas. She is currently involved in developing and implementing environmental management plan adoption strategies in the private sector. Much of Jennifer's work involves complexity, systems logic and reporting frameworks. In her recently completed PhD thesis, Jennifer analysed the relationship between sustainability objectives and contemporary decision making. During this research, she developed a method for clarifying risk in decision making trends and the effect of those risks on the equilibrium of a triple bottom line reporting framework.

Sue Stocklmayer
Director, CPAS, ANU

Sue Stocklmayer is the Director of CPAS at the ANU. She holds a BSc (London), a Grad Dip App Sci and MSc (Curtin) and a PhD in the area of science communication. She has a special interest in gender issues. At ANU, Sue is responsible for administering the graduate programmes in science communication, and for the outreach activities of CPAS to further the public awareness of science. She has written textbook materials in physics and chemistry, has made television presentations to children and to teachers, has presented at international science festivals and given numerous workshops, particularly in understanding and teaching physics and chemistry and in science communication. Her present research interests lie in the informal learning of science and in knowledge sharing. In 2004, she was made a Member of the Order of Australia (AM) for services to science communication.

Greg Walkerden
Principal, Batkin Walkerden Associates, Sydney

Greg Walkerden is a consultant who is currently developing capacity-building websites and lecturing on innovation and change management in the Faculty of the Built Environment at the University of New South Wales. Prior to this, he was Environmental Systems Manager at Wyong Shire Council, and in that role was responsible for ecosystem management strategies in the shire, a coastal catchment on the northern edge of Sydney where the population is growing rapidly. Action research – exploring ways of working innovatively with colleagues – is central to his professional practice. His focus as a researcher is on contributing to the development of practice traditions.

Acknowledgements

This book was a product of the collaboration of the practitioners and researchers who contributed to a series of workshops, email discussions and collaborative writing on the theme of social learning in environmental management. Some of these people are authors of the chapters that follow. Others gave their support with little reward except the joy of being part of a learning process aimed at improving environmental management and our social commitment to it.

This book was made possible by three sponsoring bodies. The National Institute for Environment (NIE) and the National Institute for Social Sciences and Law (NISSL) at the Australian National University (ANU) provided the finances that allowed us to run the facilitated workshops and to produce the book. The Local Sustainability Project (directed by Professor Valerie A. Brown and funded through a grant from the Australian Research Council) also provided funding for the project, as well as some of the important linkages to local and regional practitioners at the coalface of environmental management.

The intellectual seeds for this project were nurtured through our early discussions with members of the Human Ecology Forum at the ANU. This forum is committed to advancing the ideas, theories and practices by which the interrelationships between people and the environment can be understood.

The contribution of all workshop participants is acknowledged, but special thanks are due to Judy Lambert, Nicki Mazur and Greg Walkerden for their able and innovative facilitation of workshops and their critical insights. Among the many others we would like to thank are: Trish Boekel for her support, editing and wordsmithing; Rod Dunne for his creativity and wonderful illustrations; Sonya Duus and Julia Pickworth for their enthusiasm and assistance with workshops and project management; and the anonymous academic referees for their critical comments on drafts of the book. Thanks go to a number of people who were involved in the publication process including Maree Tait who gave early guidance, and Rob West and all at Earthscan.

To our families who loved us despite our absences and the continual thinking and re-thinking of ideas, book structures and frameworks – thank you. Most importantly for the social learning process, thank you to the readers of this book – it's your interest and subsequent actions which will improve the practice of environmental management.

While this book could never have been realized without the input of all of the above, and many unmentioned others, all errors and omissions remain our own.

Meg Keen, Valerie A. Brown and Robert Dyball, Canberra

List of Acronyms and Abbreviations

ANB	Australian National Biocentre
ANU	The Australian National University
CADISPA	Cooperation and Development in Sparsely Populated Areas
CPAS	The National Centre for the Public Awareness of Science
EPSRC	Engineering and Physical Sciences Research Council
ISA	integrated sustainability assessment
LETS	Local Economic Trading Scheme
LMMA	Locally Managed Marine Area
NGO	non-governmental organization
NSW	New South Wales
R&D	research and development
SLIM	Social Learning for the Integrated Management and Sustainable Use of Water at Catchment Scale
SPIRT	Strategic Partnerships with Industry – Research and Training
UNESCO	United Nations Education, Scientific and Cultural Organization
WCED	World Commission on Environment and Development

Section 1

A Social Learning Approach to Environmental Management

Social Learning: A New Approach to Environmental Management

Meg Keen, Valerie A. Brown and Rob Dyball

At a glance

- In the last 50 years, environmental management has become integral to a wide range of community, professional and government activities
- Social change is needed if society is going to adequately address the environmental challenges threatening human societies and the global eco-systems on which they rely
- We need a new approach to environmental management that supports collective action and reflection directed towards improving the management of human and environmental interrelations. We refer to this as the social learning approach
- The social learning approach has three agendas – to create learning partnerships, learning platforms and learning ethics that support collective action towards a sustainable future
- This chapter highlights three principal partnerships – with community, specialist areas and government
- The five core strands of activity integral to the social learning approach and its agendas in environmental management are reflection, systems orientation, integration, negotiation and participation.

Caring for the planet: It takes a community

There's an old adage that claims 'it takes a community to raise a child'. The community is needed because no one individual could possibly give the child all the love, knowledge and experiences needed to nurture a well adjusted adult. In the same way, all members of society are needed to nurture a healthy environment. This holds at all relevant scales, be it the local community and its immediate environment, national policy-makers concerned with national environmental resources, or even the global community concern for processes at a planetary level. At all these levels, collective action needs strong alliances and a commitment to processes that allow us to work and learn together.

This book will not devote space to arguing that on many levels much improvement in environmental management is needed. Organizations as diverse as the World Bank (2002) and the United States Research Council (1999), and events such as the Johannesburg World Summit on Sustainable Development in 2002 and the World Social Forum in 2004, along with many others, have strongly pleaded for an urgent need to change. Headline indicators such as rapidly increasing energy and material consumption, growing income and wealth disparities, and declining species diversity all show a range of signs that suggests much needs to be done – and soon.

At the last World Summit on Sustainable Development in 2002 there was a strong multinational plea for partnerships that would allow communities, professionals and governments to jointly take action against the above-mentioned trends. However, a lot of learning needs to be done to make these partnerships work. Imagine a community that is concerned about the steady decline of its inshore fishery. Catch and income have dropped, and people are leaving the town. An international non-governmental organization (NGO) offers assistance, as does the local government fisheries office, the marine studies department at the local university, the state urban planning department and the neighbouring community. Who's going to learn what from whom? Are they learning about fish, marine ecosystems, social systems, property rights, economic incentives or some combination of these? What learning processes will be used to share ideas effectively and plan for action?

Social learning is the collective action and reflection that occurs among different individuals and groups as they work to improve the management of human and environmental interrelations. Social learning for improved human interrelations with the environment must ultimately include us all, because we are all part of the same system and each of us will inevitably experience the consequences of these change processes.

In the recent past, we have been reluctant to see either local or global environmental management as an integral part of our daily affairs. In the era of the industrial revolution, people became so removed from their natural environments that they ceased to see the interconnections between social and natural resources. We eat a banana from across the globe without knowing the social or ecological circumstances under which it was produced; we wash our hands, with little awareness of the catchments from which the water comes and where the waste water will go; and we turn on the heating, lights and television with little concern about the flows of energy we induce, or how they were generated. People working as environmental managers, in any field, have to contend with these disconnections that exist within communities, as well as those between communities and their natural environment. Part of an environmental manager's job is to create learning experiences to re-establish the mental connections between our actions and environments, thus creating pathways for social change.

There is a general recognition throughout the environmental field that it is time to bring social learning and environmental management back together.

The environmental management and learning agendas

Environmental management has grown exponentially as a profession over the past half century. Originally a new and largely unwelcome idea, it has now grown to be a major branch in many, if not most, government and non-governmental organizations; and in almost all university programmes. The first 'environment management' jobs appeared in the 1950s as junior posts, typically involved in 'cleaning up the mess', whether as pollution control officers or dog catchers. At that time there were no federal, state or local government departments responsible for environmental management, and no industry would have dreamt of such a thing. Within community sectors, the environmental organizations that existed were mostly concerned with field studies and nature walks.

Environmental legislation was slowly and somewhat reluctantly introduced into a number of countries and jurisdictions. In the US it took several tries, in various guises, before the National Environmental Protection Act was passed in 1969. This act, and similar legislation that followed around the globe, required all developments likely to have a 'significant' impact on the environment to undergo an environmental impact assessment. Unfortunately the legislation did not clearly define 'significant' and assessments were considered to be 'one-off', or 'undertaken and forgotten' (Modak and Biswas, 1999; Thomas, 2001). As environmental problems mounted, environmental protection agencies were created, although they were typically not well funded and functioned primarily as reactive organizations. Without resources or power, these first agencies could not support a process of social learning or foster the necessary change process for improving environmental management and social wellbeing.

Across much of the world today there are few levels of government without environmental management units and legislation. Environmental management or services divisions are in almost all major global corporations, with many now putting into place certified environmental management systems to ensure continuous improvement in their environmental performance (Sheldon, 1997). There is a thriving profession, with its own subsets of consultants, environmental engineers, environmental health practitioners, environmental planners, environmental economists, environmental lawyers and environmental educationalists. And finally, although still reluctantly, we have agreed that global action is necessary on a number of issues. Multilateral agreements on the environment have been put in place to direct our collective actions on issues such as ozone depletion, deforestation, desertification and climate change, and most nations have endorsed a collective action plan, Agenda 21.

Modern environmental managers recognize that there is a need to address the sociopolitical causes of biophysical environmental problems, rather than only focusing on those problems. Environmental management has expanded to become environmental governance, the concern of all citizens at every scale of society. The accepted phrase for the main task of environmental managers since 1987 has been 'sustainable development', understood to be a balance between economic development, social equity and environmental sustainability (WCED, 1987). There is now a much broader concern to re-establish global ecological integrity for the future, and to create a just and healthy human future (Soskolne and Bertollini, 1998). This broader perspective is most frequently found under the banner of 'sustainability'.

These changes have meant that the traditional field of environmental management professionals, consisting of ecologists and other biologists, has expanded to include a diverse subset of people from nearly every other conceivable discipline. Associated with this diverse membership is the need for these professional and interest groups to work and learn together in collaborative transdisciplinary groups. This collaboration is recognized as a prerequisite to achieving the necessary progress on environmental manage-ment, whether understood in the context of sustainable development or the broader concept of sustainability.

Social change is now inevitable, whether or not we choose to act. Faced with the facts, most of us will want to re-orient society and our approaches to environmental management in order to sustain our planet and ourselves. Now, more than ever, we have a strong motivation for a new approach to environmental management based on three new agendas. Firstly, we need equitable learning partnerships between the combined expertise of commu-nities, professions and governments. Secondly, we need learning platforms that enable interdependent individuals and groups concerned with common environmental issues to meet and interact in forums to resolve conflicts, learn collaboratively and take collective decisions towards concerted action (Röling, 2002). Thirdly, social change requires a transformation in our thinking and in the learning values and ethics that underpin learning processes (see Figure 1.1). As noted by Einstein, 'you can't solve a problem with the same thinking that created it'.

The strands of social learning in environmental management

Social and ecological sustainability ultimately depend on our capacity to learn together and respond to changing circumstances. Many current environmental management approaches claim to be 'integrative, participatory and adaptive',

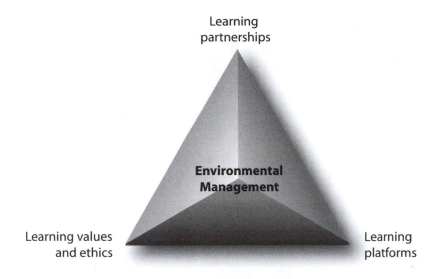

Figure 1.1 *The social learning approach to environmental management*

but there is a tendency for them to be more of the same. Partnerships occur within traditional disciplinary or managerial enclaves; actions are hampered by old institutional and social arrangements; and visions are constrained by the values and ethics that created the problems initially. The approach to social learning presented in this book is distinct and goes beyond these existing methodologies and the conventional, and problematic, traditions they bring with them.

We take an explicitly transdisciplinary approach by drawing out lessons from adaptive and participatory approaches to environmental management that are relevant to social learning. These insights are complemented with other useful concepts including those from systems analysis and organizational learning theory. Initiatives that take this transdisciplinary approach are already making a positive contribution to creating social learning partnerships, building platforms to support sustainability across multiple scales and disciplines, and fostering a social ethic of environmental care. In this book ten examples of social learning initiatives are presented from a range of sectors, such as community, government and professional. To assess these initiatives we develop and use orienting concepts, or strands of social learning.

The five braided strands of social learning that appear to be crucial to environmental management are shown in Figure 1.2. They are braided in the sense that they interact and overlap, yet each has an important role on its own. We discuss each of the five strands (reflection, systems orientation, integration, negotiation and participation) in the subsections to follow, and then combine the strands to provide a framework for analysing the case studies to follow.

Reflection
Systems orientation
Integration
Negotiation
Participation

Sustainable
Environmental
Management

Figure 1.2 *The five braided strands of social learning*

Reflection and reflexivity

Social learning is a process of iterative reflection that occurs when we share our experiences, ideas and environments with others. The importance of reflexivity – reflecting on the learning, which then leads to new learning – is a continuing theme in all the case studies that follow. Drawing on organizational psychology and adult learning theory (Knowles et al, 1998; Kolb, Osland and Rubin, 1995), the reflective learning process can be depicted as a series of learning cycles (see Figure 1.3). The cycles provide a framework for continuous reflection on our actions and ideas, and the relationships between our knowledge, behaviour and values.

The simple sequence follows the steps of diagnosing what matters, designing what could be, doing what we can and then developing a deeper understanding from reflecting on and evaluating that practical experience. Where you start in the cycle and the direction the learning takes depend on you as an individual, or on your group's needs and goals. For the environmental manager, the cycle can be used as a planning process for bringing about change and stimulating transformative learning.

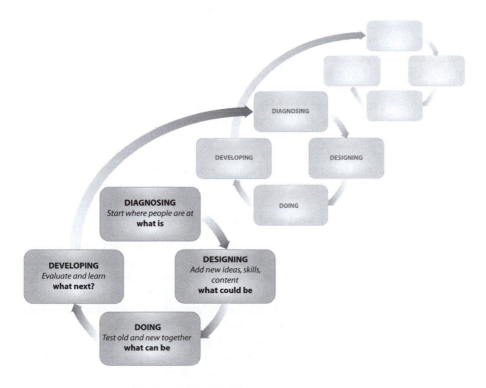

Sources: Brown et al (2003); Kolb et al (1995)

Figure 1.3 *Individual and social learning cycle framework*

Critical awareness and reflective processes, such as the one depicted in Figure 1.3, are a part of daily activities. Schön (1983, 1987) proposes that the 'reflective practitioner' engages in a learning process that continually reviews models, theories and ideas applied to the context. In practice, these reflective processes are at the:

* personal level, through setting goals and critically monitoring processes and outcomes
* interpersonal level, through briefing and debriefing within groups
* community level, through creating a common vision, identifying priorities and setting performance indicators to be assessed
* social level, through evaluating and auditing the impacts of laws, regulations and markets.

These types of reflective learning processes form the foundation of a number of social learning approaches used in environmental management. Examples include participatory rural appraisal (Chambers, 1992, 1994, 1997), participatory learning and action (Bass et al, 1995; Pretty and Chambers, 1994), participatory monitoring and evaluation (Estrella and Gaventa, 1997) and adaptive management (Gunderson and Holling, 2002; Holling, 1978; Lee, 1993).

Reflectivity in environmental management is an important lever for social change because it can reveal how theoretical, cultural, institutional and political contexts affect our learning processes, actions and values (Alvesson and Skoldberg, 2000; see also Chapter 11). To reflect on ourselves and our practices, we need catalysts that can help us see what would otherwise be invisible to us. In some cases, this is achieved through monitoring and evaluation, for example adaptive management approaches (see Chapter 3). In other cases, collaboration can provide a catalyst for reflection, challenging us to consider new knowledge and insights, or to rethink our assumptions (see Chapters 6 and 7).

Systems orientation and systems thinking

Systems theory provides a means to reflect on the links between humans and their ecosystems within an integrated framework, and gives an understanding of the change processes arising from their interactions (Costanza et al, 1993). A systems approach takes into account multiple processes that can affect learning processes, including feedback, boundary setting, communication and uncertainty (see Table 1.1). Material and energy flows and information are tightly coupled, since the information in a system controls its structure and hence the flows of energy and material necessary to support that structure.

A system orientation allows both human and non-human elements to be included as parts of a given system, with their interaction conceived of in terms of the properties the parts possess and the constraints those properties place on each other when brought together. It is these mutual constraints that cause the system to behave as it does and not in some other fashion. That is, the constraints between the parts cause the characteristic behaviour of the system as a whole. This system behaviour is also referred to as its 'emergent property', since it is exhibited only at the level of the system as a whole and is not present at the lower level of the component parts. Key concepts for this book, such as health, wellbeing and sustainability, can all be usefully thought of as an emergent property of a particular system.

Some systems may seem more 'natural' than others – a lake, a forest or a factory might seem to be self-identifying systems. However, the boundaries of any system, being the distinction between those parts and interactions that are 'inside' as against 'outside', are always subjectively determined by the human observer. Groups or individuals identifying ostensibly the same system will typically set differing boundaries and so perceive a slightly different system. A number of chapters in this book recommend that parties ensure that, as far as possible, they reach some mutual understanding, if not agreement, about what the system of interest actually is.

Further complicating our understanding of coupled human–ecological systems is the capricious behaviour of humans themselves. Humans have a capacity to learn and thus they do not necessarily respond the same way when subject to the same influences – unlike mechanical systems. Given no change to the system, a car will start when you turn the key in the ignition; however, the farmer will not necessarily react the same way each time you tell her to obey water restrictions. Human reactions can vary greatly across space and time in response to changing values, contexts, incentives or understandings.

In environmental management, when we identify a system and describe its characteristic behaviour as being 'undesirable' or 'unsustainable', we might expect to find the cause in either the properties of the system's parts and their interactions, or in the boundaries we have used to define our system from its environment. Because boundaries are largely socially constructed, we can learn about them, and also re-create them. The malleable nature of systems and their boundaries is important to recognize because a systems orientation suggests that people influence both problems and their solutions.

When striving to understand systems and our place in them, we have to accept that surprise and change are endemic to the dynamics of the systems that concern us. We are compelled to look for patterns rather than events, for processes rather than end points. Likewise, our understanding of system behaviour must be contingent on incremental, experiential learning and decision making, supported by active monitoring of, and feedback from, the effects and outcomes of decisions (Jiggins and Röling, 2002). Where we assign a goal or a purpose to systems, we must again recognize that this purposefulness is the product of subjective human values and thus always open to ongoing re-validation and negotiation.

A final lesson from a systems orientation is that given systems' inherent non-linear behaviour, which is the source of their capacity to surprise us, we must always acknowledge that a system may change its fundamental behaviour quite suddenly (Holling and Gunderson, 2002; see also Chapters 2 and 3).

Table 1.1 *Definitions of concepts used in a systems orientation to social learning*

Concept	Definition
Boundary	The borders of the system as determined by the observer
Human communication	Human communication, which has both a biological and a social basis, encompasses language, emotion, perception and behaviour. This gives rise to new properties in the communicating partners, who each have different experiential histories
Emergent properties	Properties that are revealed at a particular level of organization and are not possessed by constituent subsystems. Thus these properties emerge from an assembly of subsystems
Feedback	A form of interconnection, present in a wide range of systems. Feedback may be negative (compensatory or balancing) or positive (exaggerating or reinforcing)
Perspective	A way of experiencing that is shaped by our personal and social histories, where experiencing is a cognitive act
System	An integrated whole whose essential properties arise from the relationships between its parts. Often more accurately termed a 'system of interest', which is defined as the product of distinguishing a system in a situation where an individual or group has an interest or stake
Systems thinking	The understanding of a phenomenon within the context of a larger whole; to understand things systemically literally means to put them into a context, to establish the nature of their relationships
Trap	A way of thinking that is inappropriate for the context or issue being explored
Tradition	Literally, a network of pre-understandings or prejudices from which we think and act; how we make sense of the world
Worldview	The view of the world that enables each observer to attribute meaning to what is observed

Source: Adapted from The Open University (1999)

Unpalatable though such a message might be, believing that complex systems can always be manipulated with a high degree of certainty is simply a delusion. Often systemic change may be inevitable and the only appropriate response is adaptive change in the practice and expectation of environmental managers, decision makers and the public alike. In other words, the inherent behaviour of the systems that environmental managers seek to manage necessitates a commitment to ongoing social learning.

Integration and synthesis

Learning that allows for unforeseen outcomes, as discussed earlier, requires an openness to new relationships and fresh connections between variables. The environmental manager has to be committed to processes capable of integrating new ideas from a variety of sources and disciplines. In terms of sustainability models in environmental management, the simplest and one of the most popular is the overlapping circle diagram depicting the intersection of social, ecological and economic systems (see Figure 1.4, left). This can give the misleading impression that sustainability occurs only at the intersection of the three spheres and that each could somehow subsist without the other. The onion ring diagram (see Figure 1.4, right) goes some way to overcoming this misrepresentation by showing the various social spheres fully embedded within the ecological, thus implying their dependence. Although this particular integrative framework has the advantage of identifying links between current subdivisions, it has the disadvantage of leaving the currently dominant divisions unquestioned – and thus still part of the problem.

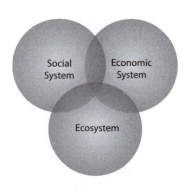

Overlapping Systems

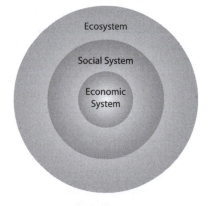

Nested Systems

Source: Lowe (1998)

Figure 1.4 *Two simplified representations of sustainable development*

The pursuit of sustainability in environmental management requires holistic and integrative frameworks from which to investigate the world, rather than ones that divide observations into a selected set of elements. Frameworks that represent links between people, roles and relationships, such as population flow charts, social mapping, professional relationships and informal networks, deal with horizontal integration. Frameworks representing scales of governance and levels of management systems describe vertical integration. Vertical, horizontal, place and issue-based integration are equally necessary for supporting social learning processes in environmental management.

Integration is so central a concept in environmental management that it has become a *portmanteau* word, covering a range of very different processes. Under some circumstances, integration has become synonymous with processes and concepts as different as coordination, collaboration, cooperation, systems, synthesis, holism, unity and consensus. Not surprisingly, these terms each have their examples in the chapters that follow, since integration of different socioecological dimensions is a recurring theme in this book. The goal is not a single consensus, nor the lowest common denominator, but a search for a rich tapestry that weaves together diverse ideas to reveal the nature of the complexity. Ison (Chapter 2) calls for transparency and coordination of traditions, Dyball, Beavis and Kaufman (Chapter 3) for synthesis through a systems orientation, Eames (Chapter 5) for critical reflection on the nature and function of social networks and social capital and Andrew and Robottom (Chapter 4) for true collaboration between communities and government.

Negotiation and collaboration

So far we have discussed the benefits of reflexive, systemic and integrative approaches to the social learning process. This could bring with it a mistaken idea that different communities, professions and agencies, with their associated values, knowledge and sets of skills, come together easily and work seamlessly in environmental management. Nothing could be further from the truth. Negotiation is needed at every interface within and between these elements of social learning in environmental management. Each group has its own identity, created by defining a core area of interest and establishing boundaries that distinguish it from the others.

For individuals, communities, specialists or organizations to work together across their knowledge and administrative boundaries is a considerable challenge, a challenge that has been met in a range of very different forms of negotiation in our case studies. Brown and Pitcher (Chapter 8) write of communities as social islands, with governments and experts negotiating their way in and out of a community across its beach. Measham and Baker (Chapter 6) take place as the basis for negotiation, while Keen and Mahanty (Chapter 7) address the difficulties of negotiating across geographic and political scales. Critchley and Scott (Chapter 9) describe the limits to negotiation within formal structures of local government.

A constructive approach to negotiation assumes that conflict generates opportunities for learning. Competing opinions and evidence are to be welcomed as creating the conditions for generating new knowledge. Every stage of the social learning cycle requires participants to embrace dialogue that addresses conflicts over ideas, potential solutions and proper practice. Brown et al (1995, p36) take a positive perspective of conflict management as follows:

- Conflict is an inevitable part of change – it is not a sign of failure of people or the system
- Conflict is a step towards a solution – it is not the signal to give up
- Conflict is shared – it is not the sole responsibility of any one person or group
- Conflict is part of a process – it is not an outcome, a barrier or an excuse
- Conflict is a matter for negotiation – it is not the end of the line.

Negotiation processes are actually built into the very fibre of society, with set terms for who consults with whom, under what conditions and according to what ground rules. Avenues that are taken for granted include voting, arbitration, commissions of inquiry, lobbying and regional development associations. At present the ground rules are shifting, since it is recognized that achieving sustainability will require the collaboration of all decision making sectors. Community consultation by researchers and government, and community conferencing in the law, have become standard practice, although the objective of full collaboration is rarely met (see Chapters 7 and 9).

Participation and engagement

Collaboration processes demand that communities engage in learning partnerships. Typologies of participation highlight that when diverse social actors engage in environmental management activities, the outcome can range from coercion to co-learning (Arnstein, 1969; Cornwall, 1995; Parkes and Panelli, 2001; Pretty, 1995; Pretty and Chambers, 1994) (see Table 1.2).

Participation typologies used in environmental management tend to break participation into discrete categories, rather than acknowledging that learning and engagement can occur through a variety of participation types spread across different stages of a project or programme, and different scales of society. For example, rather than interpreting categories in participatory typologies as a continuum from bad (coercing) to good (co-acting), there is growing acceptance that it is better to perceive these categories (with the exception of coercing) as a range of possible social learning and engagement approaches that can be combined and sequenced to achieve the outcomes best suited to the participants and the circumstances (Ross et al, 2002). In her review of Australian rangeland management programmes, Kelly (2001; see also Box 4.2, Chapter 4) found that landholders actually preferred different types of participation at different stages of the programmes, depending on their learning and management objectives.

Table 1.2 *Types of participation*

Type of participation	Description
Coercing	Token engagement within a context of large-scale power imbalance, where the will of one group is effectively imposed upon the other
Informing	Information is transferred in a one-way flow; there is no knowledge or sharing of decision making
Consulting	Information is sought from different groups, but one group (often the government) maintains the power to analyse the information and decide on the best course of action
Enticing	Different groups share information and jointly consider priority issues, but one group maintains power and entices other groups to act through incentives (such as grants)
Co-learning	Insiders and outsiders share their knowledge to create new understandings and work together to form action plans, and define roles and responsibilities. Decision making power is negotiated within institutional and social constraints
Co-acting	People set their own agenda and mobilize to carry it out in the absence of outside initiators. Knowledge is shared between the groups engaged in the activity, but knowledge flows and learning outside of this community are not assured. Power in decision making remains with the initiators of the action

Sources: Arnstein (1969); Cornwall (1995); Parkes and Panelli (2001); Pretty (1995)

From a social learning perspective, the process of participation and engagement can be referred to as single-, double- and triple-loop learning (see Figure 1.5). Single-loop learning refers to learning concerned with changing skills, practices and actions. Double-loop learning facilitates the examination of underlying assumptions and models driving our actions and behaviour patterns. Triple-loop learning allows us to question and change values and norms that are the foundation for our operating assumptions and actions. Participatory approaches consistent with multiple-loop learning thus provide a deeper understanding of the contexts, power dynamics and values affecting environmental management.

The effectiveness of partnerships and platforms is partly related to the responsiveness of social organizations and structures. Institutional structures can become so rigid that organizations cannot engage effectively with external players and learn (Pritchard and Sanderson, 2002; Senge, 1990). This can occur for a variety of reasons, including:

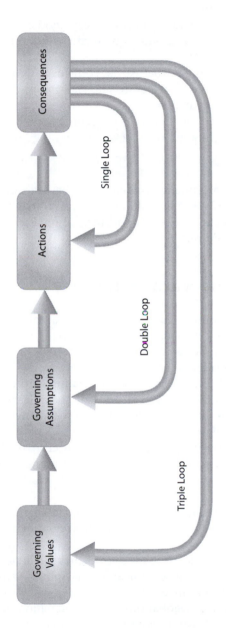

Source: Modified from Argyris (1999)

Figure 1.5 *Multiple-loop learning*

- administrative traps – institutional arrangements become inflexible and driven by narrowly defined management or efficiency considerations that are unable to take into account new information, different interests or diverse values (see Chapter 9)
- competency traps – bureaucracies become very good at what they do, but are unable to innovate and respond to new challenges requiring different approaches (see Chapter 10)
- bureaucratic traps – planning processes become captured by bureaucratic hierarchies and are unable to integrate external inputs into the decision making frameworks (see Chapter 8)
- legitimacy traps – bureaucratic processes become focused on maintaining legitimacy by servicing the interests of a narrow range of interest groups (see Chapter 4).

One of the lessons for environmental managers is that learning organizations and learning communities need flexible and adaptive structures that value change as a positive reflection of social and institutional learning processes, not as a defence against failure.

The learning journey

Social learning is, by definition, based on ethics and values about how the world should be. This book asks readers to accompany a committed group of practitioners and academics as they share the results of their own learning journey, critically considering social learning processes for sustainability. They consider ways to advance them through creating learning partnerships, platforms and values. The five braided strands of social learning provide an integrated set of processes that can guide our analyses of environmental management models and practices.

To encourage reflexivity, we suggest the readers ask themselves the following questions as they go through the book, grounding the theory in their personal and professional practice:

- What are the social learning processes embedded in current environmental management policies and programmes, and how do they relate to different ways of knowing and engaging?
- How can environmental management approaches facilitate the creation of learning opportunities that bridge different disciplines, subgroups within society and levels of governance?
- Do our present dialogues, negotiations and participation processes enable a wide variety of social learning opportunities in environmental management?
- How is our ability to act and adapt environmental management approaches affected by social structures and relationships?

- Are our processes of reflection and learning in environmental management fragmented and unable to discern the more subtle patterns of change over time and space?

In the final chapter we review our knowledge of social learning in environmental management and how the five strands of reflection, systems orientation, integration, negotiation and participation are woven into the social learning process within environmental management. However, we are all still learning, and we do not expect that all of these questions, and others you may have, can be answered definitively in the current dynamic context. The book aims to stimulate dialogues and critical reflections on social learning in a variety of fields, through unearthing some of the hidden assumptions, values and social structures that have long affected social learning in environmental management, but are not often discussed openly given the challenges of the 21st century.

References

Alvesson, M. and Skoldberg, K. (2000) *Reflective Methodology: New Vistas for Qualitative Research*, Sage, London

Argyris, C. (1999) *On Organizational Learning*, 2nd edn, Blackwell Business, Malden, MA

Arnstein, S. R. (1969) 'A ladder of citizen participation', *Journal of American Institute of Planners*, vol 35, pp216–224

Bass, S., Dalal-Clayton, B. and Pretty, J. (1995) *Participation in Strategies for Sustainable Development*, International Institute for Environment and Development, London

Brown, V., Grootjens, J., Ritchie, J., Townsend, M. and Verrinder, G. (2003) *Sustainability and Health: Working Together to Support Global Integrity*, Griffith University, Nathan, Queensland

Brown, V., Ingle-Smith, D., Wiseman, R. and Handmer, J. (1995) *Risks and Opportunities: Managing Environmental Conflict and Change*, Earthscan, London

Chambers, R. (1992) *Rural Appraisal: Rapid, Relaxed and Participatory*, University of Sussex, Brighton, UK

Chambers, R. (1994) 'Participatory rural appraisal (PRA): Challenges, potentials and paradigm', *World Development*, vol 22, no 10, pp1437–1454

Chambers, R. (1997) *Whose Reality Counts: Putting the First Last*, Intermediate Technology Publications, London

Cornwall, A. (1995) 'Towards participatory practice: PRA and the participatory process', in de Koning, K. and Martin, M. (eds) *Participatory Research in Health*, Zed Books, London, pp94–107

Costanza, R., Wainger, L., Folke, C. and Marle, K. (1993) 'Modeling complex ecological economic systems: Towards an evolutionary, dynamic understanding of people and nature', *BioScience*, vol 43, no 8, pp545–555

Estrella, M. and Gaventa, J. (1997) *Who Counts Reality? Participatory Monitoring and Evaluation – A Literature Review*, IDS, London

Gunderson, L. and Holling, C. (eds) (2002) *Panarchy: Understanding Transformations in Human and Natural Systems*, Island Press, Washington, DC

Holling, C. S. (1978) *Adaptive Environmental Assessment and Management*, John Wiley & Sons, Chichester, UK

Holling, C. S. and Gunderson, L. (2002) 'Resilience and adaptive cycles', in Gunderson, L. and Holling, C. S. (eds) *Panarchy: Understanding Transformations in Human and Natural Systems*, Island Press, Washington, DC

Jiggins, J. and Röling, N. (2002) 'Adaptive management: Potential and limitations for ecological governance of forests in a context of normative pluriformity', in Oglethorpe, J. A. E. (ed) *Adaptive Management: From Theory to Practice*, IUCN, Gland, Switzerland

Kelly, D. (2001) *Community Participation in Rangeland Management*, Rural Industry Research and Development Corporation, Canberra

Knowles, M., Holton III, E. and Swanson, R. (1998) *The Adult Learner: The Definitive Classic in Adult Education and Human Resource Management*, Butterworth-Heinemann, Woburn, MA

Kolb, D., Osland, J. and Rubin, I. (1995) *Organizational Behaviour: An Experiential Approach*, Prentice Hall, Englewood Cliffs, NJ

Lee, K. (1993) *Compass and Gyroscope: Integrating Science and Politics for the Environment*, Island Press, Washington, DC

Lowe, I (1998) 'Reporting on the state of our environment', in Eckersley, R. (ed), *Measuring Progress: Is Life Getting Better?* CSIRO Publishing, Canberra

Modak, P. K. and Biswas, A. K. (1999) *Conducting Environmental Assessment for Developing Countries*, United Nations University, Tokyo

Open University (1999) *Environmental Decision Making: A Systems Approach*, The Open University, Milton Keynes, UK

Parkes, M. and Panelli, R. (2001) 'Integrating catchment ecosystems and community health: The value of participatory action research', *Ecosystem Health*, vol 7, no 2, pp85–106

Pretty, J. (1995) 'Participatory learning for sustainable agriculture', *World Development*, vol 23, no 8, pp1247–1263

Pretty, J. and Chambers, R. (1994) 'Toward a learning paradigm: New professionalism and institutions for agriculture', in Scoones, I. and Thompson, J. (eds) *Beyond Farmer First*, Intermediate Technology Publications, London

Pritchard, L. and Sanderson, S. (2002) 'The dynamics of political discourse in seeking sustainability', in Gunderson, L. and Holling, C. S. (eds) *Panarchy: Understanding Transformations in Human and Natural Systems*, Island Press, Washington, DC

Röling, N. (2002) 'Beyond the aggregation of individual preferences: Moving from multiple to distributed cognition in resource dilemmas', in Leeuwis, C. and Pyburn, R. (eds) *Wheelbarrows Full of Frogs. Social Learning in Rural Resource Management*, Koninklijke van Gorcum, Assen, the Netherlands

Ross, H., Buchy, M. and Proctor, W. (2002) 'Laying down the ladder: A typology of public participation in Australian natural resource management', *Australian Journal of Environmental Management*, vol 8, no 2, pp205–217

Schön, D. (1983) *The Reflective Practitioner*, Basic Books, New York

Schön, D. (1987) *Educating the Reflective Practitioner*, Jossey-Bass, San Francisco

Senge, P. (1990) *The Fifth Discipline: The Art and Practice of the Learning Organization*, Random House, Sydney

Sheldon, C. (ed) (1997) *ISO 14001 and Beyond: EMS in the Real World*, Greenleaf, Sheffield, UK

Soskolne, C. and Bertollini, R. (1998) *Global Ecological Integrity and 'Sustainable Development': Cornerstones of Public Health*, WHO International Workshop, WHO

European Centre for Environment and Health, Rome Division, Rome, 3–4 December

Thomas, I. (2001) *Environmental Impact Assessment: Theory and Practice in Australia*, 3rd edn, Federation Press, Sydney

United States Research Council (1999) *Our Common Journey. The Transition to Sustainability*, Washington Research Council, Washington, DC

WCED (World Commission on Environment and Development) (1987) *Our Common Future*, Oxford University Press, Oxford

World Bank (2002) *Sustainability Report*, World Bank, New York

2

Traditions of Understanding: Language, Dialogue and Experience

Ray Ison

At a glance

- The reader is invited to reflect on how understanding arises in relation to language, metaphor and dialogue; and how, as environmental managers, we use these to interpret our learning and experience
- This chapter provides reflections on how particular understandings can become institutionalized and on the different ways 'institution', 'organization' and 'structure' can be understood in the practice of environmental management
- Together, these reflections open up ideas of how we can become aware of our own understandings when working to incorporate social learning in environmental management
- Research on social learning in the implementation of the European water framework directive is used to ground the ideas discussed in this chapter.

Creating the contexts to foster social learning

I am writing this chapter from the context of coordinating a research project on Social Learning for the Integrated Management and Sustainable Use of Water at Catchment Scale, funded by the European Union (SLIM – Contract No EVK1-CT-2000-00064 SLIM; see http://slim.open.ac.uk). It involves 30 researchers from six countries, with backgrounds spanning the social and biophysical sciences. English is used as the operational language and the research group has worked hard to engage in social learning in their research practice, as well as studying social learning using case studies and action research.

The project runs in parallel with the implementation of the European water framework directive by all European Union member states. The water framework directive has significant elements for social learning. These include the mandatory nature of public participation and demands for transparency in decision making, necessitating what Williams (2001) terms 'a joined up strategy' to bring together all those affected. Preliminary research findings suggest that in the great majority of cases studied or encountered there is little or no:

- systems orientation providing strategic and systemic thinking of the sort that might facilitate the further development of an interactive approach (that is, social learning)
- integration and synthesis creating awareness among policy-makers and catchment managers of the opportunities afforded by an interactive approach, or the growing experience of these approaches in contexts outside Europe
- participation and engagement generating capacity, in terms of extant skills, to engage with and enact interactive approaches (especially facilitation skills).

Water management and implementation of the water framework directive and associated legislation are happening mainly in a technical and instrumental context. Research and practice are radically separated and only a very limited range of knowledge sources are deemed 'legitimate' (Schön, 1995). Ends, or goals, are being pursued at the expense of any consideration of the process by which the ends are expressed and met. In the water management 'industry', goals are mainly technical, at the expense of the social and ecological context (Sterling, 2001). So long as these technical and instrumental approaches dominate, many of the demands of the water framework directive that require stakeholder participation are unlikely to be met. Thus opportunities for enabling social learning and building citizen ecological literacy are being squandered.

The long-term outcomes of enhanced water quality and its management are also threatened because, at the end of the day, achieving ecological and technical goals involves changes in the behaviour of a diverse array of stakeholders. Lack of understanding of the importance of taking social factors into account constrains the development of policies based on fostering social learning. The alternatives are not promising, since regulation is expensive and economic incentives are not always appropriate.

How can this loss of opportunity be explained? I start with the traditions of understanding within which policy-makers, water engineers, ecologists and other stakeholders in water management think and act. Thus, in the first instance it is a crisis of how we claim to know what we know. This rests, in turn, on widely entrenched distortions in what we understand as human communication, and a lack of awareness of the biological basis of language. From both of these come practices that have been conserved over time, even when the circumstances that made them necessary are no longer relevant. That is, not only do practices become institutionalized, but institutions also shape practices – institutions and institutionalized behaviours are thus self-justifying. Here I am using North's (1990) idea of institutions as 'any form of constraint that human beings devise to shape interaction'. This could be formal arrangements such as promotion procedures or organizational cultures, or informal arrangements such as the rules of a weekly touch football game.

Becoming aware of our traditions of understanding

In a book based on their fieldwork in the semi-arid rangelands of New South Wales (NSW), Ison and Russell (2000a) present a wideranging critique of the understandings that have dominated rural research and agricultural extension practice for most of the second half of the 20th century. From their co-research with pastoralists, they present an alternative model for research and development (R&D) based on understandings that come from systems theory. Their work deconstructs widespread understandings about knowledge, information, learning, extension, technology transfer and communication. However, they also offer conceptual tools and a framework for reconstruction.

The work can also be seen as a model for systemic inquiry of any set of complex issues. Figure 2.1 models one way a systemic inquiry might be conducted based on enacting soft systems methodology (see Checkland, 2001). Ison and Russell set up a structured exploration of how our understanding of R&D is developed and our understanding of change constructed. This leads to an exploration, using experiential, narrative, historical and theoretical sources, of the research context in the semi-arid rangelands of NSW, where technology was perceived to have failed (Ison, 2000a). Central to this part of their inquiry was a critical distinction based on the perceptions and actions of the researcher.

In first-order research and development, which is still the most common, the researcher remains outside the system being studied. The espoused stance by researchers is that of objectivity and, while the system being studied is often spoken of in open system terms, intervention is performed as though it were a closed system. Perception and action by researchers and those who manage and maintain the R&D system are based on a belief in a real world; a world of discrete entities that have meaning in and of themselves (Russell and Ison, 2000a, p10).

In contrast to this tradition, Russell and Ison (2000a, 2000b) stress the need for a second-order R&D in which the espoused role and action of the researcher or practitioner are very much part of the interactions being studied. In this framework, how the researcher/participant perceives the situation is critical to the system being studied. Responsibility replaces objectivity as the central ethic, and perception and action are based on one's own experiential world, rather than on a belief in a single external real world. Any move

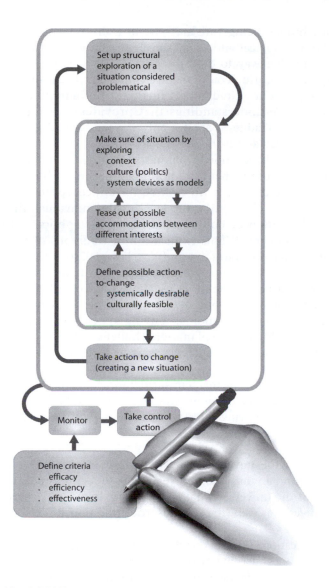

Source: Checkland (2001)

Figure 2.1 *A model of implementing soft systems methodology*

towards second-order R&D has implications for the behaviour and practice of researchers and other stakeholders in environmental issues. I propose that it is the lack of capacity to move to a second-order perspective, with its associated social learning practices of reflection, systems orientation and negotiation with the self and others, that threatens the successful implementation of the water framework directive.

As unique human beings, we are part of a lineage and our history is a product of both biological and social development, which I will call a tradition. Perhaps another way to describe this is that a tradition is the history of our being in the world. Traditions are important because our models of understanding grow out of traditions. I further define a tradition as a network of prejudices or pre-understandings that provides possible answers and strategies for action. Traditions are not only ways to see and act, but also ways to conceal (see Russell and Ison, 2000a).

Traditions in a culture embed what has been judged to be useful practice. The risk for any culture is that a tradition can become a blind spot when it evolves into practice that lacks any avenue for critical reflection. The effects of blind spots can be observed at the level of the individual, the group, the organization, the nation or culture, and in the metaphors and discourses in which we are immersed. This explication of traditions of understanding and learning is built on Maturana and Varela's (1979) biological theory of cognition, particularly that of structural coupling. Structural coupling explains how as living organisms we can never escape acting according to our context, and being acted upon by it. At one and the same time we are both independent (maintaining our own organization as a living system) and related (coupled) to our external world. This explanation challenges the common idea that we adapt to an environment, and replaces it with the idea of organisms and environments co-evolving.

A period of fieldwork in the semi-arid rangelands of NSW was one of growing awareness of this different way of understanding on my own part. I now find that the following questions posed by von Foerster (1992) best capture the choices I can make:

- Am I apart from the universe? That is, whenever I look, am I looking through a peephole upon an unfolding universe (the first-order tradition)?
- Am I part of the universe? That is, whenever I act, am I changing myself and the universe as well (the second-order tradition)?

It is these two questions I must consider when reflecting on what it is that I do. And the choice is not just one of principle, as in articulating an ethical code to be followed. For von Foerster, the answer to these questions unfolds in our living as we do what we do – it is how we experience others and ourselves. It is important to emphasize that both first-order and second-order traditions are different modes of doing R&D.

First-order research and development

The ethos and achievements of first-order R&D are characterized by disciplinary knowledge, a 'fix' mentality, and the belief that generating new knowledge is a good thing in itself (Russell and Ison, 2000a). Explicitly, it is a tradition based on a belief in an increasingly knowable world: a world capable of being understood without the need to take into account our actions as participants in creating that very world we experience. There is a basic assumption that a fixed reality is out there and that, by applying rational understanding, we will increasingly gain accurate knowledge of its elements and the laws of its functioning. In addition, most often there is no distinction between phenomena observable to the senses (such as sounds, sight and touch) and phenomena that are the products of the intellect (such as thoughts, beliefs and memories). The development of this approach has had its own phases, outlined next, all of which exemplify the fix mentality:

1   The problem is seen as a mismatch between what is scientifically known and technically feasible, and current practice. The new technology is designed by research scientists and then transferred to the end users, who put it into action to address the problem
2   Built into the belief of a technological solution is a conception of the benefits that could be derived from better farming systems or, in the case of rangelands, a return to the 'natural ecosystem' state, without considering who participates in defining 'better' or how what is perceived as 'natural' has come to be constructed
3   Social and political insights are specifically added to the R&D equation (for example most multidisciplinary research).

At its simplest, the first-order view accepts the existence of an objective reality, made up of things bearing properties and entering into relations. Such has been the success and prestige of modern science that many accept it as the best framework available for understanding how we think, which delivers a powerful social and political role to science, as understood in this form. The point of departure from the first-order view in the SLIM project saw social learning as part of an interactive approach that acknowledges we are actors in our environment and thus all our actions, including those of scientific inquiry, inevitably act on our environment.

The original SLIM project proposal argued that water catchments are conventionally understood as biophysical 'hard' systems and that problems are addressed through instrumental interventions, typically through engineering works. However, in recent years, another approach has emerged in response to the frequent failure of the instrumental and strategic reasoning of the first-order perspective. This approach is based on the idea that sustainable and regenerated water catchments are the emergent property of systems practice, of systemic inquiry (see, for example, King and Jiggins, 2002; Röling, 1994, 2002; Röling and Woodhill, 2001). That is, desirable water catchment properties arise from interactions among multiple interdependent stakeholders in the catchments and between those stakeholders and the catchments themselves. Where such an interactive approach applies, centralized policy provides a context for a dynamic local decentralized process and, in the case of large watersheds, for concerted parallel local processes. In seeking to move away from taking only a first-order approach, the SLIM project has no intention of fostering irrationality or fuzzy thinking. Rather, along with Winograd and

Flores (1987), the commitment is to developing a new ground of rationality – one that is as rigorous as the first-order tradition in its aspirations, but does not share the technical and instrumental presuppositions underlying it.

Second-order research and development

Awareness of the distinctions between first- and second-order R&D traditions has important implications for how social learning is understood, fostered and researched. In the context of the SLIM project, an interactive second-order approach has three important implications.

Firstly, it emphasizes social learning as an emergent property of collaboration. Stakeholders are considered intelligent, responsible agents who are willing to act in the collective interest. It is taken as given that they are learning about their domain of existence and are creating reciprocal arrangements. Typically, such social learning is facilitated by helping stakeholders see the water catchment (in its social and biophysical dimensions) as one system, in which they are interdependent with others.

Secondly, for social learning to emerge, stakeholders must develop shared platforms for decision making and action. A capacity for communication, shared learning processes and concerted action must be created at the water catchment level. A water catchment managing system must be developed, often within an already complex social context of existing organizations, vested interests and institutional arrangements.

Thirdly, the interactive approach has important consequences for policy. It implies a different policy basis from the customary biophysical and economic models of the catchment, one that calls for totally different instruments and practices.

At the heart of a social learning approach is some form of communicative action, so one needs to understand how human communication occurs. My concern is to provide a biological explanation, though others may find inspiration in Habermas's work (1984, 1987) on communicative action and reason or in other traditions.

Learning through language and dialogue

Living in language

The Santiago school of cognition (see Capra, 1996) suggests that all knowing is derived from doing. Our capacity as individuals to respond is inextricably linked to the interaction between our language and emotions. This interaction is what we call conversation. This is central to our reflections on what it is we do as practitioners of one sort or another in the name of sustainability. What is not clear, however, is what practices we need to engage in, individually and collectively, to address the quality of our relationship (as a species) with our environment (including other species).

Talbott (2002) sets out to chart a pathway between the advocates of scientific management and radical conservationists. Responding to the claim that 'the limits of our knowledge should define the limits of our practice', Talbott asks (p23): 'By what practice can we extend our knowledge, if we may never act without already possessing perfect knowledge?' The answer he offers is that 'We conduct an ecological conversation'. Talbott suggests three main features of an ecological conversation:

1 putting cautious questions to the other
2 compensating for past inadequacies – in the sense that in a conversation later words modify the meaning attributed to earlier words
3 recognizing that at any stage of a conversation there is never a single right or wrong response – nor is it an act of making a choice from something predetermined.

As a species, conversation is our unique selling point! To converse is to turn together, to dance – and thus an ecological conversation is a tango of responsibility. A conversation is inventive, unpredictable and always particularizing to place and people (see, for example, Shaw, 2002). Engaging with this metaphor is not to turn away from the doing of science or ecology, or any other practice. This experiential activity opens up new possibilities. It entails the responsibility of reflection, of making other distinctions and considering their consequences. It provides the basis of conducting an ecological conversation.

The role of metaphor

Metaphors provide a way to understand our understandings and how we use language. Our ordinary conceptual system, in terms of which we think and act, is metaphorical in nature. Paying attention to metaphors-in-use is one way we can reflect on our own traditions of understanding (McClintock et al, 2003a, 2003b).

Metaphors both reveal and conceal, but because we live in language it is sometimes difficult to reflect on our metaphors-in-use. The strategy of mirroring particular metaphors or metaphor clusters thus holds open the possibility for reflection and learning. For example, as outlined by McClintock (2000), the metaphor 'countryside as a tapestry' reveals the experience of countryside as a visually pleasing pattern, of local character and diversity and of what is lost when landscapes are dominated by monocultures. However, the metaphor conceals the smell, danger, noise and activity of people making a living. By exploring metaphors, we can make part of our language use 'picturable' and thus rationally visible, publicly discussable and debatable, as well as socially useful as a practical resource 'with which and through which we can think and act' (Shotter, 1993).

McClintock's (1996) conclusions contribute to an agenda for meeting demands for increased transparency and participation in environmental decision making. This, in turn, requires building social and relational capital through processes of social learning. Exploring metaphors-in-use and what they may reveal or conceal is one of many ways to explore the context of issues in the process of environmental decision making. It may also be used to explore and trigger enthusiasms – where enthusiasm is a predisposition to action (Russell and Ison, 2000b).

McClintock (1996) identified two parallel ways of working with metaphor: acting as practitioner–narrator and practitioner–facilitator. (Practitioner here can be translated as researcher, manager, community worker or government agent.) The role of practitioner–narrator includes the following steps:

1   Make initial distinctions around the metaphors-in-use (for example for landscapes, lifestyles, products, events)
2   Bring forth metaphors of the practice context
3   Explore the metaphors by considering revealed and concealed aspects
4   Judge enabling and disabling metaphors and identify alternatives
5   Iterate, involving different people, different sources of metaphors or different issues.

The role of a practitioner–facilitator is to use metaphors to create a space for understandings to emerge. A six-step process has been proposed:

1   Propose initial distinctions around metaphors and anticipate ways in which the distinctions can be meaningful
2   Consider activities for jointly bringing forth and exploring metaphors (in workshops or on farm walks)
3   Consider activities to jointly juxtapose metaphors and consider what each metaphor implies and does not imply (a proxy for revealed and concealed aspects)
4   Revisit the distinctions around metaphors and propose further distinctions around judging metaphors, choosing between metaphors, and dominant and reified metaphors
5   Consider activities to facilitate processes of moving between metaphors
6   Iterate steps 1–5.

Fostering dialogue

Debate-based communication is often grounded in situations of conflict. Dialogue differs from and contrasts with debate. The roots of the word 'dialogue' can be translated as meaning 'flowing through', while the roots of the word 'debate' mean 'to beat down' (Isaacs, 1993). Isaacs' (p45) definition of dialogue is 'a sustained collective inquiry into the processes, assumptions, and certainties that compose everyday experiences'.

Dialogue is a process that does not seek consensus, but to provide an environment for learning, to think together. This does not refer only to analysing a problem, but to sharing understandings and assumptions and the reasoning behind these assumptions in order to build richer pictures and act jointly. With these distinctions as background, Kersten (1995) devised a research process based on listening to and exploring the local context with the aid of local people. The resultant models for R&D she devised are depicted in Figure 2.2. Her research showed that dialogue meetings have to be situated in a broader approach if dialogue is to emerge.

As part of her research, Kersten set out to design dialogue workshops between scientists (mainly ecologists) and pastoralists. Her subsequent experience reflects a flaw in the overall R&D system – the ecologists were concerned only with formulating research problems from within their 'system of doing ecology'. In effect, what they tried to do was to impose their system of interest on the context, rather than allow a jointly conceived system of interest to emerge from the dialogue. This process of using dialogue to resolve conflicts and support social learning is consistent with the negotiation strand of social learning discussed in Chapter 1. Both view conflict as an opportunity to support social interactions and learning through problem definition and resolution.

Kersten found that the context and history of participants have a major influence on the possibilities for dialogue to emerge. She identified a set of nine factors that either enhanced or constrained dialogue (see Table 2.1). When situated in an overall research approach that values multiple realities, techniques such as mind-mapping and matrix ranking were found to break down the cultural barriers between the individual as 'pastoralist' or 'researcher'. These techniques opened up the possibility of each genuinely hearing the other.

Facilitating learning and dialogue: Institutional directions

Institutional factors

In recent years, I have moved my research focus from practices directly associated with biophysical phenomena to a concern with how our institutional and organizational practices mediate our relationships with the biophysical world (for example through dialogue, social learning and exploring metaphor). This shift of attention has been prompted by my experience that how humans think, learn and act in relation to the biophysical world (and other species) is the arena in most need of attention. However, there is much confusion in the literature and in everyday conversation about what is meant by organization, institution and structure (see Ison, 1994, 1996, 2000b).

North's (1990) distinctions between 'organization' and 'institution' are initially helpful but, from a systems perspective, do not go far enough. I suggest the need to recognize a further set of distinctions between the organization and structure of a system. The organization of a system is defined as a particular set of relationships, whether static or dynamic, between components that

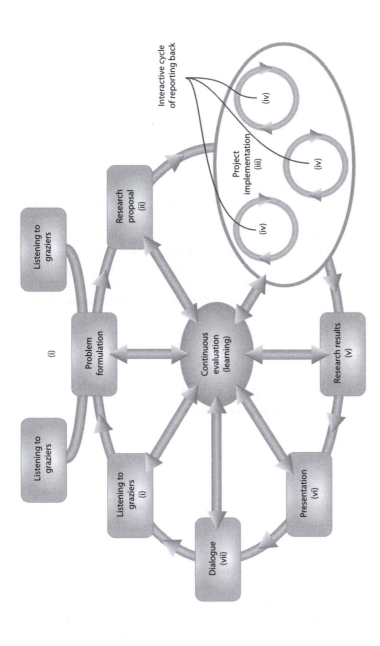

Figure 2.2 *Schemas for iterative cycles of listening and allowing interpretation by stakeholders*

Notes: (a) Research starts with a desire to listen and to build relationships (moving from steps i–ii) rather than extracting data. Problem formulation, what constitutes relevant data, and some preliminary interpretations of data are generated with stakeholders and through iterative processes (steps i–iv). These create the circumstances in a co-researching relationship for dialogue to emerge among stakeholders (step vii) having set up an ethical basis for research reporting (step ii and steps v–vi)

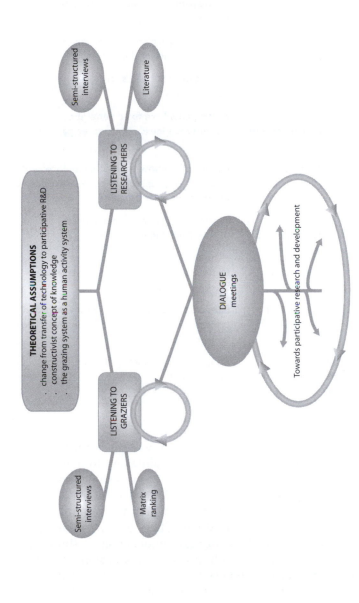

(b) The basic steps in a research process designed to foster dialogue between researchers and local stakeholders in an issue, with the aim of creating the circumstances for one or more participative R&D projects to emerge as joint ventures. The starting point is for the researcher/facilitator to be aware of his/her own theoretical assumptions

Sources: Kersten (1995); Kersten and Ison (1998, p167)

Figure 2.2 *Continued*

Table 2.1 *Issues arising from meetings between pastoralists and scientists that enhanced or restricted dialogue*

Enhancing dialogue	Restricting dialogue
Participants come to a meeting as individuals	Participants come as representatives of a group
Participants articulate their personal understanding at the meeting	Participants are at the meeting as groups and act as part of that group
Time has been spent on building relationships before the meeting and during the meeting	Little time has been spent on building relationships
Participants are prepared to relax preconceived ideas about other participants at the meeting	Participants have fixed general or stereotyped ideas about other participants
Participants do not know each other beforehand	Participants know each other beforehand and are not prepared to relax preconceived ideas about each other
Participants listen actively to other participants with an open mind that is not blocked by preconceived ideas	Participants listen to re-establish preconceived ideas
Participants are open to ideas and ask for suggestions from other participants	Participants are defending or attacking statements made
Participants respect other meanings and understandings. Multiple realities are acknowledged	Participants do not respect meanings and understandings other than their own. They believe in one reality
Participants feel they can benefit from a good discussion with people who see the same issue from different perspectives	People have the feeling they are 'being participated'

Source: Kersten and Ison (1998)

constitute a recognizable whole – a recognizable unity as distinguished by an observer. Organizational relationships have to be maintained to maintain the system – if they change, the system either 'dies' or becomes something else.

On the other hand, the structure of a system is defined as the set of current concrete components and relationships through which the organization of a system is manifest in particular surroundings. Thus for a particular R&D organization like NSW Agriculture, the key organizational relationships might be those between politicians, researchers, administrators, extension officers and agricultural/horticultural producers (experience suggests that consumers are often excluded). If these relationships cease to exist, then that which is unique to a particular organization ceases to exist. If it were a biological organism, this would mean the death of the organism. But because organizations are not biological organisms, those involved can choose to become some other organization – remember that the same organization can realize or manifest itself through different structures. Structures in this example might include particular divisions, programmes or practices.

Social learning systems in practice

In many ways the water framework directive in Europe is a unique piece of legislation and presents many opportunities for creative implementation. In the main, however, it is not being grasped creatively. The systems of interest that are beginning to be enacted in some circles can be characterized as:

- a system to ensure our minister does not face infraction (court) proceedings by Brussels (from the perspective of ministry and senior line agency staff)
- a system to establish the best possible scientific basis for water quality (from the perspective of scientists and engineers in the environment agencies)
- a system to cause minimum disruption to our current procedures and so avoid additional costs (from the perspective of English water policy-makers and ministers)
- a system to engender duplication and conflict with planning and land use management practices and legislation (from the perspective of professional planners).

Many other possible systems of interest could be formulated in the current context. None of them is right or wrong, but merely different ways of thinking systemically about the situation and beginning a process of systemic inquiry. However, this systems orientation is not much in evidence. For example, in Scotland the baseline status for the water framework directive established in-house by the Scottish Environmental Protection Agency is based on existing technical data and 'professional judgement'. For them, the goal was to meet the reporting deadline without considering:

- who learns or could learn in the process of developing the baseline data (that is, who might relevant stakeholders be and how might they be involved?)
- who, apart from professionals, may have relevant data to contribute (for example anglers, gillies, estate managers, school children)
- whether how they are enacting the water framework directive will deliver what it aspires to deliver in, say, 2020. There has been no backcasting, for example, and little consideration of whether their implementation model is sustainable in terms of human resource and transaction costs. Participation is seen as a luxury that can wait until later.

In contrast, from a second-order perspective, the creative implementation of the water framework directive could be likened to the design of a learning system

(Ison, 1994; Ison and Russell, 2000b). Table 2.2 shows some considerations for designing particular learning systems.

The elements of Table 2.2 are not prescriptions, but considerations for design that must be adapted in space and time. But adapting for design

Table 2.2 *Two independent sets of design considerations for the design of learning systems*

Nine design features of systems courses at The Open University	Ten design considerations for the SWARD project,[1] including some key starting conditions
1 Ground concepts and action as much as possible in the student's own experience	1 A perceived issue or need that has local identity
2 Learn from case studies of failure	2 Active listening to stakeholder perceptions of the issue/need
3 Develop diagramming (and other modelling) skills as a means for students to engage with and learn about complexity	3 Good staff – in this case, young, motivated and proactive women
4 Take responsibility as authors (or researchers) for what we say and do (epistemological awareness)	4 No, or very limited forms of, control
5 Recognize that learning involves an interplay between our emotional and rational selves	5 Proper resourcing, particularly in the early stages
6 Develop skills in iterating – understanding learning as emerging from processes that are not deterministic	6 A minimum number of initial group leaders who acted as 'key attractors'
7 Introduce systems concepts, tools, methods and methodological approaches to develop skills in formulating systems of interest ... for purposeful action (an example would be an exploration based on metaphors)	7 Scope for self-organization around particular enthusiasms
8 Use verbs not nouns! Verbs denote relationships and activity and are key to the process of activity modelling, one of the main features of soft systems methodology	8 An appropriately experienced participant to conceptualize systems
9 Make assessment relevant to action in the personal and professional lives of students	9 Some small 'carrots' for participants at the beginning
	10 A supportive local press creating a positive publicity network

Note: [1]A community-based R&D project in the southwest of England

Source: Ison (2002)

requires an opening up to our traditions of understanding. The same is true of designing for or facilitating social learning.

When applied to good environmental management, or even the broader concept of sustainability, social learning has been described as the process of collective action and reflection among different actors directed toward improving the management of human and environmental interrelations. The SLIM project originally proposed that the research would focus on social learning as a combination of (a) stakeholders' shared learning about the biophysical nature of the watershed (ecological parameters), and (b) stakeholders' shared learning about human collective agency. In this sense, we argued for the need for reflection, that is, learning about learning and its facilitation. Further, because social learning has remained a rather vague concept, we proposed to use the theory of partnership, as collective cognitive agency, with its emphasis on structural coupling and consistency among perception, emotion and action, as the basis for an alternative policy framework.

Despite committing from the outset to build a community of practice engaged in its own social learning, the members of SLIM have still found it difficult to articulate and reflect on existing deeply held theoretical commitments. What is more, we have found it difficult to explore and honour our differences. Recognizing this dilemma, we set up an international mid-term review of our project built around each partner's articulation of social learning and their reflections on it. This has helped and enabled us to move on, much as the reflective processes used in the social learning for sustainability workshop which produced this book helped to gain greater insights into process and allowed the organizers and the participants to move on together (see Chapter 13).

Conclusions

My intention has been to invite and trigger the reader's reflections on their own traditions of understanding, particularly how that understanding arises in relation to language, metaphor and dialogue, and how they might choose to understand learning. These reflections are designed to recognize that 'my world is different to your world and this must always be so. The common ground, which is the basis of our ability to communicate with one another, comes through the use of common processes of perceiving and conceptualizing' (Russell, 1986, p54).

I have also invited reflection on how particular understandings can become institutionalized. These reflections invite the use of a systems orientation and consideration of emergent properties (practices) that might arise from this perspective. In my experience, many line agencies, government ministry staff and expert advisers are not prepared to relinquish their perceived power and control. To engage or participate fully in a social dialogue, an emergent property of a social learning strategy for sustainability may well be enhanced citizen ecological literacy.

Acknowledgements

The support of the European Union and members of the SLIM Contract No EVK1-CT-2000-00064 SLIM (website http://slim.open.ac.uk) is gratefully acknowledged. David Russell is, as ever, a source of inspiration. My thanks to the editors for the invitation to contribute and the hard work they put in on the original manuscript.

References

Capra, F. (1996) *The Web of Life*, Harper Collins, London

Checkland, P.B. (2001) 'Presentation to a joint meeting of UKSS/OUSys', *OU Systems Society Newsletter*, February. See also www.spmc.org.uk

Habermas, J. (1984) *The Theory of Communicative Action, Vol 1, Reason and the Rationalization of Society*, Beacon Press, Boston

Habermas, J. (1987) *The Theory of Communicative Action, Vol 2, Lifeworld and System. A Critique of Functionalist Reason*, Beacon Press, Boston

Isaacs, W. N. (1993) 'Taking flight: Dialogue, collective thinking and organisational learning', *Organizational Dynamics*, vol 22, pp24–39

Ison, R. L. (1994) 'Designing learning systems: How can systems approaches be applied in the training of research workers and development actors?', in *Lectures and Debates*, proceedings, International Symposium on Systems-oriented Research in Agriculture and Rural Development, vol 2, pp369–394

Ison, R. L. (1996) *Facilitating Institutional Change*, proceedings, ANU/IIED/OFI Sustainable Forest Policy Short Course, Oxford

Ison, R. L. (2000a) 'Technology: Transforming grazier experience', in Ison, R. L. and Russell, D. B. (eds) *Agricultural Extension and Rural Development: Breaking Out of Traditions*, Cambridge University Press, Cambridge

Ison, R. L. (2000b) 'Experience, tradition and service? Institutionalised R&D in the rangelands', in Ison, R. L. and Russell, D. B. (eds) *Agricultural Extension and Rural Development: Breaking Out of Traditions*, Cambridge University Press, Cambridge

Ison, R. L. (2002) 'Systems practice and the design of learning systems: Orchestrating an ecological conversation', in *An Interdisciplinary Dialogue: Agricultural Production and Integrated Ecosystem Management of Soil and Water*, proceedings, Ballina, NSW, Australia, 12–16 November

Ison, R. L. and Russell, D. B. (2000a) *Agricultural Extension and Rural Development: Breaking Out of Traditions*, Cambridge University Press, Cambridge

Ison, R. L. and Russell, D. B. (2000b) 'Exploring some distinctions for the design of learning systems', *Cybernetics and Human Knowing*, vol 7, no 4, pp43–56

Kersten, S. (1995) 'In search of dialogue: Vegetation management in western New South Wales, Australia', unpublished PhD thesis, University of Sydney

Kersten, S. and Ison, R. L. (1998) 'Listening, interpretative cycles and dialogue: Process design for collaborative research and development', *The Journal of Agricultural Education & Extension*, vol 5, pp163–178

King, C. and Jiggins, J. (2002) 'A systemic model and theory for facilitating social learning', in Leeuwis, C. and Pyburn, R. (eds) *Wheelbarrows Full of Frogs. Social Learning in Rural Resource Management*, Koninklijke van Gorcum, Assen, the Netherlands

McClintock, D. (1996) 'Metaphors that inspire "researching with people": UK farming, countrysides and diverse stakeholder contexts', PhD thesis, Systems Department, The Open University, Milton Keynes, UK

McClintock, D. (2000) 'Considering metaphors of countrysides in the United Kingdom', in Cerf, M., Gibbon, D., Hubert, B., Ison, R., Jiggins, J., Paine, M., Proost, J. and Röling, N. (eds) *Cow Up a Tree. Knowing and Learning for Change in Agriculture, Case Studies from Industrialised Countries*, INRA (Institut National de la Recherche Agronomique) editions, Paris

McClintock, D., Ison, R. L. and Armson, R. (2003a) 'Metaphors and understandings: Building systems practice', *Cybernetics and Human Knowing*, vol 11, pp25–47

McClintock, D., Ison, R. L. and Armson, R. (2003b) 'Metaphors of research and researching with people', *Journal of Environmental Planning and Management*, vol 46, 5, pp715–731

Maturana, H. R. and Varela, F. G. (1979) *The Tree of Knowledge. The Biological Roots of Human Understanding*, New Science Library, Boston

North, D. (1990) *Institutions, Institutional Change and Economic Performance*, Cambridge University Press, Cambridge

Röling, N. (1994) 'Platforms for decision making about eco-systems', in Fresco, L. O., Stroosnijder, L., Boum, J. and VanKeulen, H. (eds) *Future of the Land: Mobilising and Integrating Knowledge for Land Use Options*, John Wiley & Sons, Chichester, UK

Röling, N. (2002) 'Beyond the aggregation of individual preferences. Moving from multiple to distributed cognition in resource dilemmas', in Leeuwis, C. and Pyburn, R. (eds) *Wheelbarrows Full of Frogs. Social Learning in Rural Resource Management*, Koninklijke van Gorcum, Assen, the Netherlands

Röling, N. and Woodhill, J. (2001) 'From paradigm to practice: Foundations, principles and elements for dialogue on water, food and environment', background document, National and Basin Dialogue Design Workshop, Bonn, December

Russell, D. B. (1986) 'How we see the world determines what we do in the world: Preparing the ground for action research', mimeo, University of Western Sydney (Hawkesbury) Richmond

Russell, D. B. and Ison, R. L. (2000a) 'The research–development relationship in rural communities: An opportunity for contextual science', in Ison, R. L. and Russell, D. B. (eds) *Agricultural Extension and Rural Development: Breaking Out of Traditions*, Cambridge University Press, Cambridge

Russell, D. B. and Ison, R. L. (2000b) 'Enthusiasm: Developing critical action for second-order R&D', in Ison, R. L. and Russell, D. B. (eds) *Agricultural Extension and Rural Development: Breaking Out of Traditions*, Cambridge University Press, Cambridge

Schön, D. (1995) 'The new scholarship requires a new epistemology', *Change*, November/December, pp27–34

Shaw, P. (2002) *Changing Conversations in Organizations. A Complexity Approach to Change*, Routledge, London

Shotter, J. (1993) *Conversational Realities: Constructing Life through Language*, Sage, London

Sterling, S. (2001) *Sustainable Education. Re-visioning Learning and Change*, Schumacher Briefings No 6, Green Books, Totnes, UK

Talbott, S. (2002) 'Ecological conversation. Wildness, anthropocentrism and deep ecology', Netfuture, www.netfuture.org/2002/Jan1002_127.html/accessed in January 2002 von Foerster, H. (1992) 'Ethics and second-order cybernetics', *Cybernetics and Human Knowing*, vol 1, pp9–19

Williams, K. (2001) 'The impact of the water framework directive on catchment-management planning in the British Isles', *Chartered Institution of Water and Environmental Management Journal*, vol 15, pp97–102

Winograd, T. and Flores, F. (1987) *Understanding Computers and Cognition: A New Foundation for Design*, Addison Wesley, New York

3

Complex Adaptive Systems: Constructing Mental Models

Rob Dyball, Sara Beavis and Stefan Kaufman

At a glance

- A systems perspective brings together otherwise disparate sources of information and synthesizes their various insights to produce a better understanding of the emerging issues in environmental management
- Adaptive systems theory provides a framework for understanding change in situations with a number of interacting variables, which is typical of social learning and environmental management
- Some of the general principles of complex systems and their implications for the practitioner are described and related to issues in social learning and environmental management
- A case study involving management adaptations to flooding and acid sulphate soils in the lower Macleay River catchment illustrates the need to integrate the biophysical and socioeconomic components of a complex system.

Systems change and renewal

This chapter argues that environmental managers may well find it useful to take a systems orientation to some of the issues and challenges they are confronted with. All environment management issues are coupled to social issues, and a systems orientation is particularly suited to understanding the complex dynamics of change that result. In keeping with the approach taken throughout this book, this chapter illustrates the concepts presented within the context of a study where environmental managers employed those concepts to their advantage. This study involves the interaction between management responses to flooding and the long-term environmental problems encountered in the lower Macleay River catchment on the mid-north coast of New South Wales (NSW).

One of the complex issues for the environmental manager to resolve here is the mismatch between knowledge, values, economic estimates and levels of trust that are apparent between stakeholders at individual, group and intergenerational scales. The required shift in personal understanding as part of the social learning process follows the ideas proposed by Ison in the previous chapter, notably the case he puts for each individual to rethink their personal boundaries. This chapter examines the principles involved in building on such rethinking, and generating a collaborative, shared, systems orientation to a sustainability issue. However, before presenting this practical example of a systems orientation, the chapter introduces some key concepts. It does this at some length, since a vast range of terms are used within the systems literature – many of them ambiguously or contradictorily – including some 163 definitions of the central systems concept of 'stability' (Grimm and Wissel, 1997).

Systems definition

This chapter adopts Newell and Wasson's (2002, p4) definition of a system as:

> *composed of discernable parts (elements, agents) that interact to constrain each other's behaviour. It is these* mutual constraints, *operating between the parts of the system, that limit the range of behaviours available to the system as a whole – and thus give rise to its 'emergent' (or synergistic) properties. In other words, the characteristic (or lawful) behaviour of the system arises from the internally-generated (endogenous) forces imposed on parts of the system by parts of the system.*

The core concepts embedded in a systems orientation are unpacked, revealing some of the power and usefulness of a systems orientation.

The concept of parts

We start with the idea that a system has component 'parts'. These might be physical things, such as animals, plants and rivers, or they might be conceptual, such as the various worldviews, attitudes, knowledge and beliefs held by different stakeholders. One of the strengths of a systems orientation is that both physical and social processes and concepts are integrated within the same framework, rather than being external to one another where they might be managed in isolation.

The parts of a system interact and place an influencing constraint on each other as a consequence of their respective properties. In the example that follows, we will see how acid sulphate soils, considered a part of the system in question, have certain properties, such as high sulphur and organic matter contents. When these properties combine with properties possessed by other parts, such as water, the properties of the two cause sulphuric acid to mobilize and be transported into local waterways. Both water and acid sulphate soils are physical things, but we can see in the example that human attitudes, values and behaviour are also crucial parts of this system – since it is when certain human disturbances occur that the natural soil and water combination responds in a way that we find problematic. So we think of the human attitudes as parts, with properties of their own, such as 'ignorance' or 'willingness to seek help'.

Both the parts and their properties that make up a system are selected by the observer. There are any number of parts that we could identify as components of the system under management in the Macleay River example, and any number of individuals, groups and attitudes too. It is the concerned individuals and groups who must negotiate which of the parts are to be included in the defined system. Likewise, for any selection of parts of a system there are almost an infinite number of properties that each might possess. The soils in question have many more properties than just their sulphur and organic matter content, and sulphur and organic matter have many other properties than just their capacity to oxidize or reduce. Yet, in the context of the issues of concern to the people of the region, these are the properties that are identified as relevant, and so this is the system that is constructed.

Systems thinkers argue that humans selectively identify systems of concern to them from myriad complex interrelations that form reality itself. It would be impossible for us to comprehend reality in its complex entirety, dwelling on all entities and all their properties and relationships simultaneously. However, as we may often select different parts and properties for the system of interest we identify, even if we call it by the same name (such as 'the Macleay River'), it is important that through social dialogues and processes of negotiation we make clear what is 'in' and what is 'out' of our system. Some of the techniques discussed elsewhere in this book help an environmental manager initiate collective understanding of our different orientations as a first step to cooperative behaviour in the face of complex issues. However, the central issue for this discussion is how people learn about and act in response to the boundaries they perceive their systems to have.

Constraints and system behaviour

We use the definition of 'system' proposed by Newell and Wasson (see p42). They deliberately use the term 'constraint', although other systems orientations talk of parts 'enabling' the system to achieve certain goals. However, this language tends to imply that the system can have a purpose or goal ascribed to it and that the parts necessarily cooperate in some way towards that goal. This is only true in a limited number of cases, often of a human-engineered kind, and less common for the messy real world cases with which environmental managers engage. However, the notion of 'constraint' invites us to consider that our system is behaving as it does because it is constrained by its parts and their relationships. Thus if we want it to behave otherwise, we need to understand how we might change the parts or their relationships, or both, so that the system is constrained to behave differently.

For some, 'constraint' has a negative connotation, associated with 'denial of freedom', but we would argue against that association. As humans we willingly enter into constraining relationships all the time – from lover to parent, from orchestral musician to soccer player. We do so because, by accepting these relational bonds, we engage ourselves with the other and are party to an experience or the creation of a whole that we could not have alone. In systems terms, our mutual constraints are causing some new behaviour or phenomena at the system level. In system literature, this is often termed 'emergent behaviour' or the 'emergent properties' of the system.

The issue of treating systems as though they had goals was touched on earlier in this chapter. As a metaphor, 'goal' has a finality that is inappropriate in most environment management situations. As many systems thinkers have argued since Vickers onwards, in most cases humans do not seek to achieve some end when they intervene in systems, but rather to maintain some process – noting that 'maintaining a process' could be considered a goal of sorts (for a discussion of Vickers, see Checkland, 1985, 2000; Midgley, 2000). In environmental contexts, this is inevitably the case.

The system we are seeking to manage does not have a fixed state that we could set as a goal to achieve or maintain. Rather, the environment consists of many component systems and subsystems, each interacting and cycling through their change processes. With no single arrangement identifiable as the environment's 'proper state', we are left to negotiate with each other on the basis of our personal values, and the case study presented here illustrates a number of conflicting values in this regard. We refer to this identification of systems in relation to our values as a 'system of interest' – the 'product of distinguishing a system in a situation in which an individual or group has an interest or stake' (The Open University; available at www.open2.net/systems/ glossary/index.html).

Another problem of setting goals as the end point of 'good' environmental management stems from the systems concept of nested hierarchies. Systems typically have subsystems and are themselves nested within broader systems. In the case study here, we can identify systems at the landscape scale, with the central actors and agents being, for example, individual farmers and fishermen and their actions. But issues at this level relate to and are influenced by issues at a high level, for example changes in market demand for different farm and fishery products. Because the complex interactions between layers of the system and their outcomes cannot be predicted, one central understanding from a systems orientation is to abandon inflexible strategies in favour of responsive and adaptive management regimes.

Feedback and control

A systems perspective describes these links between mutually influencing parts in terms of feedback loops. The effect of a feedback loop may be reinforcing, balancing or reducing, and hence act to control aspects of the relationship between parts of the system. Reinforcing feedback occurs where the influence of certain behaviour is fed back into the system, causing it to exert more of the same sort of influence. This is also called 'positive feedback', but this term is often mistakenly taken to mean 'good or beneficial' or 'upwards or growing'. If such feedback loops are uncontrolled, the behaviours (human or mechanical) tend to run away exponentially. Aggressive competitive price undercutting is an example of runaway feedback that drives the system in a downward spiral until it becomes non-viable.

Balancing or stabilizing feedback dampens the system, causing it to close at some equilibrium level. The feedback signal runs counter to the output – more feeds back less, and less feeds back more. A good example would be a farmer who regulated stocking levels in response to feed on offer in a paddock – increasing stock as fodder is available, but then reducing pressure as stock eat out reserves, thus allowing fodder levels to recover and stocking levels to increase, and so on. Balancing feedback is also termed 'negative feedback', but there is the same potential for confusion as with the term 'positive feedback'.

In real world situations, the combined pressures and responses of multiple feedback loops operating simultaneously across various scales produce highly complex patterns of change. Elements of the system are often highly sensitive to changes in their relationship with one another. Small changes in one area can rapidly produce major changes in the whole. This non-linear relationship between size of causal event and magnitude of response is one reason why unforeseen consequences are endemic to complex systems. Additionally, some pressures produce fairly rapid responses in the areas they affect, while others are subject to delay or accumulate only very slowly. This can be problematic when some short-term response is valued, for example increased crop yield under irrigation, while the response in some unwanted related variable is delayed, for example a rising water table.

System boundaries

As discussed, selecting what is 'in' and what is 'outside' systems of interest involves the subjective identification of boundaries, which will always relate to the aims and objectives of the person or group doing the identifying. This is why a crucial component of social learning is reflecting on what entities we have identified as valuable, what boundaries we have placed on the systems we are learning about, and where we have situated ourselves relative to other parts of the system. If we can recognize that problems are social constructions in combination with ecological reality, we can start to work on solutions that address both physical processes as well as the stakeholders' construction of those processes as problematic.

Ison et al (1997, p261) write:

> *The views of other stakeholders have to be taken into account and methods developed for formulating the problem 'system' as a composite of all stakeholders' version of the problem, combining expertise from outside with insider expertise from local communities. What emerges is a 'problem-determined system' rather than a 'system-determined problem'.*

We must reflect on where each stakeholder is situated, what perspective they have upon the system, what overlap exists with others and what they know or understand about the system as they experience it. From this, we move to integrate and synthesize those perspectives and understandings, seeking some agreement on the system, its boundaries and the problems that arise, together with what steps we might then take to collectively handle those problematic processes better. Inevitably, this will raise conflict – both in the system as identified and the differences as to key issues and values therein. As argued in Chapter 1, we should not eschew this conflict for it is present whether we recognize it or not, but should openly negotiate it and the perspectives and knowledges that underlie it.

Patterns of change in complex systems

The dynamics of complex adaptive systems compel us to seek patterns of change and descriptions of change processes rather than look to specific events or end points. Holling and Gunderson (2002) have recently proposed a general model that describes these patterns of change in coupled human and natural systems (see Figure 3.1). Central to this model is the concept of resilience, which they define as 'the amount of disturbance that can be sustained before a change in system control and structure occurs' (p28). The term suggests that systems enduring over long time spans are not merely resistant to external pressure, but that they absorb the pressure and in some sense recover their initial characteristic patterns of behaviour without being fundamentally changed. Holling and Gunderson suggest that, over time, all such complex systems follow an initial phase of renewal, followed by an exploitation phase of rapid growth, then a conservation phase of maturity and stability and a final phase of creative destruction – a necessary precursor to a new phase of renewal.

For each phase, Holling and Gunderson propose a relationship between what they call 'potential', which might be thought of as the amount of energy and material resources available and the degree to which those resources are connected to form some common structure. This structure might best be thought of by analogy to a forest regrowing after a fire. Immediately after the fire there is an abundance of unbound nutrient and organic material resources. As the forest recovers, these resources are progressively connected into the physical structure of the trees. In due course, nearly all the materials have been allocated to maintain the structure of the mature forest, and no further

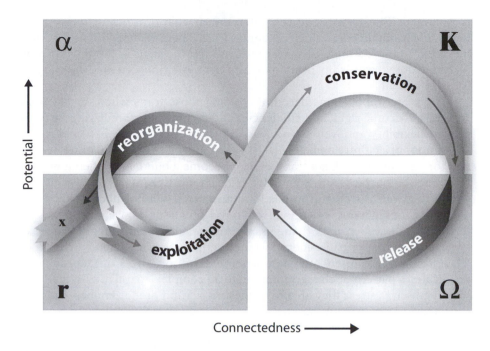

Note: The exiting x indicates system transformation

Source: Holling and Gunderson (2002). Reproduced by permission of Island Press, Washington, DC

Figure 3.1 *Stylized representation of dynamic processes in adaptive systems*

development is possible. While this has been occurring, the resilience of the system has been declining as the share of resources devoted to maintaining structure leads to increased rigidity and accompanying vulnerability. The mature system might be very stable, but it lacks resilience and, inevitably, the vulnerability of the system is exposed. Eventually, the system enters its phase of creative destruction as the structure and connectivity of the old system dissipate and the unbound resources are made available for reorganization and renewal (Holling and Gunderson, 2002).

Holling and Gunderson suggest that it is when connectivity in a system is low, during the release and reorganization phase, that a system is most likely to undergo transformational change into a completely new system, functionally dissimilar to the previous system. Hooker (no date) notes that it is important to distinguish between cyclical systemic change, where a system's resilience eventually restores pre-disturbance functions, and this transformational change into a new system that is functionally unlike the old. The former seems to demand sufficient flexibility to roll with the punches and sufficient unallocated resources to tough out the lean times until 'normal' functioning is resumed. The latter requires behavioural adaptation and redesign to innovatively obtain core valued outcomes from a new system with new normal behaviour. One example of pressure for a 'new' system is the introduction of Landcare stewardship principles into a production-oriented farming or forestry system.

There are implications here for avoiding those traps where institutional structures become rigid, and efficiencies and comfortable familiarities militate against flexibility, innovation and learning. Ison (Chapter 2, p26) notes that 'Traditions in a culture embed what has been judged to be useful practice. The risk for any culture is that a tradition can become a blind spot when it evolves into practice that lacks any avenue for critical reflection.' Ways of thinking and acting that were successful in past circumstances will not necessarily prove useful in tackling issues emerging from novel situations. So we must retain the flexibility to question underlying assumptions, values and thought processes typical of double- or triple-loop learning, as discussed in Chapter 1.

It remains an open question whether Holling and Gunderson have articulated a pattern of change common to all complex adaptive systems – and they themselves stress they are not suggesting a 'rigid predetermined path and trajectory' (2002, p51). What they do reveal is a general relationship between material and energy flows and the structure those flows support, and the effect this tends to have on system resilience. The notion that surprise and collapse are endemic to change processes in complex systems directly challenges traditions of management that assume certainty and constancy.

Instead of a search for certainty, we must foster traditions that recognize and accommodate the system behaviour and are informed by experiential learning and decision making. This can be supported by active monitoring of, and feedback from, the effects and outcomes of decisions (Jiggins and Röling, 2002). In all cases, managers will need to acknowledge that change, collapse or decay leading to reorganization is not a system aberration or the result of a failure of management, but an inevitable feature of living in this world. Nonetheless, it may be within human capacity to strategically manage a biophysical system's release phases to reduce their catastrophic effects. Further, humans can build cultural structures that see the impact of a system's change phase shared or amortized among members, rather than resting solely on those immediately affected.

As the following case study illustrates, we inherit the full consequence of previous system intervention, and of course bequeath the outcomes of the changes we make to those who come after us. We never act in the full knowledge of the consequences of our action – even if we did, the value sets of our day would influence whether we would change our actions in the light of that knowledge. However, a systems orientation encourages critical reflection on what is done and why, what structure is being maintained and in whose interest, and what parts or properties of the system are being valued or ignored in decision making processes.

Social learning in a complex human and biophysical system

In the lower Macleay River catchment on the mid-north coast of NSW, sustainable natural resource management is the focus for policy-makers, landholders and the broader community. In common with many coastal catchments of NSW and Queensland, the lower Macleay River catchment is characterized by two major environmental issues: flooding and acid sulphate soils. These issues exist against a background of pastoral and agricultural development that has included clearing forests and woodlands and draining wetlands to optimize the availability and productivity of fertile, low-lying areas. As such, stakeholders and the ecosystem provide a case study to illustrate a number of the processes discussed earlier, with sometimes incommensurate aspirations between a number of stakeholders and their relationship to, and influence on, the dynamics of change in the underlying biophysical ecosystem.

As discussed in the next section, flooding and acid sulphate soils are natural outcomes of the region's biophysical history. At present they are exacerbated by land management practices. The social learning process to adapt practices to this reality represents a complex interplay of localized and broader social and environmental processes. Significant time scales and stakeholders range from immediate daily pressures on decision making (by the community, local and state government), through to the historic role of state government policy, market processes and the long-term sustainability of the primarily natural resource-based local economy. Conceptually, it is helpful to consider the biophysical and social aspects of the study separately as mutually influencing 'coupled systems', while acknowledging that they are but components of a single systemic whole. We conclude with an integrated discussion of the natural and social system framing the social learning process occurring in the lower Macleay River catchment.

The natural system and human adaptations to date

Flooding in the lower Macleay River catchment is a response to a number of factors expressed at a whole-of-catchment scale, including:

- climate variability
- high drainage density
- a steep gradient associated with the escarpment in the upper catchment
- a funnel-shaped catchment narrowing in a down-catchment direction, with the bottleneck just upstream of the town of Kempsey.

As a result of these factors, significant rainfall events in the upper catchment of the Macleay River can result in large volumes of high-velocity stream flow to the lower catchment. Consequently, frequent flooding is a characteristic of the lower catchment. As a response to severe floods in 1949 and 1950, flood mitigation works, including the installation of levees, artificial drains, causeways and floodgates, were carried out to protect low-lying flood-prone land.

During minor to moderate floods, these flood mitigation measures retain floodwaters within the main channels below major floodgates in order to protect Kempsey and surrounding farmland. However, in severe floods, when the levees are at risk of being breached, the floodgates are opened to release pressure from the system (and hence protect Kempsey), and the low-lying areas are inundated. The presence of drains allows for rapid drainage of these areas during both floods and seasonally wet periods. This management strategy, effected over several decades, fits Holling and Gunderson's (2002) description of developing 'engineering resilience' to maintain efficiency of function during flooding.

However, the lower Macleay River catchment is also the site of extensive acid sulphate soils. These naturally occurring, highly organic soils have developed under a set of specific conditions associated with sea level change, the precipitation of hydrogen sulphides from seawater, and bacteriological activity in the presence of a high organic content. Acid sulphate soils are not problematic until they are disturbed through the construction of artificial drains, farming practices or urban/peri-urban development. When this occurs, the soils are oxidized and a series of chemical reactions produce sulphuric acid and precipitation of heavy and trace metals, including arsenic, iron, aluminium and cadmium.

During dry periods and/or when soils have been drained artificially, the acid and metals accumulate in the soil. Rainfall then mobilizes these compounds within the soil matrix, and ultimately delivers them to artificial drains and streams when soils become saturated. As a consequence, water quality in waterways can be characterized by low pH, low dissolved oxygen and toxic levels of heavy and trace metals. Detrimental impacts of this poor water quality include damage to metal and concrete infrastructure, and increased morbidity and mortality of aquatic biota. Acid sulphate soils are a major environmental hazard to oyster and other aquaculture industries.

Local resistance to the recent introduction of State Environment Planning Policy 14, which includes highly prescriptive but scientifically supported changes to land management practices, can be partly understood in relation to the following considerations. Firstly, the impact of top-down (or 'exogenous' in systems terms) decision making about flood mitigation in the past has led landowners to be sceptical of the value of these changes. Lacking trust in the science and wisdom behind the policy, landowners are now drawing on their knowledge of past events in a locally rational response to imposed costs in the face of uncertainty. Clearly, management systems for flood mitigation and acid sulphate soils do not match. Drying out and draining flood-prone areas provide ideal conditions for oxidation of acid sulphate soils.

Secondly, the values and concerns motivating action in each management system vary among different groups of stakeholders, adding another layer of complexity through potential and actual conflict. Landholders who have complied with requirements for flood mitigation over the years are now faced with new knowledge and requirements for revised land use and management practices. A willingness to comply can vary according to the risks imposed on specific landholders, and their understanding of the issues and associated consequences. A mismatch between understanding, knowledge, economic costs and levels of trust means that conflict can occur between stakeholders at individual, group and intergenerational scales, illustrating the importance of the social learning principle of negotiation and collaboration.

These key stakeholders include the land managers who, to varying extents within this group, could potentially reduce the impacts of acid sulphate soil discharges by modifying their practices, frequently at their own cost. The local community and their local council representatives have a stake because of their economic and social links with local industry, such as aquaculture and fishing businesses, and tourism. Any of the members of stakeholder groups can hold different values and understandings about how their practices affect land and water quality, and the wellbeing of other groups. Further, members of one stakeholder group are likely to hold different values and understandings about the practices of members of other groups.

For instance, a 1999 NSW Department of Agriculture survey (Woodhead, 1999) in which 90 per cent of respondents were farming on acid sulphate soils indicated that:

- only half of the farmers were aware they had acid sulphate soils on their property
- 43 per cent knew the pH of their soils
- 20 per cent knew the pH of their water
- most significantly, only 20 per cent indicated that they needed help in managing acid sulphate soils.

According to the survey, most information on acid sulphate soils was sought from industry bodies, rather than from state regulatory bodies (such as the Department of Land and Water Conservation, Environment Protection Authority and National Parks and Wildlife Service). Government help was wanted, however, to communicate 'correct' information to the media from 'well-informed and balanced consultative groups', and to develop workable policies that do not hinder farmers' ability to make money. Clearly, the rationality of different stances needs to be negotiated before integration and synthesis can occur.

A systems perspective encourages us to recognize the ways humans deal with uncertainty. This means attempting to understand the roles of free will, the perception of context and mutual constraints acting to create particular stable states in the system. Without downplaying the considerable challenge of this task, considering the interpretations of the system by the people involved is a good starting point. Research has found that people's perception of context and their actual capacity to act are fundamentally based in the 'now' and the 'local', and this determines the broader history and context (Kaufman, 2002).

Managing issues in the future and global dimensions requires management to be personally sustainable in the daily dimension. This suggests that, regardless of the broader benefits of change, if the behaviour is not sustainable in a person's daily life they are not likely to change it (Kaufman, 2002). Thus a necessary if not sufficient aspect of social learning for improved environmental management requires successfully linking personal and community behaviour with outcomes at broader scales. Awareness of this issue is also useful because human experience is a valuable heuristic in analysing 'position' within complex human–biophysical systems, although research methods for incorporating that experience into analysis, planning and practice are outside the scope of this chapter.

The social system – a social learning work-in-progress

The complement to linking different 'traditions of understanding' (Ison, Chapter 2), 'codes of rationality' (Kaufman, 2002) and 'knowledge cultures' (Brown and Pitcher, Chapter 8) is to identify and develop our own understanding of broader, non-experiential scales of interaction. It is clear that adapting to the major biophysical issues facing managers and landholders in the lower Macleay River catchment must be underpinned by processes of social learning. Within this context, communities need to align current knowledge of trends, processes and responses in order to establish good, long-term environmental management practices and, simultaneously, distribute the costs and benefits of change to make it personally viable to stakeholders. Using Holling and Gunderson's (2002) model to map biophysical and management processes in the lower Macleay River catchment suggests a simple phased sequence describing the current natural and anthropogenic systems (see Table 3.1 and Figure 3.1).

Assessment of quantitative and qualitative data indicates that these phases vary in both temporal and spatial scales, and in rate of response. Cycles of discharge can involve time steps that are linked to climate and/or tidal phases and therefore expressed hourly or daily (high-intensity, short-duration convective storm or tidal effects), weekly (low-intensity, long-duration frontal storm event), monthly (tidal effects or major flood event), seasonal, or long term (El Niño Southern Oscillation). Discharge can also occur across the whole catchment or at subcatchment, farm, paddock or smaller scales. Consequently, some phases would be contemporaneous, or at least overlapping. In this sense, a sequential phase change would not be a simple, single set of processes and responses but a nested, multi-series operating at different temporal and spatial scales. This variability of scale and process, with its associated variation in the risk exposure and the direct experiences of different stakeholders, presents a challenge for finding the necessary common ground to start negotiations and forge learning collaborations.

Table 3.1 *Transition phases in the natural and anthropogenic systems*

Phase	Natural process	Anthropogenic process
Exploitation	Formation of new coastal landscapes and associated ecosystems in response to climate and sea level changes	Clearing of timber, reclamation of wetlands, establishment of dairying industries, construction of flood mitigation works
Conservation	In low-lying areas, accumulation of sediments, sulphides, anaerobic bacteria and organic matter in soil matrix	Greater accumulation of sulphuric acid and organic matter in soil matrix, establishment of pasture grass species
Release	Mobilization of acid and heavy/trace metals into natural drainage system in response to large rainfall events after drought	Increased spatial and temporal mobilization of acid and heavy/trace metals into natural and artificial drainage network – in response to climatic and land use/management factors
Reorganization	Adaptation by some biota, changes in species composition and diversity	Adaptation by some biota (for example amphibia species), colonization of drainage network by tolerant, often exotic, plant and animal species

In addition to the biophysical processes occurring in the landscape, social and economic frameworks must be considered. In the lower Macleay River catchment, acid discharges and associated metallic plumes and/or deoxygenated water cause lost productivity in local industries (pasture, dairying, aquaculture, recreational fisheries and tourism). This may be episodic in relation to specific events, or long term. In February and March 2001, for example, a major fish kill occurred in the major tributaries of the Macleay River (Belmore River and Kinchela Creek), prompting closure of the lower Macleay River to fishing for approximately nine months. Local recreational and commercial fishing licences were cancelled, and commercial fishers had to move down the coast in an attempt to remain financially viable. This had profound impacts on the local economy. By contrast, long-term impacts are expressed through expansion of scalded areas where the ground surface remains unvegetated, and the persistence of poor water quality from acid sulphate soil 'hotspots'. These impacts have onsite costs to landholders in terms of farm productivity, and offsite costs to other commercial, industrial and environmental interests.

Decision makers and many landholders respond to these impacts by developing strategies that decrease acid discharge or mitigate its effects. Where this occurs and impacts are reduced, the process of adaptive change does not follow the Holling and Gunderson model (see Figure 3.1). The reorganization phase is not followed by exploitation, but is expanded to include a raft of changed practices that, if successful, will lead to a conservation phase, and evolving release and reorganization phases (Table 3.2).

Table 3.2 *Adapting land management to the biophysical reality*

Phase	Process
Phase 1	
Exploitation	Clearing of timber, reclamation of wetlands, establishment of dairying industries, construction of flood mitigation works
Conservation	Accumulation of oxidation by-products and organic matter in soil matrix, establishment of pasture grass species
Release	Mobilization of acid and heavy/trace metals into drainage network
Reorganization	Adaptation by some biota (for example amphibia species) Colonization of drainage network by tolerant, often exotic, plant and animal species
	Rehabilitation of wetlands through changed land tenure or land use requirements (instigated through State Environment Planning Policy 14)
	Manipulation of floodgates to introduce brackish tidal inflow to artificial drains, or to inundate pasture (salt water acts as a buffer and increases water pH)
	Opening or removal of floodgates to flush wetlands with fresh water (for example Yarrahappinni Wetlands)
	Use of mulches or liming to optimize revegetation of surface scalds
	Manipulation of groundwater levels to minimize oxidation of sulphides in soil matrix
	Design of engineering infrastructure to account for flood recession patterns, and acid sulphate soil distribution
Phase 2	
Conservation	Accumulation of aquatic biota in drainage system and pasture grasses in agricultural/pastoral zones, and increased biodiversity (as fauna and flora) in wetlands/wooded areas
	Reduced rates of accumulation of oxidation by-products in soil matrix
Release	(Decreased) mobilization of acid and heavy/trace metals into drainage network
Reorganization	Ongoing development of research and development in relation to acid sulphate soils and flood mitigation
	Ongoing development of education and communication strategies to optimize uptake of new knowledge and generate or build trust

Importantly, social learning is embedded in this process as:

- evolving technical and scientific knowledge to develop and implement new management practices
- ongoing communication of new knowledge to a broad range of stakeholders
- the challenges these present to negotiation from and across differing knowledge backgrounds and the subsequent synthesis of common purpose.

Whatever the mechanism, in this highly complex system the implementation of new practices arising from new knowledge will be possible only at a community scale. In the lower Macleay River catchment this means that stakeholders must appreciate:

- the value of rehabilitation and mitigation at both local and regional scales
- the connectivity between farm practices and land quality, onsite and offsite water quality and biodiversity
- that both flooding and acid sulphate soils have short-, medium- and long-term impacts that will have implications for current and future generations.

Clearly, there are challenges to facilitate participation and engagement across these scales and between the wide range of affected stakeholders, but effective social learning for improved outcomes is likely to be impaired if successful partnerships cannot be forged.

Communication of information relevant to these points is being increasingly addressed by researchers, state agencies, local government, local action groups and the broader community. However, a number of factors in the lower Macleay River catchment have created a dichotomy, providing the basis for acrimonious conflict and social disharmony. Some landholders will not engage in the process of reorganization and development of new knowledge. They tend to be older members of the farming community who feel threatened by a history of top-down decision making and regard current attempts to develop complex management strategies as a threat to their autonomy.

Other landholders, often representing younger generations, are more accepting of the new knowledge and engage more actively in processes of change. Although this generational contrast is not exclusive, its definition is clear enough to be recognized as an example of powerful intergenerational conflict (pers comm, Henderson, 2002). For as long as this endures, the necessary steps of combining individual perspectives of the system of interest into some common agreed system, boundary and characteristic behaviour is likely to remain stalled.

Coherent purposeful action to better handle system behaviour is essentially impossible while individuals and groups identify and relate to a plurality of incommensurable system constructs. For social learning to occur, there will have to be some means of resolving this conflict, or of building a shared commitment despite it. It is not clear yet, within the timeframes in which changes are occurring, whether the outcomes of research and management are providing positive or negative feedback loops to these community groups. It may be that the type of feedback will determine whether a system will revert to an exploitation phase or continue with reorganization and conservation. With this in mind, processes of adaptive management (see Figure 3.1) may include different components of a community simultaneously practising both a simple, sequential phase model (see Table 3.1), and a nested, multi-phase model (see Table 3.2). The relative power of each group to constrain, or provide impetus to, processes of change will affect system development and evolution.

Holling and Gunderson (see Figure 3.1) establish a model of cyclical adaptive change that suggests a linearity and two dimensionality that the lower Macleay River catchment case study challenges. In this case, given the need to integrate the biophysical and socioeconomic components of a complex system, the case study represents a multidimensional, multi-responsive and multiphase system.

Conclusions

This chapter concludes by picking up on some of the guidelines for reflection given in Chapter 1, as the purpose of concluding statements is to reflect upon what has been learned. The questions asked there were:

1   What are the social learning processes embedded in current environmental management policies and programmes, and how do they relate to different ways of knowing and engaging?

Approaching the problem from a completely top-down perspective, no matter how well resourced and informed by science and broader regional policy imperatives, fundamentally misses the opportunity and need to engage with the knowledge and behaviour of the humans intimately embedded in the system of concern. Conversely, limiting our engagement to a particular position within the system is likely to neglect significant social, economic and biophysical sustainability issues acting at non-experiential scales. It is also likely to fail to deliver necessary resources for the people involved to act.

2   How can environmental management approaches facilitate the creation of learning opportunities that bridge different disciplines, subgroups within society and levels of governance?

Somewhere between top-down and bottom-up processes, genuine social learning takes place. We have illustrated that there are multiple significant biophysical scales with which human activity interacts, and that, simultaneously, there are multiple interacting scales of social structure rationalizing, resourcing and influencing that activity. A systems orientation has been shown to be a particularly useful way to consider three disparate issues within a common framework. The lower Macleay River catchment case study and others in this book suggest that governance of the environmental and social components of our world systems, and the crucial interrelations between the two, are largely unconscious. By linking communities, resources and knowledge occupying different positions in the human–biophysical system, we can attempt to expand the conscious action of given positions into a 'messy' (meaning not necessarily rationally organized), interactive network of feedback, knowledge, resources and motivations towards a sustainable future. This means scientifically informed community practice as much as it means community science and grass-roots policy. It requires a true community of common interest to come into being, not a flailing around of conflicting and/or insulated stakeholder groups. Negotiation towards commonly identified systems of interest is a crucial step towards forging that common purpose.

3   Do our present dialogues, negotiations and participation processes enable a wide variety of social learning opportunities in environmental management?

As has been discussed in this chapter, many stakeholders can become trapped within their own traditions of understanding, from which perspectives they each construct their concept of 'the system'. This process of constructing systems involves the subjective selection of the system's boundaries and the attributes of perceived key components of the system, from which the behaviour of concern emerges. As a consequence, different stakeholders typically identify very different processes and outcomes as being 'of value' or being 'problematic' and propose different intervention measures as desirable. Because present environmental management strategies fail to consider how different stakeholders define what is assumed to be commonly understood, the necessary cooperation and agreement is frequently missing. As this chapter discusses, time and effort is essential to find sufficient agreement about the boundaries, processes and fundamental behaviour of the system. As mentioned above, this process requires negotiation and dialogue to identify and accommodate inevitable disagreements. Only then can the process of social learning be initiated.

4   How is our ability to act and adapt environmental management processes affected by social structures and relationships?

By focusing on informing and educating rather than engaging and transforming, current dialogue, negotiation and participation processes in the lower Macleay River catchment can only partially facilitate social learning. Some stakeholders involved may be in a position to internalize new knowledge into their practices, and may even choose to do so if exposed to it. However, the majority of land managers, for instance, are neither informed nor concerned about their acid sulphate soils problem. A perception of common resources and common risk – that is, identification of a common system of interest – is necessary if development activities in the region are to be designed and enacted through cautious adaptive management. Consequently, without participatory knowledge and resource sharing, little is likely to change.

5   Are our processes of reflection and learning in environmental management fragmented because they are focused on events or crises, rather than on more subtle patterns of change over time and space?

This case study offers an interesting clarification of that question. Arguably, the shift from flood management to managing floods and acid sulphate soils illustrates adaptation over time to environmental processes operating at the catchment-wide scale. However, simultaneously, while biophysical understanding has improved, it would appear that reflection and learning have not progressed beyond acknowledging the connection between land management practices and environmental outcomes. There is no evidence of an appreciation of the situated validity of land managers' choices in behaving the way they are, and in refusing to change. This is a fragmentation of understanding and empathy, not of time and space, for all that this is a spatially and temporally distributed problem. In this sense, reflection and learning for sustainable development are fragmented, not only because of a focus on individual events and crises, which we have been calling goals, but because of a failure to recognize that the maladaptive behaviour at hand is in fact itself a response to patterns of change in social and biophysical domains over time and space, that is, processes. The shift in focus from management directed towards goals to management conceived of as a process of ongoing problem handling has been discussed.

This chapter has shown that the perspective of complex adaptive systems thinking can and does provide valuable insights into the process of social learning as a form of adaptive change. Systems thinking can help understand the high-order system characteristics, such as terms like 'sustainability', as an emergent property of coupled human and environmental systems. In so doing, it helps to highlight the dynamics of change in ecosystems, noting that different stakeholders value differing and often conflicting variables, and that such variables operate across multiple scales and with undefined boundaries. Despite this complexity, a systems perspective offers a unifying structure that makes this complex interrelationship comprehensible. It enables various information and knowledge sources to be brought together to produce a greater understanding of key processes of change in the complex whole than would be possible from any partial perspective.

Acknowledgements

The understanding of systems thinking presented in this chapter owes much to ongoing conversations and contributions from Dr Barry Newell, The Australian National University.

References

Checkland, P. B. (1985) 'From optimizing to learning: A development of systems thinking for the 1990s', *The Journal of the Operational Research Society*, vol 36, no 9, pp757–767

Checkland, P. B. (2000) 'Soft systems methodology: A thirty year retrospective', *Systems Research and Behavioural Science*, vol 17, S11–S58

Grimm, V. and Wissel, C. (1997) 'Babel, or the ecological stability discussions: An inventory and analysis of terminology and a guide for avoiding confusion', *Oecologia*, vol 109, no 3, pp323–334

Holling, C. S. and Gunderson, L. H. (2002) 'Resilience and adaptive cycles' in Holling, C. S. and Gunderson, L. H. (eds) *Panarchy: Understanding Transformations in Human and Natural Systems*, Island Press, Washington, DC

Hooker, C. (no date) 'Introducing three basic concepts: System efficiency, resiliency, adaptability – their nature and roles in sustainable development', Understanding and Issues for Industry, An Occasional Series of Brief Papers to Design and Explain Key Ideas and Provoke Dialogue, Paper 1, Cooperative Research Centre for Coal in Sustainable Development, University of Newcastle, UK

Ison, R., Armson, R. and Stowell, F. (2001) 'The system revisited: System practices for managing complexity', *Systemist*, vol 23, pp29–54

Ison, R., Maiteny, P. and Carr, S. (1997) 'Systems methodology for sustainable natural resource management', *Agricultural Systems*, vol 55, no 2, pp257–272

Jiggins, J. and Röling, N. (2002) 'Adaptive management: Potential and limitations for ecological governance of forests in a context of normative pluriformity', in Oglethorpe, J. (ed) *Adaptive Management: From Theory to Practice*, International Union for the Conservation of Nature, Cambridge

Kaufman, S. (2002) 'Driving motivations: Social capital and the cultural basis of agency in carpooling at The Australian National University', honours thesis, School of Resources, Environment and Society, The Australian National University, Canberra

Midgley, G. (2000) *Systemic Intervention: Philosophy, Intervention and Practice*, Kluwer Academic, New York

Newell, B. and Wasson, R. (2002) 'Social system vs solar system: Why policy makers need history', in Castelein, S. and Otte, A. (eds) *Conflict and Cooperation Related to International Water Resources: Historical Perspectives*, UNESCO Document SC.2002/WS/53, UNESCO, Grenoble

Woodhead, A. (1999) *Acid Sulphate Soils: Farming Community Ideas about the Way Forward*, NSW Agriculture and the Acid Sulphate Soils Management Advisory Committee, Sydney

Section 2

Learning Partnerships with Communities

4

Communities' Self-determination: Whose Interests Count?

Jennifer Andrew and Ian Robottom

At a glance

- Dominant views of what constitutes appropriate knowledge reflect the values and interests of people and organizations in positions of power in our society in general, and environmental management in particular
- The centralist organizations that determine the policy and practice of sustainability regard environmental issues as matters of scientific, technological and economic knowledge, through which their power is entrenched
- Knowledge embedded within specific communities, over which centralized organizations have no control or understanding, is often afforded a secondary role
- The nature of how different groups construct their knowledge has significant consequences for how environmental management issues should be understood and addressed
- Governments and other centralized organizations need to recognize the capacity for communities to determine and control their own futures in moving towards sustainability.

Conceptions of knowledge and learning

The history of government environmental policy in Australia through the 1990s and into the 21st century demonstrates that environmental agendas in Australia ignore the differences inherent in different social contexts. They thus ignore the significant contribution, documented by Ison (Chapter 2) and by

Dyball, Beavis and Kaufman (Chapter 3), that different settings and different constructions of knowledge bring to environmental management practices. A key example is the popularity of ideas such as 'best practice', which assume that best practice, as formulated through a centralist organization such as government or industry, is compatible with all circumstances, regardless of different contexts. Such ideas are based on a belief that knowledge is not value-laden and humanly constructed, and that it can be centrally determined and controlled. They see 'effective' outcomes as being achieved through technocratic processes (underpinned by scientific knowledge), guided predominantly by scientific rather than philosophical or ethical questions.

This conception of knowledge allows for an approach to learning and capacity building that presumes a central agency knows which actions are best for the common good, and are equally desired by all, independent of culture, gender, religion and other differences among people and among or within communities. Knowledge is viewed as having one legitimate, dominant explanation. Learning lies in adopting this knowledge, with success being demonstrated through behavioural change.

A mass of policy documents and extension materials support the conclusion that governments and other organizations view learning, education and capacity building as ways of shaping the behaviour of others. Consider the following extract from *Biodiversity Conservation Research: Australia's Priorities* (ANZECC and Biological Diversity Advisory Committee, 2001, p62):

> *[The aim is to] Develop scientifically-based educational material to convey our knowledge of species, ecological communities, biophysical processes, habitats, ecosystem services, the effects of human activities, the value of biodiversity and the effects of making different natural resource management decisions... Make these materials and tools available in forms suitable for use by land holders and managers, industry, catchment and marine area management authorities, government at all levels, the community, and writers and teachers of curricula for the sciences, social sciences and economics.*

This statement clearly demonstrates a generalizable, scientific view that sees knowledge as centrally derived and determined. Further, it is assumed to be applicable to all contexts, regardless of the social, cultural and geographical arrangements associated with local settings in which the knowledge is to be used. The statement also separates the act of generating knowledge from the sectors that will potentially use it, and assumes the knowledge will be digestible to specific audiences as long as it is packaged appropriately.

The term 'capacity building' has gained considerable currency in many environmental programmes and policies of late and is used in association with learning opportunities. Yet despite the popularity of the term, there are still problems with its usefulness as the source of a platform for learning. An immediate issue that comes to mind is: Who determines the agenda of capacity building? Is it self-determined by people who have decided they need further understanding to tackle a local environmental issue, or has it been determined for them by others? Examples of expressions of capacity building demonstrate that it is seen as a form of information transfer. It is also seen as an instrument for achieving particular goals set by organizations that deem what information is appropriate and whose capacity should be built through adopting that information. Through this conception, is it scientific, technocratic and economic information and knowledge that is deemed to be fundamental to resolving environmental issues?

A scan of current government and organizational policy demonstrates that it is this generalizable, context-free knowledge that is valued as being relevant to environmental improvement. For example, consider the following extract from the Rivercare programme of the Framework for the Extension of the Natural Heritage Trust, a major programme directing Australia's natural resource management and sustainability efforts:

> *Rivercare, in conjunction with all other Trust programmes, will contribute to the following Trust priorities:*
>
> – *to provide land-holders, community groups and other natural resource managers with understanding and skills to contribute to biodiversity conservation and sustainable natural resource management... (Commonwealth Government, 2002).*

The view espoused here tends to assume that landholders, community groups and other natural resource managers need to build their understanding and skills through Natural Heritage Trust programmes. It is taken for granted that they require guidance in biodiversity conservation and sustainable natural resource management and that this guidance, as described through the trust's goals, is appropriate to their context. Context-dependent knowledge is afforded very little status or is considered secondary to the generalizable knowledge that supports government and other centralized views of capacity building – precisely because it is specific to a particular context and is not generalizable. Yet, as the case studies in this chapter attest, resolving environmental issues is as much about knowing the context as it is about applying discipline-based, generalizable knowledge.

If contextual knowledge is seen as paramount to resolving localized environmental issues, centralized organizations that invest considerable tax dollars into generalizable knowledge-based 'solutions' (such as scientific, technocratic and economic learning) should rethink their focus. They should invest in localized solutions directed by and for those people whose practices are most affected by environmental change. Additionally, if environmental issues are seen as existing within different social and cultural contexts, surely they would be advanced by centralized organizations gaining a greater understanding of the context of a particular environmental issue, and debating the issue within that context with those most affected.

Scientific, technical and economic aspects of land management form only one part of a more comprehensive process undertaken by land managers.

Within real contexts, land management involves a complex process where social, cultural, political, geographical and historical aspects of the setting play some part in establishing what best practice might be within a specific context. However, generalizable aspects appear to take precedence over context-dependent ones. Most current reporting of environmental programmes aimed at achieving the sustainable management of natural resources or ecosystem recovery, such as the Australian Natural Heritage Trust, clearly demonstrates this. So what is documented tends not to provide a complete picture of what has taken place within real situations.

Consider the following extract from a story written by a farmer, John Weatherstone, about his property, Lyndfield Park (2003, pp6–8):

> *Despite having tapped into the best advice available during the 1960s, 70s, and early 80s, we were starting to see evidence of some deep seated environmental problems beginning to emerge. Prior to the drought, however, these problems were either unrecognized or ignored ... at that time the whole focus of scientific research and government policy was production oriented. The word 'sustainable', if it was used at all, was only used in an economic context...Traditional farming practices were placing large stresses on the land, and limiting its ability to cope with environmental stresses such as drought. We wanted to reduce the pressure we were placing on the land so that it would become more resilient to stress, while at the same time caring more for the assets of the farm upon which our enterprises were based: the soil, the nutrients it contained, the vegetation that held it in place and the native life that was part of its natural cycle.*

Clearly, there is a conflict between how the farmer and the government conceptualize the issues of sustainability, and thus between the type of information, learning and behavioural change that each views as necessary. The farmer's conceptualization is strongly based on his own experiences and belief system, which are paramount to the practices he ultimately sees as helping to resolve his land management issues. This example also demonstrates the contested nature between the different conceptualizations of land management and resolution of land use issues.

The plethora of environmental development projects being conducted through programmes such as the Natural Heritage Trust acknowledges the need for local participation in environmental change. Yet government processes determining the direction of that change and the theory underpinning the advocated practices are set in advance. In the case of the Natural Heritage Trust, funding is negotiated at the state and Commonwealth level. This not only politicizes the process but also negates the ability of local groups to determine their own futures. The following 1996 interview response from a South Australian farmer involved in a vertebrate pest management programme funded by the Commonwealth Government demonstrates this power differential, as well as the difference in conceptualizing how to resolve issues:

'I don't blame the politicians. They come out with a view that comes from a very strong scientific/technocratic view of the world. They put that view to a meeting of farmers believing their position is right; while they might just be talking about an aspect of farming.'

As illustrated by the five strands of social learning (see Chapter 1), negotiation and collaboration are integral to social learning for social change, leading towards improved environmental management practices. This is particularly so where they are used to redress the over-representation of more powerful sectors in theorizing about environmental and sustainability policy. Yet the negotiation and collaboration apparent in most government-based programmes, such as the Natural Heritage Trust, tend to occur at the governmental level where policy (theory) is devised for land managers (practitioners). This means that what is deemed legitimate practice is considered to be so because it matches the theories of the people (and their institutions) who created it. It may not necessarily coincide with the theories of land managers in specific contexts.

An alternative can be found in the principles of action research. An important underlying principle of action research is that practices are shaped, guided and constrained by the theories of practitioners themselves, and of others who are part of the organizational arrangements and relationships within which the practitioners work. This means that environmental issues or problems are viewed within the context in which they take place, and environmental improvement is seen as social, rather than solely or even mainly scientific, in nature.

So how should we respond to these issues? The case studies to follow shed light on some processes and ways forward for environmental improvement and learning.

Characteristics of environmental/ sustainability issues

We all relate to the environment (however we construct it) in certain ways. Therefore we are all affected by changes to our environment. Proposals for changing the environment are nearly always met with differences of opinions about if and how the environment we relate to ought to be changed. These differences of opinion result in an environmental issue of some kind. The educative exploration of such environmental issues is an important part of social learning, aimed at an improved understanding of our relationships with the environment.

Initiatives and interactions, such as those reported in the following case studies (Boxes 4.1 and 4.2), show that the environmental and sustainability issues are complex and contextual, contentious and difficult, and politically and socially constructed.

Box 4.1 Cooperation and Development in Sparsely Populated Areas (CADISPA)

The CADISPA project is based in the Department of Community Education in the Faculty of Education at the University of Strathclyde in Glasgow, UK. The project is currently coordinated by Geoff Fagan of the Department of Community Education.

The project is distinctive in its interest in sustainability and participatory process. According to a recent brochure (December, 2001), the CADISPA project is concerned with developing a definition of sustainability that will help local people and the economic community. The emphasis on sustainability and localness is clear:

> For CADISPA, all economic and social regeneration must stem from within a framework of sustainable economic, environmental and social factors.
>
> CADISPA builds social capital by non-formal education, active engagement and local decision making.
>
> CADISPA uses standard community development techniques to enable people in individual communities to own, understand and act upon their own preferred sustainable agenda (CADISPA, 2001).

The aim behind the CADISPA model is to help local people identify their development needs and support them to pursue their collective agenda and form partnerships with economic development agencies and local authorities (Hampson and Fagan, 1997).

CADISPA builds rural partnership groups by seeking agreed entry into local communities and always working with existing community groups, then publishing with them a development agenda for their locality. It starts with local people and their vision of the future – gradually building the picture and extending the consultation and partnership base until each feels confident with the potential development and its appropriateness, extent, cost and cultural ambience (Hampson and Fagan, 1997).

At its simplest then, CADISPA seeks to help local people make their community more sustainable. This help should not intervene in the control of local people who, according to Mohan and Stokke (2000), are pivotal to the identification and prioritization of their own agenda.

CADISPA staff adopt a facilitation role. They identify project opportunities; establish links among community groups and support agencies and funding bodies of various kinds; set up articles of association and companies limited by guarantee to provide a measure of legal protection to the community groups; and supply a positive and supportive spirit to the work of projects that are always complex and often problematic. CADISPA staff attend many community group planning meetings, though their role is generally low-key and responsive rather than highly visible and directive. Through the capacity building support of CADISPA, community groups are encouraged to 'make a statement' that is sustainable and lasting. This is often in the form of a community edifice of some kind that, owing to its bricks and mortar characteristics, has both immediate functional and lasting iconic value in communities. The CADISPA project team works with communities in developing a series of case study reports. These reports describe the natural and social history of a community, its current structure, and social, economic and environmental issues. There is an iterative process by which these case study reports are fed back to community committees.

This process is briefly exemplified by one of the development projects supported by CADISPA on Easdale Island off the west coast of Scotland. The most immediate development on Easdale Island is the refurbishment and expansion of the derelict drill hall of significance to the community. The trust has succeeded in winning a major grant (UK£700,000) to carry out the capital improvements and employ a manager for two years. Part of the funding agreement is that the operations of the hall are for the benefit of island residents (not, for example, for tourism in the first instance). Yet if the hall is to succeed in generating enough revenue to be economically sustainable in the middle to long term, it must also be available for renting out to off-island groups on a commercial footing. An issue is that should the hall succeed in generating needed revenue by attracting external visitors, there is the potential that the very qualities (isolation; sparse population; peace and quiet...) that attracted residents to the island in the first place will be threatened. In short, steps to ensure economic sustainability have the potential to threaten environmental and social sustainability. This is a concrete expression of the so-called essential tension of sustainability, and in a sense illustrates its self-contradictory nature.

These issues are not matters of transferable knowledge and skills. Rather, they take place within complex contexts that are likely to have multiple levels of governance seeking to control how an issue is resolved. For example, at one CADISPA site where the community is attempting to redevelop its community hall there are four bodies involved in governance: the village hall trustees (the leaseholders of the hall); the village hall committee (responsible for day-to-day operations of the hall); the village community company; and the community council. Even an issue as seemingly straightforward as vertebrate pest management (see Box 4.2) can involve the federal government as the funding agency, the state government and its agricultural extension officers and local landholders.

Another layer of complexity involves the multiple stakeholders in the community. Each has an individual vision and interest in the issue, and there is generally only partial agreement on a common vision for resolving the issue.

For example, the CADISPA case study shows that, in addition to the bodies formally involved in governance, individual residents, casual tourists, local and regional government bodies and funding agencies have some 'stake' in the outcome. In the Southwest Queensland example (see Box 4.2) there were also multiple stakeholders who had to negotiate the learning agenda, including researchers and local landholders.

These complex social systems, with their accompanying social structures and relationships, require serious negotiation among environmental, social, cultural, commercial and political interests. This negotiation can take years, for example, as in the experience of some of the CADISPA initiatives. The Southwest Queensland example, with its history of disquiet between government and landholders, also required serious and long-term negotiation to examine and expose interests. In this case, a cyclical learning process between the researchers and landholders helped to establish which understandings were common to the two groups, and which differed. A collaborative and iterative inquiry process was set up to help resolve the different understandings. The data to be collected and the method of collecting the data were negotiated, and the meaning of the results collaboratively considered. Once a common understanding could be established from the first iteration of the learning cycle, further cycles could occur. This joint learning process not only helped to establish common ground on which further learning could occur, it also built trust between the groups, a key component of social learning (see Chapter 5).

As noted in Chapter 1, this negotiation process is not without significant challenges. The two case studies presented in this chapter, and many similar cases, experienced communication problems within planning groups and between these and the governing and/or funding agencies. This was clearly an issue for landholders in Southwest Queensland, where differences in knowledge, values and experiences were accentuated by the distances between properties, forming a multifaceted communication barrier for land-holders. When learning communities are divided by space, the rapid flow of information and sharing of knowledge across diverse groups are hindered. This potentially slows down the learning process, unless these barriers can be overcome. In today's communication age, the options are blossoming, for example e-discussion groups, video- and teleconferencing, newsletters, and so on. However, new technologies still need to be managed and communications carefully facilitated for successful learning to occur. Even within supposedly homogeneous groups, there may be significant communication differences, for example between government staff and extension officers, as briefly highlighted in our second case study.

Owing to the diversity within and among groups it is important that social learning processes allow the expression of differing understandings of the concept of environmental issues and sustainability. These understandings are shaped in part by the educational, political and cultural history of the location and the state. For example, landholders and government agents in the Southwest Queensland case study clearly hold different concepts of

Box 4.2 Achieving social learning through action learning: A case study of feral goat management

Designing programmes and activities that encourage social learning, including integrating different knowledge systems, is a challenge faced by many agricultural extension officers around Australia. An evaluation of several agricultural and natural resource management projects in Southwest Queensland highlighted a number of success stories (Kelly, 2001). Here we report on a project to control feral goats on rural properties as an example of one way to facilitate social learning (Thompson et al, 1999).

This project is characterized by collaboration and ongoing critical inquiry of actual problems as they arise in the project cycle. Graziers, government extension officers and researchers jointly defined problems, allowing the stakeholders' different values and knowledge to emerge early in the process. The research agenda was negotiated through facilitated small group meetings, with graziers and researchers acting as equal partners. At regular project implementation points, key stakeholders critically reviewed the results and considered how they could be best used in practice and in furthering the research agenda. This collaborative planning process reflected the four stages of the action learning cycle – plan, implement, observe and evaluate (see Figure 4.1, and the discussion in Chapter 14 using the terms 'diagnose', 'design', 'do' and 'develop'). Evaluation is used to support critical and self-critical reflection on the results to plan for the next cycle of action (Dick, 1996; Zuber-Skerritt, 1995, 1996). Collaborative planning processes incorporate the philosophy that knowledge is created from concrete experience, common to both experiential learning and action learning. However, it goes further than simply experiential learning. Kolb's (1984) original experiential learning cycle was extended by Revens (1982), who emphasizes that action learning is useful when 'no expected solution' exists and those involved in learning will advocate different courses of action according to their different value systems, past experiences and future plans (King, 2000).

Collaboration is difficult when parties are negative about others' knowledge systems. This was the situation between graziers, researchers and government staff in the feral goat project. Negativity had developed over many years, with distrust between government and landholders. This distrust was also related to the stakeholders' different views of the world in general, and different perceptions and priorities about feral goats in particular (see the similar discussion in Chapter 3). However, in-depth interviews in Southwest Queensland revealed an underlying recognition that both types of knowledge are needed to advance sustainable land and pest management, as government officers from Charleville explained:

'It's offering more alternatives to problems, rather than our thinking that we [government] know the only way; and their thinking they [landholders] know the only way' (state government officer 1, Charleville).

> 'Landholders anchor things in reality I think. You know, we [government] can come up with these ideas on paper ... but [landholders] are there to make sure that there's realism in what we're trying to do' (state government officer 2, Charleville).

Landholders also valued both knowledge systems and understood the benefits of integrating their localized understanding of the landscape with the more generalized scientific knowledge:

> 'We want somebody from outside looking in, we are inside looking out ... local knowledge is used as well as scientific knowledge' (landholder, Group S, Southwest Queensland).

Once there was mutual recognition of the value of different types of knowledge, a process was needed to integrate them. In this case, landholders treated scientific knowledge as a hypothesis, wanting to test out the scientific ideas in their specific context and asking questions such as: 'But will it work in my type of country?' As one landholder said:

> 'I know I would take any research if they do it in a hands-on manner in partnership with someone on their place [with a landholder on their property] ... because somebody has got to make a living on the results' (landholder, Group G, Southwest Queensland).

The process of inquiry that emerged was one of social learning. It was based on a participatory action learning cycle used at a micro-level, such as in meetings, and at a macro-level as a project framework where the cycle was repeated annually (see Figure 4.1).

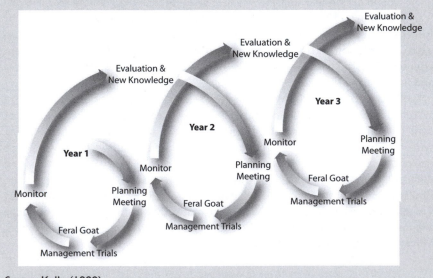

Source: Kelly (1999)

Figure 4.1 *Learning cycles in feral goat management in Queensland*

This process and the facilitation methods encouraged people to be open about their preferences, goals and values. Discussions were predominantly about the content, such as how to build goat yards, mustering techniques and aerial survey methods; but the process and framework for the project were also discussed. Many landholders had a learning agenda and knew what information they wanted to gather; others voiced their preferences about learning styles, including the reluctance to write. Specific methods and frequent negotiations are needed to facilitate groups where people have a variety of goals, learning styles and different value systems. Some of the methods and negotiations undertaken in the feral goat management project are outlined in Table 4.1.

Table 4.1 *Methods and negotiations undertaken in feral goat management project*

Examples of methods and techniques	*Outcomes and evaluation*
Define the problem	Graziers felt their knowledge respected and valued.
Acknowledge different worldviews and develop multiple project goals	Grazier interest and practice change was maintained beyond life of project.
Facilitate semi-structured interviews to define the problem and to elicit goals, values and context. For example, graziers explained their situation and government staff asked questions to clarify	Clear understanding of context by researchers

Limited dominance of scientific discourse over local, experiential and contextual knowledge

High level of enthusiasm, energy and commitment from graziers |
| Small group meetings | High level of ownership by graziers |
| Processes explicit and transparent, with critical questioning and continual negotiation encouraged | High level of trust between everyone

Limited conflict; problems addressed quickly |
| Specialist panel to provide expert scientific information; graziers assisted in developing questions for the panel | Limited dominance of scientific discourse over local, experiential and contextual knowledge |

The outcomes of this project indicate that negotiated learning agendas are possible, though implementation can be difficult. For example, despite attempts to ensure landholder knowledge was valued in the project, landholders themselves sometimes deferred to the scientists and neglected their own experience. The insidious nature of the dominant discourses in society is sometimes difficult to recognize and even more difficult to ensure that all types of knowledge and points of view are adequately represented.

Sources: Dick (1996); Kelly (1999, 2001); King (2000); Kolb (1984); Revens (1982); Thompson et al (1999); Zuber-Skerritt (1995, 1996)

sustainability that are likely to be influenced, at least in part, by their educational, political and cultural histories. Structured negotiation can help to find mutually acceptable processes to define the problem and move forward.

Understandings of 'good' environmental management practices are often tied up with a range of ideas associated with concepts of sustainability and these ideas are also affected by the size of the community. Some communities have very small populations; others are larger, but with little diversity of expertise. This is also exemplified by the Southwest Queensland case study, where landholders tend to share expertise in the same profession – that of grazing in the mulga lands. Issues partnerships can be invaluable in broadening perspectives and deepening the understanding of sustainability. These partnerships need not only be with research or government organizations. Clear benefits have been demonstrated from linking different communities experiencing similar issues to learn collaboratively (see Chapter 7).

However, collaboration inevitably gives rise to contention, as was discussed in Chapter 1. Any issue (environmental or otherwise) consists of differing opinions held by humans. According to the *Macquarie Dictionary* (Dellbridge et al, 1997), an issue is 'a point in question or dispute, as between contending parties in an action at law', and 'a point or matter the decision of which is of special or public importance'. In these definitions, the 'contending parties who dispute the point and who imbue it with special or public importance' are parties of humans. Hence an environmental event (or proposal relating to such an event) becomes an issue only when it is in contention and when people judge that it is important to resolve it. Because issues reside in the debates and arguments among stakeholders, such issues cease to exist when differences are resolved. In other words, issues are only issues as long as people disagree – once people agree, an issue no longer exists. In this sense, environmental issues are entirely human–social constructs that have meaning within particular social, cultural and political contexts; they do not exist independently of human consciousness, and are not something possessing an independent ontological existence (Robottom, 2000, p229).

Sustainability is also a difficult and contentious concept, owing largely to the essential tension inherent in sustainability initiatives – the tension between economic and environmental interests. Sustainability issues share characteristics with other environmental issues in that they are also, by definition, essentially contested. The experiences of each of the initiatives represented earlier in this chapter show that an engagement of environmental issues needs to include consideration and discussion of a range of social, cultural and political concepts such as equity, participatory democracy, and generational and intergenerational human rights. These discussions, debates, arguments and contestations are desirable and should not be considered in any way pathological. They are the means by which a more complex and sophisticated understanding of the respective communities' notion of sustainability is negotiated. The difficult nature of these negotiations is attested by Barkin: 'Sustainability … is about the struggle for diversity in all its dimensions' (2000, p172).

This often-difficult process of resolving diverse dimensions is itself educative and requires critical thinking skills:

> *Interpretations of sustainability are, therefore, value-laden, and serve particular social and economic interests; all need to be critically assessed... An important role for environmentalists and environmental educators searching for educational pathways supporting social transformation is one in which we contest with these interests in order to make spaces for our students and communities to find their own pathways (Fien, 1997, p23).*

The experience of the CADISPA and Southwest Queensland projects is that as communities strive to develop a shared or common vision of development for their own specific sustainability project, they can be expected to demonstrate what Diduck (1999) refers to as four enduring themes in resource and environmental management: change, complexity, uncertainty and conflict.

The fact that on-the-ground efforts in developing sustainability projects and initiatives are difficult and problematic is a function of what is being attempted – a practical reconciliation of two somewhat opposing interests (economic and environmental). It is not a measure of inadequacy of those mounting the efforts, nor of the concept of sustainability itself. The difficult and problematic nature of sustainability projects in fact suggests the value of practical reconciliation of contesting interests. It also suggests that endless armchair theorizing about the concept of sustainability may be futile.

Barkin (2000) comments on the essentially contested nature of sustainability projects, stressing the need for local participation and control in determining the direction of the projects. He also makes the important point, evident in a number of the CADISPA settings, of the need to adopt a politicized perspective – one in which the role of the relatively more powerful 'elite' is understood and questioned as local groups determine their own futures. He (p170) makes a telling point about the need for reorganizing political and economic power structures and relationships in contexts seeking sustainable solutions to their social, economic and environmental interests:

> *To be successful [sustainable development policies] require the direct participation of the intended beneficiaries and others who might be impacted. But there is also generalized agreement that this participation must involve more than a mere consultative role. For such an approach to work, it requires that the elites become aware of the need to integrate people into real power structures in order to confront the major problems of the day; this entails a redistribution of both political and economic power, a fundamental prerequisite for any program for sustainability...*

The CADISPA and Southwest Queensland cases reinforce Barkin's perspective that we need to adopt a view of sustainability that is politicized (recognizing the need for changing power structures and relationships). They emphasize the necessary involvement of a network of local people in a process of ongoing reconciliation of economic, social and environmental interests that amounts to a struggle for cultural survival.

Conclusions

In summary, an analysis of the two case studies presented in this chapter and some of the relevant literature suggests that environmental and sustainability issues:

- are complex in structure
- express themselves within specific contexts
- involve a wide range of stakeholders, who are likely to express a wide range of values and interests
- need a politicized perspective to be resolved
- require negotiation and reconciliation to be resolved, and these are usually difficult and challenging processes
- have a process of resolution that is a function of social, cultural, political and environmental elements, and is often a case of 'cultural survival'
- above all, are socially constructed – some of their key substantive elements of environment, ecosystem, environmental issue and sustainability are all socially constructed concepts and need to be recognized and treated as such.

For social learning that is attempting to educate about environmental and sustainability issues, the subject matters do not exist objectively as factual material to be transmitted but, instead, are human constructions to be explored. This indicates a strong role for discussion and debate among people about how they conceive of solutions to environmental and sustainability issues, expressed in a manner that appreciates the different and legitimate views of individuals.

References

ANZECC and Biological Diversity Advisory Committee (2001) *Biodiversity Conservation Research: Australia's Priorities*, Commonwealth Government of Australia, Canberra

Barkin, D. (2000) 'Overcoming the neoliberal paradigm: Sustaining popular development', *Journal of Developing Societies*, vol XVI, no 1, pp163–180

CADISPA (2001) *Cooperation and Development in Sparsely Populated Areas*, University of Strathclyde, Glasgow, UK

Commonwealth Government (2002) 'Framework for the extension of the Natural Heritage Trust, attachment A, Rivercare' available on Natural Heritage Trust website, www.nht.gov.au/publications/framework/rivercare.html

Dellbridge, A., Bernard, J. R. L., Blair, D., Butler, S., Peters, P. and Yallop, C. (eds) (1997) *Macquarie Dictionary*, 3rd edn, Macquarie Library Pty Ltd, Victoria

Dick, B. (1996) 'Action learning and action research', AREOL (action research and evaluation) resource archive, available at www.scu.edu.au/schools/gcm/ar/arp/actlearn.html

Diduck, A. (1999) 'Critical education in resource and environmental management: Learning and empowerment for a sustainable future', *Journal of Environmental Management*, vol 75, pp85–97

Fien, J. (1997) 'Stand up, stand up and be counted: Undermining myths of environmental education', *Australian Journal of Environmental Education*, vol 13, pp21–26

Hampson, I. and Fagan, G. (1997) *Local People, Partnerships and Rural Sustainable Development*, University of Strathclyde, Glasgow, UK

Kelly, D. (1999) 'Extension theory, practice and process', in Thompson, J., Reithmuller, J., Kelly, D., Boyd-Law, S. and Miller, E. (eds) *Feral Goat Management in South-west Queensland*, Final Report to the Bureau of Rural Sciences, Queensland Department of Natural Resources, Brisbane

Kelly, D. (2001) *Community Participation in Rangeland Management*, Rural Industry Research and Development Corporation, Canberra

King, C. (2000) 'Systemic processes for facilitating social learning', PhD, Swedish University of Agricultural Sciences

Kolb, D. (1984) *Experiential Learning: Experience as a Source of Learning and Development*, Prentice Hall, Englewood Cliffs, NJ

Mohan, G. and Stokke, K. (2000) 'Participatory development and empowerment: The dangers of localism', *Third World Quarterly*, vol 21, no 2, pp247–268

Revens, R. (1982) *ABC of Action Learning*, Chartweli-Bratt (Publishing and Training) Ltd, London

Robottom, I. (2000) 'Environmental education and the issue of coherence', *Themes in Education*, vol 1, no 3, pp227–241

Thompson, J., Reithmuller, J., Kelly, D., Boyd-Law, S. and Miller, E. (eds) (1999) *Feral Goat Management in South-west Queensland*, Final Report to the Bureau of Rural Sciences, Queensland Department of Natural Resources, Brisbane

Weatherstone, J. (2003) *Lindfield Park: Looking Back, Moving Forward*, Greening Australia, Land & Water Australia, Canberra

Zuber-Skerritt, O. (1995) 'Models of action research in postgraduate education', paper presented at the 1995 Action Learning and Action Research Conference, University of Queensland

Zuber-Skerritt, O. (1996) *New Directions in Action Research*, Falmer Press, London

5

Partnerships in Civil Society: Linking Bridging and Bonding Social Capital

Rory Eames

At a glance

- 'Social capital' is the term used for the networks, values and trust that enable communities to act together effectively to pursue shared objectives
- Social capital is a useful way of thinking of the resources of the community available to support environmental management
- In trying to understand the complexity of the water management issues of the Swan–Canning catchment, mobilizing social capital is a means by which the community may interpret and handle the complexity for themselves
- In a region such as the Swan–Canning catchment, there can be a conflict of interest between bonding social capital (shared interests and networks that hold groups together) and bridging social capital (shared interests between groups across the catchment), requiring social learning processes to link the two
- While bonding social capital can help a group take responsibility for its own section of the catchment, catchment health is a whole-of-society issue and its management asks for horizontal and vertical networking between the community and external actors, that is, bridging social capital.

Context

The last decade of the 20th century saw a proliferation of interest in social capital as a way of understanding aspects of either the healthiness, dynamics or characteristics of society in general. Through themes such as civic participation, community development, state–society relations and social change, key researchers have applied and developed the concept in a wide variety of social, economic, political and geographic contexts, and at equally varied scales of social research, from individuals to organizations and nation-states (Woolcock, 1998, p155; Krishna, 2001; Rydin and Holman, 2004). The concept of social capital refers to the networks, values and trust that enable communities to act together effectively to pursue shared objectives for environmental management. It has emerged as a popular and useful idea for approaching some of the complex issues that affect all of society. The complexity that arises when multiple actors with different interests interact typifies many of the problems that confront environmental managers, and so the approach is particularly useful in this context.

Taking to heart the warning that we must acknowledge the perspective from which we use the concept of social capital (Wall et al, 1998), this chapter revisits the idea of social capital using social learning as a critical perspective in environmental management. The other warning, that social capital can be considered only in its social context, also needs to be taken aboard by practitioners in all fields. This chapter grounds ideas about social capital within a case study of multisource water pollution in the Swan–Canning catchment of southwest Western Australia. The usefulness of this is not trivial. Almost all of the dimensions of the social learning process described by Brown and colleagues in Chapter 13 can be found in the water issues of the Swann–Canning catchment. This includes individual learning; learning from working within an affinity group; learning from working with or observing other groups; and learning from the experience of the whole encompassing population. These same dimensions can be identified in the people developing social capital theory. By using social learning as the conceptual framework, the social capital approach can usefully be applied by practitioners whose field involves them in the changing field of environmental management. The aim of this chapter is to explore how social capital theories might serve as useful tools for environmental managers handling complex practical problems, such as those occurring in the Swan–Canning catchment.

Case study: Widespread water pollution in the Swan–Canning catchment

In the southwest of Western Australia, the rivers and tributaries of the Swan–Avon and the Canning catchments are under considerable stress from poor quality water entering these aquatic systems (among other factors). Water quality is affected to a large degree by fertilizers (phosphorous and nitrogen), and to a lesser degree by heavy metals being picked up and absorbed by overland flow and run-off water. These accumulated pollutants are concentrated in tributaries and rivers of the Swan–Canning catchment.

The effect of this polluted, nutrient-rich water is significant in economic, ecological and social terms.

The most visible effect is extensive toxic blue–green algal blooms along stretches of rivers in the catchment. The risk, intensity and spread of bloom events are exacerbated during summer, when river levels are low, movement of water is slow, evaporation rates are high and sunlight is seasonally strong. Other less obvious effects are fish kills, resulting from the lack of oxygen and toxicity from the algal blooms, subsequent loss of biodiversity in marine environments, and health risks to humans and domestic animals who come into contact with the water during an algal bloom event. Long-term effects of nutrient-rich and polluted water entering the waterways of the Swan–Canning catchment are changes to the biotic community that lead to reduced biodiversity. This loss of biodiversity extends to riparian (river bank) vegetation, which is essential for minimizing erosion of stream banks and further degradation of waterways, which can lead to loss of farming efficiency and reduced farming income.

The social allocation of responsibility for both cause and remediation of the polluted waterways is a complex matter that frequently leads to heated social debate. The sources of pollutants and nutrients entering the water system in the Swan–Canning catchment do not arise from any single source but are diffuse across a range of geographical or temporal scales. Sources of fertilizers, heavy metals and other pollutants are not limited to one particular land use, but stem from a multitude of land uses, varying from rural production (primarily horticulture and dairying) to rural residential and urban settlements. These settlements increase in density and culminate in the Perth metropolitan area on the lower Swan and Canning rivers.

Run-off from agricultural land uses has been identified as a significant source of phosphorous and nitrogen, although these same nutrient-rich pollutants have also been identified as coming from urban land uses, such as urban lawns, public greens and ovals. In addition to this, a combination of infrastructure development and biophysical characteristics of the Swan–Canning catchment creates many ways that polluted, relatively nutrient-rich water can enter the water system. Primary avenues are stormwater run-off in agricultural and urban landscapes via drains, roads and gullies, while others may be groundwater seepage, direct absorption of stormwater via ponds, or direct overland flow from specific primary production activities on rural and semi-rural land.

The combination of a variety of pollutants, a disparate array of sources over time and space, and a great many avenues for polluted water to enter into the water system of the Swan–Canning catchment creates a textbook example of the problematic physical and social nature of non-point source water pollution. Not only does the poor quality water harm the ecological integrity of the environments upon which human and non-human populations and biodiversity depend, but it also challenges the economic and social futures of the region.

To add to the complexity, environmental change is happening con-currently with social change in this area. The social and political contexts in which communities in the Swan–Canning catchment are participating in environmental management and decision making are changing, with a community no longer consisting predominantly of rural landholders, but now comprising a heterogeneous membership. This change is producing subtle but important shifts in the reasons why community groups and individuals get involved in issues, and what they expect from environmental management and decision making.

Volunteer and community-led catchment management groups have increasingly become a fundamental part of collective action for sustainability for a great variety of reasons. This sector supplies environmental education, locally appropriate environmental action, community monitoring of environmental change, strategic involvement of community groups in land use planning and priority setting in state and privately funded environmental action (Raynor, 1999; Swan Catchment Council, 2002). On the ground, these changes are presenting challenges to existing and previously invisible or uncontested social boundaries – knowledge boundaries, action boundaries, jurisdictional boundaries and communication boundaries.

Where water pollution management might once have been considered to be the charge of engineers or state utility agencies, it now presents a wide variety of environmental and health issues affecting the whole of society. This social change is a fundamental step in any movement towards environmental (and therefore social) sustainability. This means that the process of learning goes well beyond the individual, to incorporate institutional and social learning as a fundamental part of effective collective action. It is in this area of collective action that social capital can be examined within our critical perspective of social learning. After introducing and critically reflecting on the concept of social capital, this chapter applies the themes of bonding and bridging social capital and their boundaries to social learning processes aimed at achieving sustainable environmental management.

What is the social capital of the Swan–Canning catchment?

Definitions of social capital have progressed from being simplistic and detached (Woolcock, 1998) to acknowledging the importance of identifying the context in which they are being used (Johnston and Percy-Smith, 2003; Wall et al, 1998). This breadth of meaning allows for continual development and refinement of social capital as a useful conceptual research tool for any given context in environmental management. In the Swan–Canning catchment, it means that it is important to identify the range of groups whose practices affect the waterways, and the relationships between them. It also makes the task of defining the term satisfactorily for all participants in any given region inherently difficult.

The seminal works of Robert Putnam (1993, 1995a), Pierre Bourdieu (1986) and James Coleman (1988), and the applications of the term by

Fukuyama (1995) and Portes (1998) have led the discussions on the merits, weaknesses and conceptual development of social capital. These authors developed social capital into a sociological term, away from an earlier economic focus on quantitative measures of physical infrastructure, social consumption expenditures and government investment in social programmes (O'Connor, 1973).

The concept of social capital has shifted from a phenomenon to be estimated by a cost–benefit analysis and used as a purely market economy decision making tool to its current manifestation as the glue that binds social interaction in and between groups concerned with a given issue. The latter perspective allows for environmental resources such as water to be overtly acknowledged as contributing to social wellbeing – for example, by being appreciated as part of a community's sense of place, as a distinct social 'good'. It also allows consideration of the contribution of social wellbeing to economic wellbeing, rather than the reverse, which was the focus of the earlier conceptualization.

From solely economic to the full set of social resources: Bourdieu and Coleman

As part of a larger body of work attempting to understand culture as a dynamic, creative and yet structured phenomenon, Pierre Bourdieu developed social capital as the term for one of many forms of capital – economic, cultural, scholastic and linguistic (Schuller et al, 2000). Bourdieu's idea of social capital is that it is the social resources available to a society, including strategies, for an individual to maintain or change their relative position in a hierarchical social structure (Wall et al, 1998, p306). Bourdieu still uses financial metaphors to explain the nature of social capital, by stressing the value of 'investment costs' and 'returns' in building and maintaining social capital (Warner, 1999, p376). Giddens (1999, p78) develops the theme further in the social realm:

> [Social capital] refers to trust networks that individuals draw on for social support, just as financial capital can be drawn upon to be used for investment. Like financial capital, social capital can be expanded – invested and reinvested.

Pretty and Frank (2000) suggest that social capital and social learning are critical to the effective functioning of community-based natural resource management. From the understanding of social capital as a capital resource described by Bourdieu, this function of social capital can be regarded as a crucial factor in the existence, continuity and effectiveness of individual community members and the groups within which they work. In the Swan–Canning case study, this Bourdieuian sense of social capital is of a resource to be drawn upon by individuals to achieve their individual goals, such as social interaction or employment. However, it is also crucial to the achievements of the group to which they belong, such as riparian revegetation projects, fencing, and habitat restoration. It is also essential in building the group's larger social capacities, such as the economic capacity, responsibility and accountability of the community group.

A refinement of the definition of social capital is provided by Coleman, who writes from an educational studies perspective with a strong interest in the relationships between educational achievement in adolescents and social inequality (Schuller et al, 2000). His definition is:

> *Social capital [is] the set of resources that inhere in family relations and in community organization and that are useful for the cognitive or social development of a child or young person [we could add 'or citizen'] (Coleman, 1994, p300).*

Bourdieu and Coleman each regard social capital as the social relations that individuals have access to, and therefore part of each society's distinctive social structure (Foley and Edwards, 1999).

We can regard the status of environmental and human health in the Swan–Canning catchment as the outcome of the decisions and actions of community members who regard the region as 'their place'. For example, a rational choice approach from economics would classify water as a transferable, utilitarian economic 'good'. In this rational economic perspective, the boundaries between the social roles of people (for example technical specialist, government official and farming family), and those between people and their environment (regarded as separate social and biophysical entities) are well defined and strongly held.

Coleman's challenge to the use of rational choice theory calls into question the fixed nature of this 'boundedness'. By interpreting social capital as the full set of social resources utilized by individuals and groups, water can be interpreted not only as an economic contribution and identified as an ecosystem service to society, but equally as providing aesthetic, recreational, intergenerational and intragenerational, psychological and physical health contributions to the common good. So rather than a solely economic conception of rational choice determining the relationship communities have with their environment, social capital becomes the set of resources found throughout the social relations among individuals.

Networking, bonding and bridging: Robert Putnam

Bourdieu's and Coleman's social capital is fundamentally tied to the relationship between the choices of individuals and their social relations. Since the early 1990s, Robert Putnam has sought to establish social capital as part of the structure of all associational life: 'networks, norms and trust, that enable participants to act together more effectively to pursue shared objectives' (Putnam, 1995b). Putnam's approach would have the observer estimate social capital through examining social events and trends such as local voting patterns, newspaper readership, sports and other recreation, cultural associations, landcare, service organizations and catchment management groups. Each individual contribution provides a kind of moral resource to the whole, reflecting a system of values, especially social trust. Putnam links 'human associations', understood as face-to-face interpersonal relations between individuals, to the production of networks, trust and norms of recipro-city, understanding the system as a whole constituting social capital.

Putnam also stresses the need to consider the dimensions of power and equity as inherent in the notion of social capital, something that earlier conceptualizations failed to address (Cox, 1995; Schuller et al, 2000, p10). This led to the development of the ideas of 'bonding' (within groups) and 'bridging' (between groups) social capital. In our example of the Swan–Canning catchment, bonding social capital is formed by the links between members of comparatively homogeneous subgroups (for instance farmers, teachers, conservationists and small business owners). Bonding social capital is underpinned by some agreed sharing of identity or purpose, acting within communities to bolster the ties between members, and reinforce loyalty and support within the group (Putnam, 2000). The ties may be choice of occupation, as in the earlier examples, or more deeply embedded factors such as ethnicity, religion and identity. The tendency is to encourage inward-looking groups.

Bridging social capital, on the other hand, is the building of networks, relationships and connections among the bonded groups, linking heterogeneous groups with shared interests. Consequently, bridging social capital breeds outward-looking networks and brings together people from a variety of backgrounds ... a sociological lubricant of sorts (Evans and Syrett, 2003, p11). Bridging social capital's connections are often assumed to be weaker and more fragile than those of bonding social capital. They are certainly no less important. This assumption of inherent fragility would lead those involved to expect any association of groups for the purposes of water management, such as catchment management groups, to be tentative and short-lived. While there is some evidence to that end, there are also strong and long-lasting local associations between farmers, researchers and government agencies (Brown, 1995).

However strong the bonding within or between groups, there will always be some inherent tension between bridging and bonding social capital. One bonded group may perpetuate a longstanding problem, such as the expectation of water as a limitless resource, when other groups are committed to water conservation. Loyalty to one's closest affinity group can be challenged by the need to work with the full range of stakeholders in the region. For those involved in environmental management who are trying to develop bridging capital, there will often be a history of distrust between the bonded groups, needing to be overcome by skilful remedial action. Bonded groups can also form their own alliances for their own purposes, not necessarily the objective of sustainable water management.

The links between bridging and bonding therefore become an equally important component of any social learning programme designed by the

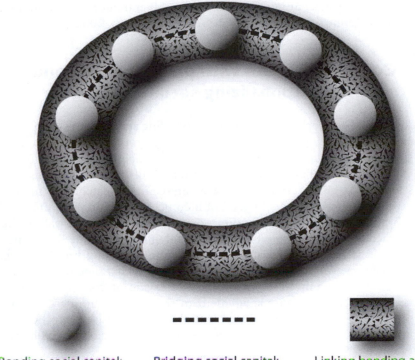

Bonding social capital:
homogeneous groups

Bridging social capital:
linking heterogeneous
groups

Linking bonding and
bridging social capital:
social networks

Source: Putnam (2000)

Figure 5.1 *Linking bonding and bridging capital*

environmental manager. Those links can be regarded as ad hoc and temporary, created to overcome a short-term problem, such as community response to flooding or cyclone damage. They can refer to the long-established systemic relationships between government agencies, local industry, specialized advisers and residents in any one region. This system can be expected to be hierarchical in nature, with government and local industry as the more powerful players. However, in practice this system is as context-dependent as Putnam's recommendation about social capital itself.

Another, and possibly more useful way to approach the links between bridging and bonding social capital in any given region is to consider them as a rich complex of networks, often invisible to those outside that particular community system. Mentoring, patronage, kinship, age cohorts, marriage and neighbours form a web that both cuts across and strengthens the links between the bonding and bridging, the within and between group relationships. Case studies of environmental management issues and responses have identified these linking networks cutting across the formal hierarchical system in urban, rural and indigenous communities alike (Nicholson et al, 2002).

Conceptual issues with understanding and operationalizing social capital

The conceptual development of the ideas of bonding and bridging social capital and the network linking the two in any given region is a useful management tool. It allows for the consideration that there can be both good and bad forms of social capital, and that they can be distributed differently according to the status and reach of the groups. In the Swan–Canning catchment there are exclusive communities, linked by level of income, length of time in the district and political affiliation, where bonding social capital acts like a wall to those outside each particular group, but like a sociological superglue for members within each group. A frequently used example of strong bonding social capital, albeit one with dubious social effects, is the Mafia. The same elements of bonding social capital are equally characteristic of community groups involved in water pollution management in the Swan–Canning catchment. The durability of such groups depends highly on the trust, reciprocity and common rules created by, and in turn creating, such sociological superglue (Pretty and Frank, 2000).

It should be apparent from these examples that social capital is not necessarily good or bad, but an expected social phenomenon in any established community. These attributes depend upon context, value and history. Bourdieu (1986) notes that groups or classes within society or a social structure can use social capital, along with other forms of capital, to solidify their relative power and wealth over other groups within society. This proposition may be understood as bad, destructive and alienating social capital or equally to be carefully fostered as a necessary step in achieving major change. The corollary of bad, or negative, social capital in a community sustainability programme might be that there is evidence of general social distrust, increasing juvenile delinquency and domestic violence.

Distinguishing between bonding and bridging social capital raises the question as to whether one is meant to be understood as better or more valuable than the other. It is also important to establish whether one creates, inhibits or decreases the other. The relationships between the two forms of social capital may be as crucial as those within. On the surface it could be assumed in the Swan–Canning catchment that the tighter the bonding within industry, farming and administrative entities, the less likely they are to open their boundaries sufficiently to work together as a single community. The success of the landcare movement, in which communities throughout Australia combined in the stewardship of their locally shared environmental resources, demonstrates that just the opposite can be the case (Brown, 1995; Carr, 2002). On the other hand, the history of the fragmented catchment management strategies in every state confirms that the risk is real (Brown, 1995).

A social learning approach in environmental management invokes the need to involve the full spectrum of interests in the region, the different layers of federal, state and local government, the range of industries and occupations, as well as different locally bonded groupings. Any change in the system to meet the requirements of sustainable environmental management will by definition involve the multiple strands of social learning: reflexivity, systems orientation, integration, negotiation and participation. There is little work in the literature on how bonding and bridging are internalized in the individual or the group as trust, confidence, involvement, purposefulness and worth. The need to answer questions on the nature and existence of bonding and bridging social capital and on the need to establish links between the two in any given region will be part of the responsibility of the environmental manager, researcher and community developer (Foley and Edwards, 1999, p148; Wall et al, 1998, p315).

Whether social capital can be measured qualitatively or quantitatively is still hotly debated among many social capital theorists. For example, trust levels in a social context, such as communities involved in water quality management in the Swan–Canning catchment, can quite easily be understood as being in some way related to the amount of social capital present in the networks that make up that community to begin with. Putnam's characterization of social capital as connections among individuals, the social networks and the norms of reciprocity and trustworthiness that arise from them fails to determine which is cause and which is effect. In considering trust, is it generated by, or the foundation for, the strength of the social capital involved? Chicken or egg? This is yet another example of the central place of systems thinking in environmental management, explored earlier in this book.

Conclusions

It appears that ideas for the complex research, education, practical remediation or policy development involved in rescuing a water catchment such as the Swan–Canning from escalating broad-based pollution can well be clarified by exploring the status of the region's social capital. One aim of a social learning process that contributes to any of these activities is to make the boundaries inhibiting social learning more permeable, thereby permitting the strengthening of social capital. These boundaries determine not only bonding and bridging social capital, but the potential for establishing lasting links between the two. Here the five strands of social learning become critical processes for environmental management.

On reflection, making ideas of social capital part of the social learning process is a critical part of environmental management. Trust and cooperative learning facilitate both recognition and transcendence of knowledge, action and communication boundaries. Each environmental management project using social capital as an interpretive tool will need to be extremely sensitive in its application, as there are few hard and fast general rules and the crucial importance of context always applies. Nevertheless, a few conclusions can be drawn:

• Widespread water pollution is a whole-of-society issue, and therefore its re-mediation necessarily involves the distribution, quality and connectedness of social capital
• The distribution and quality of social capital is related to the types of boundaries that determine individual, own group, other groups and whole-of-community status
• Social learning has been described as dependent on achieving permeability between individual and group knowledge boundaries, and so different sets of bonding capital must be addressed differently, and so must bridging and bonding social capital
• Skills in introducing the social learning strands of reflectivity, systems thinking, integration, negotiation and partnering in strengthening social capital will need to be extended to strengthen the network linking bridging and bonding social capital in any given region.

In the Swan–Canning catchment, these conclusions suggest that the idea of building social capital offers a valuable and sensitive approach to social change for improved environmental outcomes. They also suggest that change strategies intended to reduce water pollution that expect to work within only one scale, and on only bonding or bridging capital, could well be counterproductive. In addition, they may explain the successes and failures of current and past social change programmes.

A final point is that a consideration of the role of social capital in environ-mental management asks for deeper consideration of the application of the social learning strands presented in Chapter 1 and throughout this book. For example, systems orientations at a catchment level are well developed, as adaptive management systems coupled with ecological approaches have been practised for decades (Carpenter et al, 1999; Christensen et al, 1996). Likewise, partnerships between community, industry and government are also a regular component of catchment strategies (Leach and Pelkey, 2001; Robinson and Wallis, 1991). Integration is another common element as catchment approaches are routinely recommended precisely because of their capacity to integrate social, economic and ecological resource use. So three strands of social learning are integral to the very idea of sustainable water catchments, and have been used for decades. Why then is there not a consistent history of success?

It may be useful to explore the relative absence from catchment manage-ment of the other two social learning strands – collaboration and reflection. Collaboration among different groups and at different scales is often taken for granted, rather than considered a matter for well-designed intervention. The other missing element is the lack of mutual reflection within and between groups on the construction and maintenance of boundaries between them. As argued elsewhere in this book, it may well be that introducing a process of reflection on these boundaries and developing appropriate methods of negotiation across such boundaries may create avenues that bring considerations of social capital into the mainstream of water management.

References

Bourdieu, P. (1986) 'The forms of capital', in Richardson, J. (ed) *Handbook of Theory and Research for the Sociology of Education*, Greenwood Press, New York

Brown, V. A. (1995) *Landcare Languages: Talking to Each Other about Living with the Land*, Department of Primary Industries and Energy, Canberra

Carpenter, S., Brock, W. and Hanson, P. (1999) 'Ecological and social dynamics in simple models of ecosystem management', *Conservation Ecology*, vol 3, no 2, www.consecol.org/vol3iss2/art4/

Carr, A. (2002) *Grass Roots and Green Tape: Principles and Practices of Environmental Stewardship*, Federation Press, Annandale, NSW

Christensen, N., Bartuska, A., Brown, J., Carpenter, S., D'Antonio, C., Francis, R., Franklin, J., MacMahon, J., Noss, R., Parsons, D., Peterson, C., Turner, M. and Woodmansee, R. (1996) *The Report of the Ecological Society of America Committee on the Scientific Basis for Ecosystem Management Ecological Applications*, vol 6, no 3, pp665–691

Coleman, J. (1988) 'Social capital in the creation of human capital', *American Journal of Sociology*, vol 94 (supplement), ppS95–S120

Coleman, J. (1994) *Foundations of Social Theory*, Belknap Press, Cambridge

Cox, E. (1995) *A Truly Civil Society*, ABC Books, Sydney

Evans, M, and Syrett, S. (2003) *Generating Social Capital? The Social Economy and Local Regeneration*, Regional Studies Association Conference: Reinventing Regions in the Global Economy, Pisa Congress Centre, Pisa, Italy, 12–15 April 2003. Available at www.regional-studies-assoc.ac.uk/events/pisa03/evans.pdf

Foley, M. and Edwards, B. (1999) 'Is it time to disinvest in social capital?', *Journal of Public Policy*, vol 19, no 2, pp141–173

Fukuyama, F. (1995) 'Social capital and the global economy', *Foreign Affairs*, vol 74, no 5, pp89–104

Giddens, A. (1999) *Reith Lectures 1999*, BBC, http://news.bbc.co.uk/hi/english/static/events/reith_99/default.htm

Johnston, G. and Percy-Smith, J. (2003) 'In search of social capital', *Policy and Politics*, vol 31, no 3, pp321–334

Krishna, A. (2001) 'Moving from the stock of social capital to the flow of benefits: The role of agency', *World Development*, vol 29, no 6, pp925–943

Leach, W. and Pelkey, N. (2001) 'Making watershed partnerships work: A review of the empirical literature', *Journal of Water Resources Planning and Management*, November–December, pp378–385

Nicholson, R., Stevenson, P., Brown, V. A. and Mitchell, K. (eds) (2002) *Common Ground and Common Sense: Community-based Environmental Health Planning*, Commonwealth Department of Health and Ageing, Canberra

O'Connor, J. (1973) *The Fiscal Crisis of the State*, St Martin's Press, New York

Portes, A. (1998) 'Social capital: Its origins and applications in modern sociology', *Annual Review of Sociology*, vol 24, pp1–24

Pretty, J. and Frank, B. (2000) *Participation and Social Capital Formation in Natural Resource Management: Achievements and Lessons*, proceedings, International Landcare 2000 Conference, Melbourne

Putnam, R. (1993) *Making Democracy Work: Civic Traditions in Modern Italy*, Princeton University Press

Putnam, R. (1995a) 'Bowling alone: America's declining social capital', *Journal of Democracy*, vol 6, no 1, pp65–78

Putnam, R. (1995b) 'Tuning in, tuning out: The strange disappearance of social capital in America', American Political Association John Gaus Lecture, available at 'The American Political Science Association Online, www.apsanet.org/PS/dec95/putnam.cfm

Putnam, R. (2000) *Bowling Alone: The Collapse and Revival of American Community*, Simon and Schuster, New York

Raynor, L. (1999) *Local Government and Landcare in Western Australia*, WA BankWest Landcare Conference, Fremantle

Robinson, S. and Wallis, R. (1991) 'Integrated catchment management: The Western Australian experience', *Environment*, vol 33, no 10, pp31–34

Rydin, Y. and Holman, N. (2004) 'Re-evaluating the contribution to social capital in achieving sustainable development', *Local Environment*, vol 9, no 2, pp117–133

Schuller, T., Baron, S. and Field, J. (2000) 'Social capital: A review and critique', in Schuller, T., Baron, S. and Field, J. (eds) *Social Capital: Critical Perspectives*, Oxford University Press, Oxford

Swan Catchment Council (2002) *The Swan Region – A Natural Resource Management Strategy*, Swan Catchment Council, Midland, Western Australia

Wall, E., Ferrazzi, G. and Schryer, F. (1998) 'Getting the goods on social capital', *Rural Sociology*, vol 63, no 2, pp300–323

Warner, M. (1999) 'Social capital construction and the role of the local state', *Rural Sociology*, vol 64, no 3, pp373–394

Woolcock, M. (1998) 'Social capital and economic development: Toward a theoretical synthesis and policy framework', *Theory and Society*, vol 27, no 2, pp151–208

6

Combining People, Place and Learning

Tom Measham and Richard Baker

At a glance

- All those involved in environmental management can benefit greatly from thinking of environments as 'places' and acknowledging the different ways people engage with their environments
- Understanding environments as places integrates their social, cultural, biological, physical and economic dimensions
- Thinking of environments as places also helps to explain our experiences of those environments, link environments at different scales and understand human behaviour and change
- Thinking about people and places together allows us to move beyond the boundaries that we construct as it involves us switching our focus to relationships
- All cultures have built up an understanding about particular places, as illustrated by a case study of the Yolngu people of the Northern Territory
- Co-management can help us acknowledge and validate how different people interact with environments as places
- Spending time in environments and listening to why they are important to people helps us to respect them as places.

Learning to see environments as 'places'

The need to increase our understanding of how we interact with our environments is a fundamental learning step towards more sustainable environmental management. The theme of this chapter is to think of environments as being made up of 'places'. The essence of this concept is that locations and contexts carry with them a range of different meanings, which vary between individuals and between cultures (Massey, 1994; Relph, 1976). The notion of place is not new, but has received renewed interest as one of a range of concepts with potential value when it comes to integrating different aspects of sustainable environmental management practice as they manifest at different scales (Cantrill and Senecah, 2001; Cheng et al, 2003). A rainforest may be a particular ecosystem or catchment, but it is also a place of significance, a source of livelihood or inspiration.

The idea of place is concerned with the significance of different locations to different people, hence no single way of understanding place is universally valid. Implicit to the concept is the notion that identities of places change over time – they evolve or adapt or are re-created (Relph, 1976). In turn, the way we understand places – or our identity with places – also develops and changes throughout our lives. This inherent dynamic quality is fundamental to why the concept of place is so important to learning about sustainable environmental management practices.

Equally crucial is the concept of place as being inherently integrated. Thinking of environments as places facilitates acceptance of their cultural and spiritual aspects, as well as their biological and physical dimensions (Williams and Patterson, 1996). It also facilitates acceptance of difference. Though they may be connected, no two places are the same. This chapter proposes that learning to manage environments sustainably means accepting people and their cultures as integral parts of the environments we want to learn about. Attempting to learn about ourselves or our environments in isolation runs the risk of overlooking how they are interconnected.

Conceptual background

The concept of using place as a means of considering environmental issues emerged in the 1970s as a response to the portrayal of environmental concerns as technical issues (Relph, 1976; Tuan, 1974). Humanist and political geographers argued that environments are more than biological and physical entities. In response to the rise of quantitative spatial analysis, Relph (1976) argued that environments are more than mere coordinates on a map – they are lived-in places constituting the settings and situations around us. Environments, be they forests, cities or deserts, are areas of cultural significance and Relph perceived a strong need to learn to respect them as such.

Since the 1970s, the concept of place has been informed by successive waves of theoretical rethinking. A notable shift in focus involved acknowledging the political dimensions of place – the social and political influences operating throughout society that shape the identity of places. Places are constructed from many points of view, including gender, class and ethnicity. As such, they have contested identities that reflect power dimensions. Furthermore, the identities of places are not fixed at any given temporal or spatial scale as their defining characteristics are the subject of contestation and change. By being contested, they are continually updated or re-invented, reflecting shifts in power relations (Huggins et al, 1995; Johnson, 2000; Kemmis, 1996; Massey, 1994).

Recently, theorists have emphasized an ecological rationale for viewing environments as places. While human geographers in the 1970s argued that we were diminished as humans by excluding the human dimensions to environmental issues, Plumwood (2002) has argued that the concept is fundamental to human survival, and that western approaches to natural resource management are philosophically flawed. Central to her argument is that our search for technical solutions to environmental problems has endorsed an artificial distinction between humans and nature. She argues that human survival depends on a radical rethinking of the way we connect with each other and the ecosystems that support us. Critical of the philosophical roots that isolate human culture and nature, Plumwood (2002, p239) argues that 'We must counter those maladaptive forms ... in order to develop a communicative, place-sensitive culture which can situate humans ecologically and nonhumans ethically'.

A further aspect to the theory of place is that human beings are social agents who go out and make meaning in their environments. Our environments are not backgrounds where we conduct life. It is fundamental to human existence that we engage with our surroundings – they are a reflection of our actions and our aspirations. Moreover, the places we interact with are dynamic – the relationship between person and location that defines place is one based on continuous dialogue and developing understanding. For this reason, place is a valuable context for learning about sustainable environmental management practices (Williams and Patterson, 1996).

Social and cultural dimensions to sustainability

One of the most important challenges for learning in natural resource management is to find ways to integrate the different dimensions of sustainable environmental management – the social, cultural, biological, physical and economic dimensions of the environment. The way this issue has been expressed, the so-called triple bottom line, seeks to deliver environmental, social and economic outcomes (Spiller, 2000). However, in distinguishing these outcomes, the triple bottom line continues to endorse the distinctions among these dimensions. Conceptualizing environments as places means to think of them as unique examples of different ways these dimensions are expressed. As Cheng et al (2003, p96) explain, 'The environment is not an inert, physical entity "out there" with trees, water, animals, and the like, but a dynamic system of interconnected, meaning-laden places'. Places integrate not only the biological, physical, social and economic dimensions of sustainability, but the histories and aspirations of the people who are connected with and a part of these environments (Cantrill and Senecah, 2001; Moore, 1997).

Place and moving beyond boundaries

A central issue raised in the first three chapters of this volume was that we need to move beyond the boundaries that we construct around our spheres of interest or concern if we are to better understand and cooperate in handling the complex environmental issues we face. This is an issue geographers have grappled with extensively, asking whether it is appropriate, or even possible, to indicate the boundaries of places. This has been influenced partly by increasing interest in the role of globalization, which has focused attention on relationships between places over great distances. Considering her home suburb of London, Doreen Massey (1994) shows how a distinct part of London is defined by its relationships with other places all over the world – by the people of many cultures who live there, the cars that pass through its streets on their way to somewhere else and by the products for sale in its shops that were designed and manufactured in various places around the world.

The same could be said for almost any place, including an outback region of Australia. Consider, for example, the area known as the Gulf of Carpentaria. It is defined in part by its relationship with a particular boundary – the Australian coastline. But it is also defined by its relationships with the rest of Australia and the world through industries such as fishing, beef and mining, which connect the region to a global economy. The region is connected to other places in countless ways, such as the rivers and roads that traverse it, the cultures of the people who live and visit there and their histories and mythologies that span time and space. It is through acknowledging these relationships that we can move beyond the limits that boundaries impose or, as Massey (1994, pp154–5) puts it:

> *Instead of thinking of places as areas with boundaries around, they can be imagined as articulated moments in networks of social relations and understandings ... this in turn allows a sense of place which is extroverted, which includes a consciousness of its links with the wider world, which integrates in a positive way the global and the local.*

There are further reasons for moving beyond the limits of boundaries and starting to think of environments as places, including issues such as scale, changing behaviour and linking theory with practice.

Scale

The issue of scale is fundamentally tied to better understanding and handling environmental management issues, as was discussed and illustrated by Dyball, Beavis and Kaufman (Chapter 3). The relationship between the global and the local has been a prominent discourse in recent years, and various attempts to consider appropriate scales for dealing with sustainability have included concentrating on scales such as the bioregion and catchment (McTaggart, 1993; Wittayapak and Dearden, 1999). It is important to emphasize that the concept of place is not fixed at any one of these scales, but is concerned with the inherent relationships among them (Massey, 1994). As such, thinking of environments as places involves an amalgam of global change and local identity (Stoll-Kleeman and O'Riordan, 2002).

People think at different scales according to different issues. Thinking in terms of places can help them link these scales so that a paddock, for example, sits within some larger scale such as a catchment or bioregion. The idea of 'places within places' is inherent in the concept, with Relph (1976), for example, demonstrating that a house is a place in a street, and a street is a place in a suburb, and so on. The relationships among places at different scales attracted the interest of Cheng et al (2003). They have identified that the geographic scale of place can influence people's group identification and affect the outcomes of natural resource issues. People may adopt a general position on an issue depending on their political persuasion; however, they may think differently as an individual landholder directly affected by a decision.

Behaviour and change

One of the reasons people have taken an interest in the concept of place is related to a broader interest in understanding how people change their attitudes and behaviour. This has emerged from extension research, which has led to a new focus on trying to understand how people engaged in natural resource management view and value their world. Central to this interest is a focus on the human propensity and capacity to change towards more sustainable approaches to engaging with environments. What the concept of place can provide is a means to understand and characterize existing constructions of environments and, moreover, an opportunity to study the influences and processes that underpin these constructions (Cantrill and Senecah, 2001).

Place links theory with experience

Place is a context in which people can base their learning in the reality of experience and relate the general to the particular. As Kolb et al (1995) have indicated, while generalization gives meaning to the concrete instance, it is the instance that delivers this meaning to make it usable (see also discussions by Keen and Mahanty – Chapter 7 – and Harris and Deane – Chapter 11). When it comes to learning about our interaction with environments, the context for people to relate the principles of environmental management to the reality of experience is the places where they live and work. It is for this reason that, in terms of the four-stage cycle developed in Chapter 1 (Figure 1.3), the concept of place is most relevant to the 'doing' stage of learning. To borrow an expression from Relph (1976), people relate the general to the concrete in their 'lived-world' – the places where we live out our lives.

Furthermore, research has shown that rationalizing experience is crucial to adult learning, in terms of both learning motivation and learning process. In terms of motivation, Knowles et al (1998) have shown that adults are more willing to learn about issues they see as relevant to their experience of life. Learning that is life related makes it easier to connect generalizations with experience. To put it differently, learning that helps us to explain or enhance our experience of our environments is both a source of knowledge as well as being crucial to motivating us to engage with those environments in a more sustainable fashion. But it is important to emphasize that what is relevant to learning about our relationship with environments varies between cultures (see the example of Yolngu learning in Box 6.3).

How do we learn to see environments as places?

Learning to respect people and place is not a straightforward process. More than any particular activity, it requires a disposition to accept that other people may think differently from oneself. Beyond this starting point, we now look at some general principles.

Inclusiveness and engagement

Learning to respect people and place can be helped by working with people to develop networks and coalitions. Such alliances can be an important way to include a voice for people affected by local aspects of sustainability. But to be effective, it is important to be inclusive in defining the processes with which groups are engaged. Drawing on her experience of working with indigenous peoples on wildlife management in southern Africa, Suchet (2001) cautions against basing alliances on western stereotypes in favour of more flexible networks emphasizing commonalities of experience and aspirations for managing land. To respect people and their relationships with place, it is important to acknowledge our own understandings and avoid imposing these on others who may think differently. It is also important to engage with people to try to gain insights into how they understand their environment. While it may not be possible to fully understand how another person or culture views and understands their land or related concepts, it is important to make an attempt to listen to and understand them (Chapters 2 and 4; Suchet, 2001).

Time in place

Learning to respect people and place requires taking the time and effort to go and meet people and get to know places (see Box 6.1). It involves listening to people talk about their land or sea country. Learning to respect place also involves some level of learning about that place, and this is greatly helped by actually being in a place for a time. One of the most important ways to learn about people and what makes places so significant is to walk or drive around the places that are special to these people and ask them to explain what is significant around them. This has important implications for those policy-makers who develop policy without leaving the office. Current research is

Box 6.1 Learning to respect and interpret place in the Atherton Tablelands

Research in progress into learning about place in the Atherton Tablelands has provided insight into how people develop a respect for place, which is related to an enhanced ability to 'read' or interpret place. In this case study, the ability to interpret place involved not only learning *about* place, but also learning *from* place. In each of the interviews where this ability was discussed, the theme of time in place was prominent. People could describe different levels of understanding that corresponded to stages in the time they had been in a place. Some participants had developed this literacy over a very long period and it had become tacit knowledge, which was difficult to describe. Other relatively recent arrivals in a place could describe the process of developing this literacy more explicitly, because they were aware of recent shifts in their understanding. One of them describes this change:

> '...the first time I ever drove in here I thought oh my God you know it's dry and really dusty and quite harsh looking. I thought how could anyone possibly want to live here? There's nothing that would attract you that's what I thought first. Then I started noticing the finer details and it somehow ... it's an emotional issue, became really, really attractive to me.'

The finer details these participants described included the movement of water through the country (including below the surface), and flowering events and how these interacted with animal behaviour. Over time, these participants became aware of these aspects and this experience was linked to developing a much stronger affinity with the place. With this process still fresh in their minds, they could identify processes that would otherwise have been tacit understanding. For example, fundamental to their adapting to the country was seeing it change through the seasons:

> '...in time I've actually grown to love it and when I go away for a little while I come back and I just have this really strong feeling in my heart when I see it coming down the range ... it's like coming home, beautiful although I think seeing it through the changes of the seasons too really helps. Being here and I think spending time here like not just coming here for little bits. For me it was necessary to actually endure the hardship of being here as well...'

For many of the participants who described developing an ability to read and respect their place in the Atherton Tablelands, continuity was crucial to developing this strong understanding and respect for place — either in terms of the duration of visits, or the frequency of visits to the places they described. In addition, some participants described seeing country under different conditions (such as climatic conditions or disaster events) as a trigger for deepening their understanding and respect for these places.

Source: Tom Measham, unpublished PhD thesis, The Australian National University

showing that many people in rural regions are frustrated by the fact that they are affected by policy generated by people who have never been to their region. They argue that such policy is based on a poor understanding of what it means to live in the places affected by the policy. Simply spending time in the regions, meeting the people and listening to their concerns, would greatly improve policy.

Wisdom sits in places

Indigenous cultures around the world have developed deep and intensely local understandings of place. Such cultures often stress the importance of understanding the stories local places have to tell. As in pre-literate European societies, landscapes and not books are key texts that need to be read, for they embody central cultural understandings.

Many indigenous cultures would concur with the Western Apache belief that wisdom sits in places (Basso, 1996). For the Western Apache, particular places embody moral codes that guide behaviour, and wisdom comes from learning the stories places have to tell. As one Apache man puts it (Basso, 1996, p70):

> *'wisdom sits in places. It's like water that never dries up. You need to drink water to stay alive, don't you? Well, you also need to drink from places. You must remember everything about them. You must learn their names. You must remember what happened at them long ago. You must think about it and keep on thinking about it.'*

Rather than seeing such knowledge as characteristic only of indigenous cultures, it is important to stress that all cultures have built up understandings about particular places. For example, as Box 6.2 highlights, many non-indigenous Australians share with indigenous Australians an ability to read the landscape for the stories it can tell.

The connections between indigenous and non-indigenous Australians' reading of landscapes are the results of individuals in local places learning about the environment and passing on this information. In both cases, oral traditions and continued access to country are vital for such information to be passed from generation to generation.

While local environmental knowledge can be found among both indigenous and non-indigenous Australians, there is a stark contrast in how such knowledge is valued within the different cultures. Within western society, the local knowledge of people like Doug Nash has been undervalued in the face of the privileged status of 'scientific' understandings. Western science privileges universal laws over specific local observations and science over folklore. As a result, local understandings of place tend to be excluded from the scientific enterprise of natural resource management.

Indigenous environmental knowledge systems have been even more marginalized from mainstream systems of knowledge. However, within indigenous

---

Box 6.2 A personal story

In the early 1990s I made the transition from working for the Northern Territory Museum with Aboriginal people to the National Museum of Australia, working with mainly non-indigenous farmers in southern Australia, documenting sense of place. On my first field trip I found myself standing in a paddock with an elderly farmer whose family had farmed the area for over 120 years. It was an uncanny experience for me as his eloquent afternoon-long description of the landscape around us had so much in common with rewarding days I had spent with traditional Aboriginal people in my previous job. Like Aboriginal stories of country, Doug Nash's knowledge was deep and rooted in the landscape itself. Doug had lived his whole life on farms in the region and grew up hearing stories from his parents and grandparents about the places they farmed. The country itself was a rich text that he was more than happy to read aloud to me. He pointed out to me features such as:

- the first ten acres that were cleared
- the dam that was literally full of rabbits when rabbits arrived in the region in 1902
- the paddock that grew the region's first lucerne crop in 1906
- the paddock that he and his cousin sowed on a Saturday in April 1936, the day before his cousin's daughter was born
- numerous other telltale small signs I would never have noticed that illustrated where and how people had once farmed or lived.

Inspired by Doug and many other farmers who could read their landscapes, I focused the National Museum's first major travelling exhibition around the theme of how all Australians needed to develop greater land literacy skills. While individual farmers have developed skills to read their landscapes through long family association with places, as a wider community we are very limited in our land literacy skills. The travelling exhibition attempted to develop broader senses of place across the Murray–Darling Basin by focusing on examples such as Doug's local land-reading skills.

Source: Richard Baker, The Australian National University

Australian cultures such local environmental knowledge is of central cultural value. Individuals with deep environmental knowledge and the capacity to pass on this knowledge to subsequent generations are key community leaders. Further, such knowledge is at the heart of their religious and economic systems and, as Box 6.3 highlights, can influence how they perceive learning itself.

Yolngu approaches to learning can provide many lessons for sustainable environmental management practices. Firstly, all learning occurs in a particular context and is relevant only if it helps you to understand and function in

Box 6.3 Yolngu learning

The Yolngu people live in the Northern Territory and are traditional owners of northeast Arnhem Land (Dhimurru Land Management Aboriginal Corporation, 2003). In their community school, they teach traditional knowledge and traditional ways of knowing that are quite distinct from western philosophical approaches to knowledge.

In considering the cultural differences in approaches to learning, Marika-Mununggiritj and Christie (1995) have pointed out that in English we describe the 'discovery' of knowledge – something that was previously hidden which comes to light. By contrast, Yolngu learning focuses on being educated in the ways of the ancestors. Their metaphors for learning focus on the concept of *galtha* – a connecting spot or place where people gather for negotiating special activities such as hunting or ceremonies. 'Anywhere there is a ceremony, there will be a galtha. Every ceremony must be different, because its art lies in creating that ceremony to specially reflect the participants and the place and the time' (Marika-Mununggiritj and Christie, 1995, p60). Implicit in the concept of Yolngu knowledge is that *galtha* is everywhere and possible wherever people are acting properly.

For the Yolngu people, learning includes a sense of how to interpret their environment by reading such things as animal tracks, tides and the imprints of their elders and spiritual beings. In the process, they learn to recognize what they see in the environment and how it can help them. The Yolngu also learn how to identify patterns of their ancestors. This entails seeing the journey of their ancestors, which involves identifying the land and the people they have interacted with and how this fits in with the whole web of meaning that makes up Yolngu life. These things are visible in the land and have been passed down to younger generations through songs. The Yolngu learn to live in the present in a way that is consistent with the lessons of the ancestors:

> Yolngu education is learning to love and understand our homeland and the ancestors who have provided it for us, so as to create a life for ourselves reworking the truths we have learned from the land and from the elders, into a celebration of who we are and where we are in the modern world (Marika-Mununggiritj and Christie, 1995, p61).

Yolngu learning is not about discovering something that was previously hidden. It is about developing the knowledge and the skills to be truthful to the culture of the past and re-invent it in the context of the present.

Source: Richard Baker, The Australian National University

that context. What is considered appropriate to learn in any context varies according to location and culture. By thinking of environments as places, it is possible to integrate the links between culture and location. Furthermore, it facilitates accepting that environments or places have a cultural history that needs to be respected and learned if we are to continue to live with them sustainably.

Another lesson concerns time. There is a strong lesson that keeping the essence of places alive does not equate to conserving culture 'like a museum piece'. Instead, it means being educated in the lessons of the past and re-inventing places in such a way as to be consistent with these lessons (Marika-Mununggiritj and Christie, 1995). Finally, the Yolngu approach to learning demonstrates the strong links between learning, culture and place. These three are mutually dependent – keeping culture alive relies on learning the lessons of the past and applying them to the present. These lessons are inherently linked to place, to Yolngu traditional country. Place, in turn, is meaningless without culture. It is the country where the ancestors have developed what it means to be Yolngu, and how this is interpreted in the present.

Collaborative management

The potential for collaborative management (co-management) to play a significant role in social learning is elaborated on by Keen and Mahanty (Chapter 7, as illustrated in Figure 7.1). Here we suggest that co-management can help to acknowledge and validate the way different people interact with environments or places. However, it is important to point out that co-management arrangements offer both an opportunity and a challenge in learning to respect people and place. As argued earlier in this chapter, the notion that the identities of places are contested and changing is fundamental to the concept of place. Robinson and Mununggurit (2001) explain that co-management arrangements can play a significant role in contesting, decolonizing and localizing conventional understandings of places.

Yet while the idea of co-management has considerable potential, existing attempts to develop co-management have thus far fallen short of supporting respect for people and place in Australia. The design of these arrangements has so far failed to acknowledge the importance of traditional country. Rather than support shared understanding, the arrangements have tended to undermine indigenous resource use and traditional environmental knowledge (Robinson and Mununggurit, 2001). Instead of empowering indigenous peoples, co-management arrangements have often excluded them from decision making authority, or assigned management roles, rather than negotiating such roles.

In response to these sorts of problems, indigenous groups have established organizations to manage their natural and cultural resources and promote their understanding of place. These organizations, such as the Dhimurru Land Management Aboriginal Corporation in Yolngu traditional country, aim to tie collaborative arrangements to indigenous relationships with their traditional country (Dhimurru Land Management Aboriginal Corporation, 2003; Robinson and Munundguritj, 2001).

Conclusions

Learning to see environments as places has many implications. It means learning to accept that we are part of the environments we are trying to sustain – that our survival and prosperity depend on the way we interact with them. It further means that we need to learn to accept diversity. What for one person is a pristine natural environment, for someone else may be a place of tradition and creative re-invention of what it means to interact with a place. The rationale for learning to respect people and place is clear – it is at the heart of learning to manage environments sustainably. Thinking of environments as places involves thinking about them in terms of relationships instead of boundaries. This is crucial to sustainable environmental management practices because relationships are easier to change than boundaries. When it comes to how we learn to respect people and place, there are some insights – but few concrete answers. The discussion in this chapter has hopefully gone some way to conveying the rationale for increasing respect for diversity and the spirit of collaboration.

References

Basso, K. H. (1996) 'Wisdom sits in places: Notes on a Western Apache landscape', in Feld, S. and Basso, K. H. (eds) *Senses of Place*, School of American Research Press, Santa Fe, NM

Cantrill, J. G. and Senecah, S. L. (2001) 'Using the "sense of self-in-place" construct in the context of environmental policy-making and landscape planning', *Environmental Science and Policy*, vol 4, nos 4–5, pp185–203

Cheng, A., Kruger, L. E. and Daniels, S. E. (2003) ' "Place" as an integrating concept in natural resource politics: Propositions for a social science research agenda', *Society and Natural Resources*, vol 16, no 3, pp87–104

Dhimurru Land Management Aboriginal Corporation (2003) home page, http://members.iinet.net.au/~dhimurru/about.html, accessed 10 January 2005

Huggins, J., Huggins, R. and Jacobs, J. M. (1995) 'Kooramindanjie: Place and the postcolonial', *History Workshop Journal*, vol 39, pp165–181

Johnson, L. (2000) *Placebound: Australian Feminist Geographies*, Oxford University Press, South Melbourne

Kemmis, D. (1996), 'Community and the politics of place', in Brick, P. D. and McGreggor Cawley, R. (eds) *A Wolf in the Garden: The Land Rights Movement and the New Environmental Debate*, Rowman and Littlefield Publishers, Lanham, MD

Knowles, M. S., Holton, E. F. and Swanson, R. A. (1998) *The Adult Learner: The Definitive Classic in Adult Education and Human Resource Development*, 5th edn, Butterworth-Heinemann, Woburn, MA

Kolb, D. A., Osland, J. S. and Rubin, I. M. (1995) *Organizational Behavior: An Experiential Approach*, 6th edn, Prentice Hall, Englewood Cliffs, NJ

McTaggart, W. D. (1993) 'Bioregionalism and regional geography: Place, people and networks', *Canadian Geographer*, vol 37, no 4, pp307–319

Marika-Mununggiritj, R. and Christie, M. J. (1995) 'Yolngu metaphors for learning', *International Journal of the Sociology of Language*, vol 113, pp59–62

Massey, D. (1994) *A Global Sense of Place, Space, Place and Gender*, Polity Press, Cambridge, pp146–156

Moore, S. A. (1997) ' "Place" and sustainability: Research opportunities and dilemmas', in Vanclay, F. and Mesiti, L. (eds) *Sustainability and Social Research: Proceedings of the Conference of Australian Association for Social Research*, Charles Sturt University, Wagga Wagga, NSW

Plumwood, V. (2002) *Environmental Culture: The Ecological Crisis of Reason*, Routledge, London

Relph, E. (1976) *Place and Placelessness*, Pion Limited, London

Robinson, C. and Munungguritj, N. (2001) 'Sustainable balance: A Yolngu framework for cross-cultural collaborative management', in Baker, R., Davies, J. and Young, E. (eds) *Working on Country: Contemporary Indigenous Management of Australia's Lands and Coastal Regions*, Oxford University Press, South Melbourne

Spiller, R. (2000) 'Ethical business and investment: A model for business and society', *Journal of Business Ethics*, vol 27, no 1/2, pp149–160

Stoll-Kleeman, S. and O'Riordan, T. (2002), 'Enhancing biodiversity and humanity', in O'Riordan, T. and Stoll-Kleeman, S. (eds) *Biodiversity, Sustainability and Human Communities: Protecting Beyond the Protected*, Cambridge University Press, Cambridge

Suchet, S. (2001) 'Challenging "wildlife management": Lessons for Australia from Zimbabwe, Namibia, and South Africa', in Baker, R., Davies, J. and Young, E. (eds) *Working on Country: Contemporary Indigenous Management of Australia's Lands and Coastal Regions*, Oxford University Press, South Melbourne

Tuan, Y.-F. (1974) 'Space and place: Humanistic perspective', *Progress in Geography*, vol 6, pp211–252

Williams, D. R. and Patterson, M. E. (1996) 'Environmental meaning and ecosystem management: Perspectives from environmental psychology and human geography', *Society & Natural Resources*, vol 9, pp507–521

Wittayapak, C. and Dearden, P. (1999) 'Decision-making arrangements in community-based watershed management in northern Thailand', *Society & Natural Resources*, vol 12, pp673–691

7

Collaborative Learning: Bridging Scales and Interests

Meg Keen and Sango Mahanty

At a glance

- Our capacity to collaboratively learn about and respond to changing circumstances in our biophysical and social environments is vital for successful environmental management
- Collaborative management attempts to realize these goals, but often focuses on project cycles and processes of participation rather than on the learning processes
- This chapter focuses on processes of collaborative learning within co-management
- Case studies from the South Pacific highlight that collaborative learning can help bridge the social differences between interest groups and scales of management
- Co-learning processes can encourage negotiation of learning agendas, clarification of roles and responsibilities and reflection on the distribution of social power and the diverse ways of knowing.

Learning our way towards sustainable environmental management

Environmental management aimed at achieving social and ecological sustainability will depend on our ability to collectively recognize and respond to changing circumstances and unfamiliar trends. Resolving complex environmental problems such as global climate change, fisheries decline or soil salinity requires learning across disciplines, cultural and social divides and levels of governance. This social learning process involves groups, communities and organizations collaboratively taking action based on a joint analysis of problems, their causes and solutions, and entering into learning partnerships to apply their knowledge innovatively (Holling et al, 1998; Jiggins and Röling, 2002). This chapter looks at the challenges and opportunities posed by the dual aims of collaboration and learning.

Environmental management involving the participation of multiple stake-holders is the basis of the collaborative management or co-management approach. Co-management involves a partnership between different stake-holders for an area or set of resources for which common goals have been established (Renard, 1997). Co-management recognizes the value of different types of knowledge (for example scientific and local) and integrates local and higher-level management systems (Berkes et al, 1991; Borrini-Feyerabend, 1997). While co-management is generally framed around an adaptive management or 'learning by doing' philosophy (Borrini-Feyerabend et al, 2001), the mechanics of how this learning can occur in practice have not been well examined. For this reason, we have chosen to focus on the learning aspect of co-management, which can be referred to as collaborative learning or co-learning (Daniels and Walker, 1996).

In this chapter we discuss the issues that are central to resolving different values and beliefs in developing a co-learning agenda. We examine case studies of environmental management initiatives from the South Pacific, highlighting the challenges in co-learning. In particular, we consider how co-learning processes can encourage negotiation of learning agendas, clarification of roles and responsibilities and reflection on the distribution of social power and the diverse ways of knowing.

We start by looking at where some of the central challenges in co-learning lie.

Challenges in co-learning

Co-learning involves a range of social actors negotiating and agreeing on the nature of the required learning and actions, their respective roles and respon-sibilities and the processes of reflection that will occur over space and time. It is best viewed as an iterative process of collaboration and negotiation between actors that is strongly affected by dynamic social networks, relationships and structures. Figure 7.1 provides an overview of the co-learning process. It shows the need for tools and approaches that facilitate multi-stakeholder engagement in defining, analysing, negotiating, organizing, implementing and reflecting on activities aimed at achieving sustainable environmental manage-ment. In practice, the different stages can interact with each other and are not strictly cyclical, for example reflections can occur at any stage. Thus the simplified cycle can be seen as a wheel, with the co-learning hub at the centre. While the outer cycle is dominant, interactions occur across the wheel.

Co-learning processes are embedded in a web of complex and evolving social relationships and structures (see Chapter 3). Social relationships such

Figure 7.1 *Co-learning: Collaborative and adaptive management with a learning focus*

as power relations, cultural norms, and communication networks can support or hinder co-learning processes. They are supportive when the co-learning processes incorporate these social relationships and use them as a means to advance the learning process. However, there are times when the act of learning can reveal the weaknesses of existing social relationships and thus challenge present practice. Resistance to change can create tensions within a social system, but out of this tension can come great benefits – if managed well. The same applies for social institutions such as knowledge systems, government agencies and formal and informal rules that enable or constrain people in their decisions and choices (for more on social relations and structures see Cohen, 1989; Giddens, 1991). The cases discussed later in this chapter demonstrate both the difficulties and importance of addressing these relationships and structures.

Co-learning processes involving multiple interest groups often result in conflicts that need to be negotiated. These negotiations have to address contested understandings, activities and values that shape preferred learning and management strategies. This calls for a reflexive learning agenda that allows participants to consider how they have developed their knowledge, their learning preferences and the relationship of their knowledge to that of others. In negotiating a learning agenda, consideration should be given to instrumental goals (such as learning new skills and facts), as well as transformative goals that allow participants to understand, engage in and change social networks, structures and relationships that enhance or hinder their activities.

To sum up, the challenge in effective co-learning is to enable key stakeholders to collaboratively define the learning agenda and jointly shape the learning process – important prerequisites for true learning partnerships in planning, decision making and adaptive management. Using case studies from the Pacific, we can examine these processes and related issues in greater detail, and flag innovative approaches to working through them.

Social relationships in learning processes

Learning can be conceived of as a social phenomenon, reflecting our own deeply social nature as human beings (Wenger, 2000, 2001). The relationships and social structures that affect communications and interactions between people and their environments provide the scaffolding on which learning occurs. These relationships between actors are particularly critical in co-management, where parties come together to negotiate learning and management regimes that are subject to continual review (Borrini-Feyerabend et al, 2001).

Two cases studies, both involving the Biodiversity Conservation Network, are discussed next (see Box 7.1). These studies highlight the influential role that the nature of the relationship between individuals and key social actors can play in defining a project's management focus and learning outcomes. In the first case involving local marine management in Fiji, it has been possible to define a shared agenda where relationships between stakeholders are on a more equal footing because of tenure and other economic and political factors. However, in the example of the Arnavon and Kalahan projects, the actors holding the purse strings largely defined the learning agenda. The first case demonstrates that when communities are engaged in designing and implementing the learning process, their commitment is strengthened because they are able to ensure that the monitoring and other data collection processes are directly relevant to local decision making and resource management. Where this learning partnership is missing, as it is in the second example, local project staff grudgingly collected what seemed to be esoteric data for a remote donor agency. Because the data was not directly relevant to their interests and management needs, they did not engage in a learning process, or adjust their management practices.

Box 7.1 Participatory adaptive management in the Biodiversity Conservation Network

The Biodiversity Conservation Network was an innovative programme operating from 1993 until 1999, which supported 20 projects in seven countries throughout the Asia–Pacific region. The projects displayed a wide spectrum of collaborative learning, from limited local involvement to more extensive engagement in learning processes, highlighting the importance of social relationships in co-learning.

The programme used a learning and adaptive management framework to analyse factors that can contribute to the success of enterprise-oriented approaches to community-based conservation. Like the Locally Managed Marine Area (LMMA) Network (see Box 7.2), the programme aimed to document and apply new learning about the integration of conservation and enterprise-based approaches to environmental management. Projects were required to monitor their social, economic and biological impacts. Staff then developed conceptual tools, provided training and developed a common analytical framework to enable comparison between sites, and devoted considerable resources to documenting and disseminating learning from experience.

The Biodiversity Conservation Network programme shaped the learning agenda at project sites in a number of ways. It selected projects on the basis of compatibility with the key questions driving the programme and developed a programme-wide analytical framework to provide a structure for project-based monitoring. The participatory adaptive management experience in the Biodiversity Conservation Network highlights the need to openly negotiate learning agendas in order to ensure that the information gained from monitoring processes can be shared and used by stakeholders.

An example of a Biodiversity Conservation Network project that was successful in facilitating strong local engagement in developing monitoring systems and the learning agenda was the Verata Tikina project in Fiji. This initiative later extended to a broader programme for locally managed marine areas in Fiji and had a very similar approach of defining learning objectives and methods with local stakeholders (see Box 7.2). John Parks, the person facilitating the training of villagers in monitoring techniques, reported a high degree of 'buy-in' at the village level to the concept of monitoring, and in defining monitoring indicators. An example of this was the community's selection of the salt water cockle as an indictor of environmental health, as it is also a resource highly valued by the community (Biodiversity Conservation Network, 1998b). Social factors that contributed to the reported high degree of community engagement and cooperation include customary tenure over marine resources, the strong commitment of community leaders to monitoring and sustainable resource use and a high degree of community cohesion and engagement.

In contrast to the success of the Fijian project, the Solomon Island's Arnavon Islands Marine Conservation Area biological monitoring programme was much more limited. As only low local engagement was achieved, a more limited learning outcome resulted, and this was geared more to the interests of the research and professional community than the local community. This programme was designed and implemented by scientists from the International Centre for Living Aquatic and Marine Resources and The Ecology Lab Pty Ltd (an Australian-based consulting company), in consultation with staff from the Solomon Islands Fisheries Division of the Ministry of Agriculture and Fisheries, and conservation officers working with the project. It aimed to assess the effects of protection efforts on the abundance and distribution of particular marine species within the protected area, as well as train government and project staff in survey techniques.

The management committee for the project approved the monitoring programme in 1994, but members later commented that survey findings were expressed in quite 'technical' terms, and had not yet been used in their decision making. Furthermore, the monitoring programme used the abundance of some key marine species as an indicator of resource recovery, but did not assess growth rates. The latter would have helped the management committee and participating communities to design a system of sustainable harvest for marine resources in the wider Arnavon area. The failure to address questions of sustainable harvest meant that the results lacked relevance for future management. Furthermore, the failure to communicate in terminology and vernacular that was meaningful to villagers hindered the extent of social learning. The monitoring programme therefore did not serve a direct management purpose or share learning across social domains or levels of governance.

Sources: Biodiversity Conservation Network (1998a, 1998b, 1999); Mahanty (1999, 2002); Mahanty and Encarnacion (1999); Mahanty and Russell (2002); Mahanty et al (1999); Margoluis and Salafsky (1998); Salafsky and Margoluis (1999); Salafsky and Wollenberg (2000); Salafsky et al (1999)

Drawing on the Biodiversity Conservation Network programme, some key requirements to be considered in co-learning include the need to:

*   provide adequate resources – including physical, technical and human resources for negotiating and implementing a learning process
*   seek a wide range of ideas and knowledge – important when defining the learning agenda, determining appropriate methods and interpreting the meaning of data and its implications
*   negotiate the learning agenda – agreeing on the learning focus and ways to collect, analyse, interpret and communicate information
*   reflect on what has been learned – the implications of learning may be useful for future actions at the local or broader scales.

Collaboration needs to occur in all of these areas for co-learning to occur. Where local stakeholders and project staff just contribute resources or implement a predetermined learning agenda, they are unlikely to fully engage in the learning process.

A flexible approach is needed to achieve whole-of-community learning processes. Lin (2001) notes that social networks that span levels of society can enhance the flexibility of systems and reduce the costs associated with information exchange and communication. Networks between stakeholders can thus be of fundamental importance in supporting co-learning, as highlighted by the Locally Managed Marine Area Network case study (see Box 7.2). In this instance the learning process is tiered to ensure that participation is sustained across scales, and is designed to meet diverse needs. Communities define issues to be addressed, devise a monitoring programme to help judge the effectiveness of their actions at the local level and then do the monitoring with minimal outside assistance. However, such diverse monitoring programmes at the local level may not be directly comparable with findings from other communities. In Fiji, community monitoring is supported by university researchers with relevant expertise and the ability (and incentive) to collect and manage data across communities and over time.

In the Locally Managed Marine Area Network, this kind of integration is facilitated to some extent through capacity building for interested community members. A small number of respected community members are given training to increase their understanding of relevant external resources, research institution and non-governmental organization (NGO) activities and programmes and scientific monitoring and evaluation techniques that may benefit their community. In return, they provide valuable insights into their community's values and resource use patterns, and enable a better flow of information between their community and the network staff (pers comm, J. Veitayaki and I. Korovulavula, University of the South Pacific, February 2003). This community commitment is matched by the indigenous staff members (or people familiar with community vernacular) from tertiary institutions or NGOs who visit the communities regularly to learn about the outcomes of their monitoring and the social and ecological issues of concern to them. On these visits, they share the results of their own research.

For outsiders, the incentives to sustain the learning partnership are the information they gain and the ability to ground their research. For the community, the incentives are the human resources and social networks they can use to support local development and conservation. Both the locals and outsiders have a common goal, the sustainable development of the local fisheries and ongoing learning through monitoring and adaptive management. The learning partnership is thus founded on networks between social groups with different interests, knowledge and languages, and provides a platform on which different types of knowledge can be shared and synthesized. A key element of this learning process is the nurturing of facilitators from two very different communities who enable an improved flow of ideas and knowledge between social groups.

Box 7.2 Creating co-learning partnerships: Fiji Locally Managed Marine Area Network

The Fiji Locally Managed Marine Area Network is a collaborative initiative aimed at bringing together different stakeholders including local communities, conservation practitioners, government officials and researchers. It is based on a learning portfolio, which is a system to track and record common learning experiences across several projects. By putting in place mechanisms to support each other in collecting, testing, interpreting and communicating information, participants use a common strategy to improve marine resource management in Fiji. The network now covers six districts in Fiji, or 10 per cent of Fiji's total inshore marine area.

Each project follows a process that involves describing: typical conditions at the sites, types of LMMA Network strategies in use, assumptions of how using these strategies will change prevailing conditions, and information to be collected to test assumptions (Locally Managed Marine Area Network, 2003, p1–4). The similarities between this process and the simplified learning cycle described in Chapter 1 are evident (see Figure 1.3). The goal of the learning portfolio is to make the learning process more efficient by sharing learning experiences across projects.

Ideas and experiences are exchanged through multi-stakeholder workshops and reports to help stakeholders critically reflect on practice and anticipate future challenges. In this way, isolated experiments and learning experiences that are usually separated by geographic spaces and barriers among communities, conservationists and researchers are being synthesized. This is contributing to a wider social learning process at a regional and international level. Examples of the types of projects being implemented and monitored include replanting and rehabilitating mangroves, removing the invasive Crown of Thorns starfish, designating protected areas and implementing district licensing systems. Despite the diversity of projects, they are intended to share a common learning framework that promotes:

- common objectives – such as the integration of conservation and development
- common monitoring categories – these are broadly defined to allow flexibility and responsiveness to local ecological and livelihood concerns
- a common language – the use of the local vernacular is encouraged, and technical and academic jargon is avoided
- common values – for example commitment, transparency, empowerment, respect, fun and a belief that practitioners can make a difference.

A mix of scientific and traditional knowledge contributes to the success of these measures. For example, traditional knowledge of the location and structure of mangroves is combined with scientific knowledge of rehabilitation.

Traditional resource management practices are implemented, but monitored by the community using simple biological, social and economic methods that they have chosen. This increases the likelihood that learning from monitoring will be used to adapt community practice, and to influence external decision making processes.

As noted in the Biodiversity Conservation Network case study (see Box 7.1), community-led monitoring can sustain a high level of commitment to the learning process and behaviour change. The disadvantage is that the community may define the learning process narrowly. In some cases, the community-driven monitoring process has resulted in some omissions of important data for the overall assessment of the programme. For example, little information has been collected on the economic and social costs and benefits of the initiatives and most of the monitoring has focused only on those marine species deemed important to the community and their livelihoods.

However, the overall strength and success of this innovative initiative has been widely recognized. The United Nations International Coral Reef Action Network has chosen it as a demonstration site for its new projects in the region. The World Summit on Sustainable Development chose it as one of six recipients of the United Nations Development Programme's Equator Initiative: The Innovative Partnership Awards for Sustainable Development in Tropical Ecosystems. Most importantly, the communities continue to support locally managed marine areas, with more districts involved in discussions to join the programme and widen the learning network.

Note: Organizational websites: www.fosonline.org, www.lmmanetwork.org

Sources: Veitayaki et al (2002); pers comm, Joeli Veitayaki, Senior Lecturer, University of the South Pacific, 5 February 2003

Power relations in learning processes

The process of building partnerships reveals imbalances in the power individuals and groups hold in society. There is an old adage that 'knowledge is power', to which one could add that certain knowledge tends to wield greater power than other types. Co-learning initiatives that aim to be participatory and adaptive need to directly address the relationship between power and knowledge. In the case of locally managed marine areas, the power and value of local knowledge has been increased through documenting and presenting data in forms understandable and acceptable to decision makers and funding bodies. Interest in and resources for locally managed marine areas in Fiji increased significantly when locals presented their long-term monitoring data formally to government officials using graphs and trend diagrams. Conversely, those wishing to work with the communities need to convey their interests or research in terms understandable to the community. With the government now keen to adopt the Fiji Locally Managed Marine Area framework, an interesting issue arises about how uneven power relations between government and communities will be negotiated, and whether the communities can maintain their interests and independence.

When external development agencies dominate learning processes associated with development, there is often an implicit assumption that the learning is one-way, from external agents to communities, and is limited to imparting skills and discretely packaged information. A more participatory and critical view of the development process and associated learning agendas can encourage negotiation of the costs and benefits of engaging in a learning approach to environmental management.

To establish environmental management founded on co-learning, we need to question the 'one-way' learning model. Throughout the Pacific, communities are beginning to demand that the nature of the development process, and associated learning partnerships, be agreed in advance and documented. The aim of these agreements is to ensure that mutual obligations and benefits are discussed and agreed in advance. Core principles and goals are defined, while innovation and flexibility for learning approaches and activities are maintained. For example, in a Samoan fisheries project supported by the Australian aid agency, AusAID, formal and informal agreements are being used to define roles and responsibilities that affect learning processes in fisheries management. The LMMA Network also uses agreements between stakeholders covering access to monitoring data, capacity building and management responsibilities. These agreements reduce the transaction costs of sharing knowledge through complementary monitoring networks, shared project officers and joint workshops involving communities from diverse geographic localities and practitioners from different agencies.

Projects like the Biodiversity Conservation Network and Locally Managed Marine Area Network work with pre-existing leadership structures. This allows adaptive management to occur because those with the power to act are formally engaged with the project. The weakness of such an approach is that marginal groups within the community may remain marginal to the social learning process, and the learning process may become flawed because important knowledge of marginal groups is neglected. Ultimately, learning is political and affects power relations however it is structured, and thus learning agendas will have to be negotiated on a case-by-case basis with a critical awareness of social relationships and structures. Over time, as trust and experience are built, more space opens up to reflect critically on the values, assumptions and social structures affecting resource management.

This discussion highlights that power is not just about domination, but more subtly it is about the power to act (Dowding, 1996). Wenger (2000) notes that power is derived not only from the resources we command and the knowledge we hold, but also from belonging. We gain power and knowledge from the social groups with whom we associate, provided we can maintain agreement on core values and principles, or re-negotiate the nature of our belonging to that group. An adaptive and collaborative approach ultimately demands that people are open to re-negotiating interpretations and understandings that are dominant in their social groups. The adaptive and collaborative approach involves incremental change, allowing the system to adjust over time. This adjustment will still give rise to tensions, but these tensions are an important catalyst to producing new meanings and innovative learning.

Communicating meaning and knowledge

Co-learning needs tools that allow us to transcend our different values, perspectives, languages and meanings, and begin to build bridges between social groups that do not commonly interact or communicate with each other. If communication is a process of 'creating meaning' (Ticehurst and Ross-Smith, 1998), then communication has a central role to play in learning processes that create knowledge across social divides. Pritchard and Sanderson (2002, p156) claim that communication across social divides can be challenging because, 'Just as we can fail to perceive the accents with which we speak, we can fail to recognise the distinctiveness and the limitations of the discourse we use'.

Knowledge systems can create filters through which we selectively view the world. The positivist, scientific mode of inquiry underpinning the adaptive management framework has emphasized modelling, and gathering measurable and objective data on the impacts of specific actions (Jiggins and Röling, 2002; Zanetell and Knuth, 2002). A tension has emerged between this focus and that of local stakeholders, whose knowledge often stems from experience and detailed knowledge of the local context (Zanetell and Knuth, 2002). In the Arnavon case (see Box 7.1), the technical mode of monitoring and analysis dominated, resulting in data and findings that were not meaningful to most local participants. The Locally Managed Marine Area Network case and the Biodiversity Conservation Network project in Fiji, on the other hand, have been better able to blend local and technical perspectives. Combining knowledges can reveal the hidden assumptions that are embedded in research and used to filter information. It can lead to learning about ourselves and our professions, as well as about our management practices (Berardi, 2002). But how much scope is there for blending the positivist and interpretive modes of understanding, whether they be characterized by local–expert, social–science or other divisions in society?

While the Biodiversity Conservation Network conducted both quantitative and qualitative monitoring and research, the final programme analysis privileged a quantitative approach. All of the findings of qualitative studies were translated into numerical rankings to facilitate comparison of various qualitative factors across the board. Quantification was embraced in the interests of comparison and standardization, but the richness of experience and information is lost in this process. The Biodiversity Conservation Network case highlights that, far from always being a gap between technical and community stakeholders, gulfs between knowledge systems can also exist among professional advisory staff, and that breaking down and levelling these differing perspectives within donor agencies can be equally as important as bridging the local–technical gap.

Zanetell and Knuth (2002) cite participatory appraisal methods as one important contribution to building a partnership among knowledge systems and challenging the historical dominance of positivist technical knowledge. Participatory approaches establish bridging networks that facilitate information and influence flows among different groups (Lin, 2001). Participatory methods such as participatory rural appraisal (Chambers, 1990, 1992, 1997), participatory learning and action (Pretty, 1995) and participatory monitoring and evaluation (Estrella and Gaventa, 1997) have been used to pull together a suite of tools that help to create integrated communication and learning processes. For example, participatory rural appraisal involves field workers or 'experts' learning with local people with the aim of facilitating local capacity to analyse, plan, resolve conflicts, take action and monitor and evaluate according to a local agenda (Jackson and Ingles, 1995).

The tools associated with participatory methods are process-oriented, aimed at creating dialogues through different mediums that can incorporate diverse constructs and languages. In many cases the communication methods jointly create symbols, shared experiences and agreed histories. Typical tools include:

- community mapping of resources to understand current interactions between people and their environments
- diagram drawing by different social groups to reflect the social relationships affecting interactions between people and their environments (Venn diagrams)
- timelines to reflect the interactions between human activities and system responses
- transect walks to allow outsiders to see and understand the environment through the eyes of another
- collective matrix ranking to work with communities to prioritize their problems and/or potential management options (for more information on participatory appraisal see Mosse, 1994; Pretty et al, 1995).

By synthesizing information through multi-stakeholder workshops, stakeholders can potentially understand the system in all its complexity, as a basis for planning actions and monitoring programmes. In theory, the different tools overcome language barriers and communication styles. In practice, the value of the techniques depends on the skills of the facilitator and the willingness of the groups involved to share their experiences. However, true understanding between stakeholders at different scales requires more than techniques. It also depends on a commitment of time and an attitude of humility on the part of technical experts, which help to develop mutual understanding and trust (Poffenberger, 2000). This is encapsulated in the words of a former project manager in the Arnavon project on the need to work with a 'beginner's mind', which is open to new perspectives and ideas (Mayer and Brown, no date).

The tools and techniques we use to encourage co-learning are themselves an extension of the cultures and knowledge systems from which they have been derived. Some tools may serve to democratize the learning process, while others may simply reinforce pre-existing learning hierarchies and knowledge frameworks. Making generalized moral judgements out of context about the value of different tools and approaches is unlikely to be helpful. It is more prudent to collaboratively evaluate the characteristics of the learning approach and possible tools within a given context.

Conclusions

Core questions associated with the five strands of learning outlined in Chapter 1 provide a useful starting point for assessing co-learning. Does the learning approach or tool:

- encourage reflection?
- promote a systems orientation?
- generate integrated analyses?
- facilitate negotiated processes and outcomes?
- enhance the broad participation of stakeholder groups?

While examples of innovative institutional arrangements have been discussed in this chapter, there are many others that fail to bridge knowledge and cultural divides. In some cases, the arrangements are foreign to the very people they are designed to serve, imposing cultures of compliance and governance that require skills and values not present in the relevant communities (Sesega, 2000). These arrangements hinder the flow of information and the building of common experiences and learning. Decision making, management and monitoring processes all need to be negotiated and contextually relevant if learning is not to be disregarded as belonging to another group.

The six main stages of co-learning shown in Figure 7.1 attempt to address the five strands of learning and foster an inclusive and negotiated learning process. At each of the six stages there is an opportunity to nurture and extend social networks by increasing the understanding across groups of interests, knowledge and values affecting learning and management processes. The double-headed arrows across the wheel highlight the importance of flexibility in environmental management processes. Sometimes we need to go back to a previous stage and review our decisions, at other times we need to consider where we are going in order to better inform our decisions. All of this is part of a collaborative learning process.

Establishing and maintaining strong collaboration throughout the co-learning cycle is challenging, as the co-learning process is not always synchronized at each stage of the cycle. The Locally Managed Marine Area Network tries to overcome problems of pre-existing weak collaboration by using organizational arrangements (such as learning portfolios and political partnerships) to facilitate interactions between levels of government and diverse communities. In a recent World Bank (1999) comparative study of coastal resource management in the Pacific Islands, one of the core lessons learned was that stronger partnerships among communities, government and practitioners were needed to build capacity, skills and social relationships, and structures supporting sustainable coastal management. Without partnerships across scales, national and local levels begin to operate in isolation from each other, using information and experiences that are relevant only to their own particular context.

Co-learning encourages participatory and adaptive approaches in environmental management, which involve diverse social actors negotiating and synthesizing knowledge over time. Fundamental to co-learning is the negotiation of learning agendas, including the roles and responsibilities of participants, taking into account power relationships and different ways of knowing and communicating. By addressing these issues transparently, the 'politics of learning' associated with different types of knowledge, different modes of learning and relationships among stakeholders can be more openly addressed.

For co-learning to be successful, bridges among the diverse actors involved in learning processes need to be built. The bridges can be built by facilitators with skills to communicate across social groups, institutional structures that facilitate learning among knowledge communities, or learning processes that transcend disciplinary and social divides and create new tools and symbols. Building knowledge partnerships is partially about finding methods that enable different perspectives to be taken into account, but it is also about social relationships, social networks, trust and humility. By strengthening social networks across social divides, learning opportunities can be created through the improved flow of information and communications.

More attention must be given to whether the assumptions underlying analyses are biased towards a given perspective (scientific, customary, local, technical) or a given social group (males, high-income earners, decision makers). Monitoring and reflecting on our assumptions and our actions can help to reveal patterns of thinking and acting that either support or undermine environmental management. It is only when we learn to build these bridges and recognize these patterns that we can achieve social learning that ensures sustainable environmental management.

References

Berardi, G. (2002) 'Commentary on the challenge to change: Participatory research and professional realities', *Society and Natural Resources*, vol 15, pp847–852

Berkes, F., George, R. and Preson, R. (1991) 'Co-management: The evolution of theory and practice of the joint administration of living resources', *Alternatives*, vol 18, no 2, pp12–18

Biodiversity Conservation Network (1998a) *Analytical Framework and Communications Strategy*, Biodiversity Support Program, Washington, DC

Biodiversity Conservation Network (1998b) *Lessons from the Field, No. 1: Keeping Watch: Experiences from the Field in Community-based Monitoring*, Biodiversity Support Program, Washington, DC

Biodiversity Conservation Network (1999) *Synopsis of the BCN Results Dissemination Workshop*, 4 February 1999, Environmental Education Center, Miriam College, Manila, Philippines, Biodiversity Conservation Network

Borrini-Feyerabend, G. (ed) (1997) *Beyond Fences: Seeking Social Sustainability in Conservation*, The World Conservation Union (IUCN), Gland, Switzerland

Borrini-Feyerabend, G., Taghi Farvar, M., Nguinguiri, J. and Ndangang, V. (2001) *Comanagement of Natural Resources: Organising, Negotiating and Learning-by-doing*, The World Conservation Union (IUCN) and GTZ, Gland, Switzerland

Chambers, R. (1990) 'Rapid and participatory appraisal', *Appropriate Technology*, vol 16, no 4, pp14–31

Chambers, R. (1992) *Rural Appraisal: Rapid, Relaxed and Participatory*, University of Sussex, Brighton, UK

Chambers, R. (1997) *Whose Reality Counts? Putting the First Last*, Intermediate Technology Publications, London

Cohen, I. (1989) *Structuration Theory: Anthony Giddens and the Constitution of Social Life*, Macmillan Education, Basingstoke

Daniels, S. E. and Walker, G. B. (1996) 'Collaborative learning: Improving public deliberation in ecosystem-based management', *Environmental Impact Assessment Review*, vol 16, pp71–102

Dowding, K. (1996) *Power*, University of Minnesota Press, Minneapolis

Estrella, M. and Gaventa, J. (1997) *Who Counts Reality? Participatory Monitoring and Evaluation – A Literature Review*, IDS, London

Giddens, A. (1991) 'Structuration Theory: Past, Present and Future', in Bryant, C. and Jary, D. (eds) *Giddens' Theory of Structuration: A Critical Appreciation*, Routledge, London, www.iucn.org/themes/spg/Files/beyond_fences/beyond_fences. html#contents

Holling, C. S., Berkes, F. and Folke, C. (1998) 'Science, sustainability and resource management', in Berkes, F. and Folke, C. (eds) *Linking Social and Ecological Systems: Management Practices and Social Mechanisms for Building Resilience*, Cambridge University Press, Cambridge

Jackson, B. and Ingles, A. (1995) *Participatory Techniques for Community Forestry: A Field Manual*, Technical Note 5/95, Nepal Australia Community Forestry Project, ANUTECH, Canberra

Jiggins, J. and Röling, N. (2002) 'Adaptive management: Potential and limitations for ecological governance of forests in a context of normative pluriformity', in Oglethorpe, J. A. E. (ed) *Adaptive Management: From Theory to Practice*, The World Conservation Union (IUCN), Gland, Switzerland

Lin, N. (2001) *Social Capital: A Theory of Social Structure and Action*, Cambridge University Press, Cambridge

Locally Managed Marine Area Network (2003) *Learning Framework for the Locally-Managed Areas Network*, LMMA Network, Suva, Fiji

Mahanty, S. (1999) 'Case study of the Arnavon Islands Marine Conservation Area: The Arnavon Management Committee, Solomon Islands', unpublished report to the Biodiversity Conservation Network, Washington, DC

Mahanty, S. (2002) 'Building bridges: Lessons from the Arnavon Management Committee, Solomon Islands', *Development Bulletin*, vol 58, July, pp88–92

Mahanty, S. and Encarnacion, W. C. (1999) 'Case study of Kalahan Educational Foundation, Philippines', unpublished report to the Biodiversity Conservation Network, Washington, DC

Mahanty, S. and Russell, D. (2002) 'High stakes: Working with stakeholders in the Biodiversity Conservation Network', *Society and Natural Resources*, vol 15, pp179–188

Mahanty, S., Russell, D. and Bhatt, S. (1999) *What's at Stake? Overview Paper on Stakeholder Organisations in the Biodiversity Conservation Network*, report to the Biodiversity Conservation Network, Washington, DC

Margoluis, R. and Salafsky, N. (1998) *Measures of Success: Designing, Managing and Monitoring Conservation and Development Projects*, Island Press, Washington, DC

Mayer, E. and Brown, S. (no date) 'The story of the Arnavon Marine Conservation Area', unpublished paper, Biodiversity Conservation Network Washington, DC

Mosse, D. (1994) 'Authority, gender and knowledge: Theoretical reflections on the practice of participatory rural appraisal', *Development and Change*, vol 25, pp497–526

Poffenberger, M. (1997) 'Local knowledge in conservation', in Borrini-Feyerabend, G. with Buchan, D. (eds) *Beyond Fences: Seeking Social Sustainability in Conservation*, Volume 2, The World Conservation Union (IUCN), Gland, Switzerland and Cambridge

Pretty, J. (1995) 'Participatory learning for sustainable agriculture', *World Development*, vol 23, no 8, pp1247–1263

Pretty, J., Guijt, I., Thompson, J. and Scoones, I. (1995) *Participatory Learning and Action: A Trainer's Guide*, IIED, London

Pritchard, L. and Sanderson, S. (2002) 'The dynamics of political discourse in seeking sustainability', in Gunderson, L. and Holling, C. (eds) *Panarchy: Understanding Transformations in Human and Natural Systems*, Island Press, Washington, DC, pp147–172

Renard, Y. (1997) 'Collaborative management for conservation', in Borrini-Feyerabend, G. with Buchan, D. (eds) *Beyond Fences: Seeking Social Sustainability in Conservation*, Volume 2, The World Conservation Union (IUCN), Gland, Switzerland

Salafsky, N., Cordes, B., Parks, J. and Hochman, C. (1999) *Evaluating Linkages Between Business, the Environment and Local Communities: Final Analytical Results from the Biodiversity Conservation Network*, Biodiversity Support Program, Washington, DC

Salafsky, N. and Margoluis, R. (1999) *Greater than the Sum of their Parts: Designing Conservation and Development Programs to Maximize Results and Learning*, Biodiversity Support Program, Washington, DC

Salafsky, N. and Wollenberg, E. (2000) 'Linking livelihoods and conservation: A conceptual framework and scale for assessing the integration of human needs and biodiversity', *World Development*, vol 28, no 8, pp1421–1438

Sesega, S. (2000) 'Necessary and sufficient conditions for sustaining community based conservation area projects: Experiences from the South Pacific Conservation Programme', 19th Annual Pacific Islands Conference, Success Stories, Continuing Challenges and Realistic Solutions, American Samoa

Ticehurst, G. and Ross-Smith, A. (1998) 'Professional communication, organisation, and management', *Australian Journal of Communication*, vol 25, no 2, pp1–12

Veitayaki, J., Aalbersberg, W., Tawake, A., Rupeni, E. and Tabunakawai, K. (2002) 'Mainstreaming resource conservation: The Fiji locally managed marine area network and its influence on national policy development', Resource Management in the Asia Pacific Working Paper

Wenger, E. (2000) 'Communities of practice and social learning systems', *Organization Articles*, vol 7, no 2, pp225–246

Wenger, E. (2001) *Communities of Practice: Learning, Meaning and Identity*, Cambridge University Press, Cambridge

World Bank (1999) 'Voices from the village: A comparative study of coastal resource management in the Pacific Islands', Pacific Islands Discussion Paper, No 9: East Asia and Pacific Region, Papua New Guinea and Pacific Islands Country Management Unit

Zanetell, B. and Knuth, B. (2002) 'Knowledge partnerships: Rapid rural appraisal's role in catalyzing community-based management in Venezuela', *Society and Natural Resources*, vol 15, pp805–825

Section 3

Learning Partnerships with Government

8

Linking Community and Government: Islands and Beaches

Valerie A. Brown and Jennifer Pitcher

At a glance

- Communities provide the basic social learning unit in the transition to global sustainability: they form islands of decision making in the larger sea of government and civil society
- A government-initiated social change programme to reduce greenhouse gases provides examples of negotiations between government and individual communities
- Government and community decision making are each built on five sectors of knowledge – individuals, local communities, specialist advisers, government agencies and holistic coordination
- The social learning in the programme involved all five constructions of knowledge being negotiated between the government agency and each community
- Successful outcomes required a neutral zone, like the beach around an island, where government agencies could negotiate with community members.

Where can we find community?

This chapter explores the contribution of government-sponsored whole-of-community social learning to restoring global ecological integrity. We can agree that a community is the basic unit through which desired social and environmental changes can be introduced. But we then need to ask: What is a community and how does it learn? One way to describe a community is to think of it being to people as a pod is to whales, a pack is to wolves or a flock is to birds. Separate individuals are held together by shared rules and meanings to form a cooperative group. At its simplest, a community is a set of people who are brought together by choice or force of circumstance, and who have learned to live, work and play together. The creation of a community and social learning are thus inseparable.

One of the chief characteristics of a community is the continuous adjustment of rules and meanings to ensure continuity (Douglas, 1973). The community's ultimate sustainability relies on the ability of those rules and meanings to respond to internal and external dynamics of change. A chance to study those changes is provided by 22 communities involved in a three-year government-sponsored greenhouse gas abatement programme. The basic assumptions behind the study are that community is the essential social learning unit on which to base global change towards a sustainable planet, and that community reconstruction of knowledge is the essence of social learning.

Any society carries within it systems of ethics, rules for behaviour and permissible ways of gaining knowledge, embedded in a shared language and a shared understanding of reality (Levi-Strauss, 1958). The experience of community adds a further, and crucial, dimension to society and to each individual's social learning. Being brought together by something shared, and feeling a sense of commitment and empowerment through being part of establishing one's own rules, creates subsets of people who form the rich warp in the weave of the organizational structures of a society. While each community can be (and more usually is) a subset of society, they can also individually cross and even dissolve social boundaries, like the whole-of-community support for the local football team, or the cross-sectional parents' committee of the local high school. Thus we can talk of multicultural communities, radical communities and marginalized communities, as well as of mainstream communities.

The Cool Communities case study provides an example of the many and varied forms a community can take (see Table 8.1). The 22 communities involved can be:

- place-based, formed by people who live or have lived in a specific locality
- values-based, as in a body of people with a common religion or profession, even though they may have never met in person
- occupation-based, from the same workplace or the same profession
- events-based, as in an immigrant community or a self-help recovery group
- skills-based, as in hobby groups and the fellowship aspect of trade unions
- intentional, as in the way of life in monastic, socialist, self-sufficient and sustainable communities (Ife, 1995). The link can be sharing resources, as in food and services cooperatives like the successful LETS (Local Economic Trading Scheme), or sharing space, as in a neighbourhood.

One usually thinks of small, face-to-face communities with about 60 members (the size of the 'tribe' through which ancient humans appear to have evolved into social beings). However, communities meeting the criteria of having rules and meanings that enable shared knowledge, skills and values can form at any scale. The United Nations aims to represent the global human community, and sometimes speaks successfully on its behalf. The European Union is far more than a trading group; it is a body of nations unified by some common interests and values, while separated by others. At the other end of the scale, local communities are linked together through their place-specific local knowledge, and their shared construction of a combined social, economic and ecological reality.

Kelman (1975) suggests that there are three stages in becoming involved with a new community as an adult. The first is through compliance, formally and explicitly accepting community rules and behaviours, as in signing on to a political party or a bushwalking group. Later comes identification, implicitly adopting the ways of the community as one's own behaviour and values, such as in recruiting others or taking responsibility for group maintenance tasks, accompanied by increasing trust in the community. Finally, through internalization, the community member incorporates their community's constructions of the world into their own identity and sense of external reality. This may happen implicitly or explicitly. Implicit adoption of the full set of rules involves the unquestioning trust that accompanies religious conversions and strong professional identities. Explicitly, knowingly, taking part in social change involves a critical reflection on the process that is the essence of self-determined social learning. It is this last process and its relationship to ecological integrity and sustainability that we are concerned with here.

Nested knowledges and whole-of-community learning

How is it possible to study the process of social learning in a range of individual communities so as to draw out lessons that can be used by other communities? And equally important, to learn lessons that can be shared by each community's decision making system of citizens, experts, industry and government agencies, without whose collaboration the change cannot continue? The process selected for study here is the negotiation of knowledge relationships within communities involved in the shifts in reality required in moving towards sustainable environmental management. The precise changes are the social, economic and physical outcomes of each community's decision to reduce emission of the greenhouse gases, carbon dioxide (from energy use) and nitrous oxide (industrial output).

In order to become a community in the first place, each community's version of reality has established its unique balance between local, specialized and organizational knowledge, with individual change agents and holistic thinkers as negotiators of change. Each community can be considered an island of these interacting knowledges, with new knowledge relationships waiting to cross the beaches that surround each island, hoping to negotiate the required change. Changes in energy use and technical tools go to the heart of the pre-existing social, economic and physical dimensions of the community involved.

Since the middle of the 20th century, it has been widely accepted that our knowledge (our interpretation of how the world works, our construction of reality) is not stored somewhere in libraries nor issued as an edict from some expert source. Knowledge is socially constructed individually within each human head. Berger and Luckmann's 1967 classic, *The Social Construction of Reality*, drew attention to how powerful ideas such as health, environment, time and progress are developed through individual experience and mediated through social interaction, until they can be quite differently interpreted from group to group.

Since the 16th-century Age of Enlightenment, any academic discussion on the construction of knowledge has been increasingly dominated by the many constructions of reality of the different expert fields (Toulmin, 1977). In a community, however, we have a pattern of reality constructed by the shared experience of the local community, the sum of the specialist interpretations, and the strategic thinking of local organizations including local government; and the contributions of individuals and the holistic perspective offered by the goal of sustainability (see Figure 8.1). So in the Cool Communities Program we have to consider the separate realities between communities, and between community and government. Within each community, we can expect to find a mix of separate realities.

Examined from this perspective, the greatest impediment to social learning for sustainability is the failure to recognize that all five constructions of knowledge are being called into play. The key decision making sectors are routinely fragmented (Berlin, 1998). For instance, take rates of resource consumption as an environmental management issue. Individuals adopt high consumption lifestyles regardless of the specialist advice that this is a danger to both their own health and that of the environment. Local knowledge supports over-consumption to protect local livelihoods, knowing that this is at the cost of the wider resources affecting human health and the environment. Specialist advisers give conflicting advice consistent with their various knowledge frameworks, and information that may be irrelevant to both local conditions and political priorities. Lack of consistent specialist advice and of community concern for the issue leads to a lack of political will and therefore lack of strategic direction. Absence of a holistic understanding of the community's shared vision of the future, coupled with the compartmentalization, means there may be no connections between all these (Brown, 2001a, 2001b).

A recent study of the contributions from the five constructions of knowledge listed in Figure 8.1 to regional decision making in the Murray–Darling River basin found an equal commitment to future regional sustainability. Significantly, the study found that the five groups used different languages

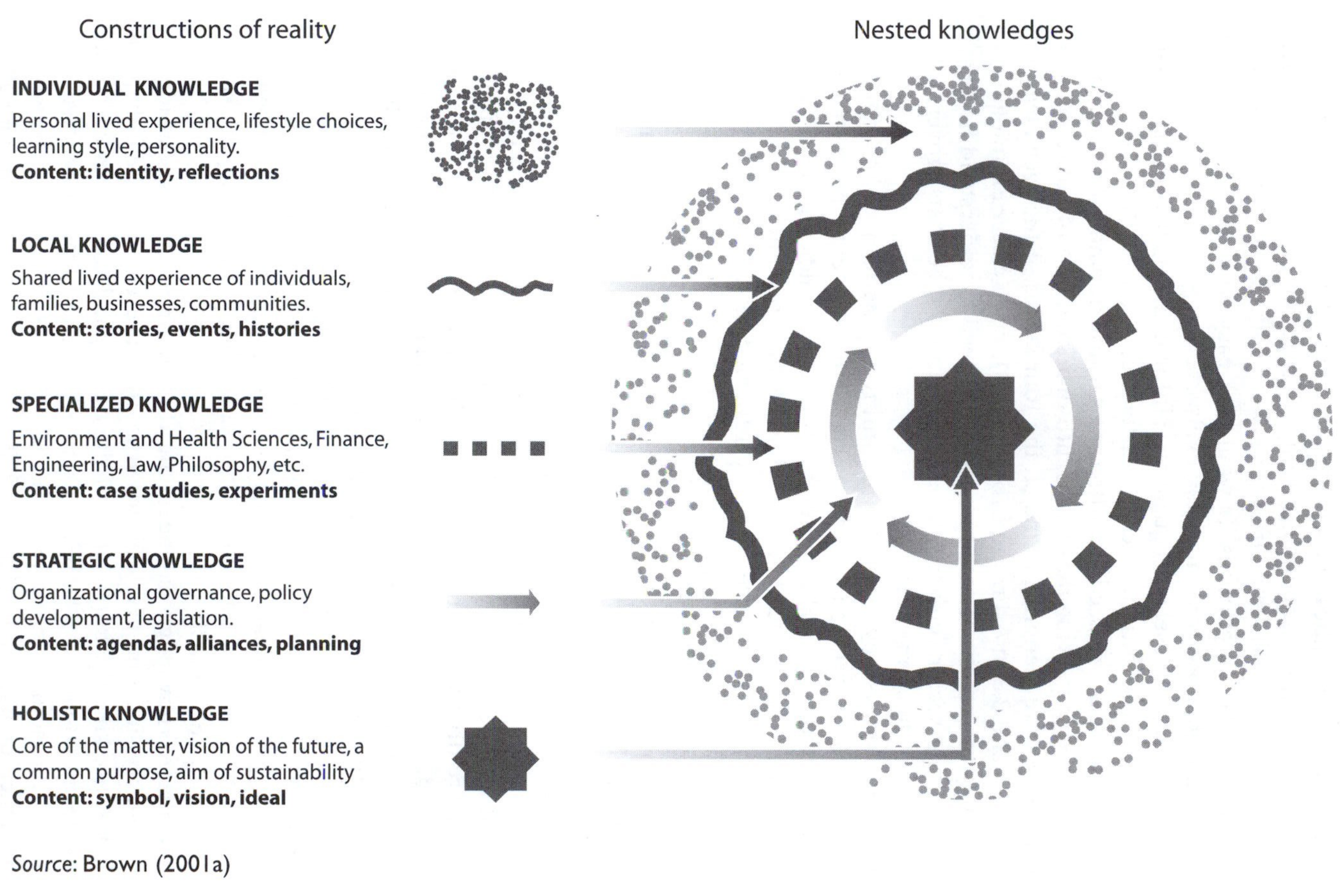

Nested knowledges

Constructions of reality

INDIVIDUAL KNOWLEDGE
Personal lived experience, lifestyle choices,
learning style, personality.
Content: identity, reflections

LOCAL KNOWLEDGE
Shared lived experience of individuals,
families, businesses, communities.
Content: stories, events, histories

SPECIALIZED KNOWLEDGE
Environment and Health Sciences, Finance,
Engineering, Law, Philosophy, etc.
Content: case studies, experiments

STRATEGIC KNOWLEDGE
Organizational governance, policy
development, legislation.
Content: agendas, alliances, planning

HOLISTIC KNOWLEDGE
Core of the matter, vision of the future, a
common purpose, aim of sustainability
Content: symbol, vision, ideal

Source: Brown (2001a)

Figure 8.1 *Knowledge cultures within Western decision making systems*

to describe distinctly different priorities among environmental management issues, and different choices among potential remedial practices and applied different performance indicators. They also identified different opportunities for, and impediments to, their different interpretations of good practice (Aslin and Brown, 2003). The differences were sufficiently great to amount to different knowledge cultures. It would be easy to conclude that these knowledge contributions were mutually exclusive.

To the contrary, each set was equally well informed, valuable and necessary for a comprehensive solution. Once the differences were on the table, synthesizing processes that engaged the different groups in whole-of-community processes were able to bring the groups into dialogue. Over 40 different tools of engagement were identified to match the four stages of the social learning (see Figures 1 and 2.3 in Aslin and Brown, 2003). For a closer examination of the case study of greenhouse gas reduction, we need to understand how each decision making sector (citizens, local community, specialists, government and holistic coordinators) functions.

Figure 8.1 shows how a whole-of-community pattern of knowledge is constructed and the relationships between the components. Note that each form of construction of local community knowledge builds on the one before. All learning starts in the head of individuals, which becomes the collectively shared community experience of place, informed by advice from specialist contributions, and shaped by the strategic directions set by the local power systems of governance. A holistic interpretation, agreement on the essence of the matter, allows the other constructions to work towards a common goal. The result can be represented as a set of nested knowledges.

Each of the nested knowledges has its own core body of content, ways of checking for truth, and well-defined knowledge boundaries. Each of these forms within set boundaries and determines what is included as true or rejected as false for that particular knowledge culture. The boundaries in Figure 8.1 are drawn so as to represent the limiting determinants of each of the knowledges. Individual knowledge is as varied as the number of people in a community. It is harnessed through shared experience and socialization into local common sense knowledge, giving each community its own identity and its own reality. The boundaries to the community decision making sector are thus unpredictable and diverse, matching their locally idiosyncratic base. Social learning for sustainability will need to address the traditional knowledge held deeply within each individual community. It can only really be known from the inside (Sahani, 2003).

Specialized knowledge has been the dominant form of knowledge in western society since the 17th century. It is often presented as the only 'true' knowledge, masking the importance of the others, and sometimes even their very existence (Bohm, 1994). While originally derived from individuals and local knowledge sources, it is repackaged into a series of separate frameworks, each with their own rationale (Kuhn, 1972). These remain compartmentalized unless linked through interdisciplinary, multidisciplinary or transdisciplinary frameworks, such as adaptive management systems. Each compartment seeks to establish a generalizable reality, valid for that framework. Boundaries are firmly defined and maintained through educational segmentation and peer review. From the specialist perspective, sustainability is traditionally divided into separate social, economic and environmental components of reality, and then further subdivided into separate disciplines (Costanza and Jorgensen, 2002).

Organizations, either industry or government, construct their realities strategically, building on information from individuals, local knowledge and specialist advisers. The information is harnessed towards designing the organization's own given direction and organizational and political pro-grammes. Knowledge transferred from other sectors is merely information to the sector that receives it, until it is reprocessed in that mode. Validity is established for strategic knowledge through the capacity of the information to contribute to meeting policy agendas (Ralston Saul, 1992). Policy goals determine the strategic purpose. For industry, it is financial advantage; for government, it is the fulfilment of their policy and platform, tempered by the priorities of their voting community. The strategic knowledge boundary is represented in Figure 8.1 as cyclical and directional. The aim of the Cool Communities Program is to make greenhouse gas abatement one of the continuing strategic goals of a diverse number of communities.

Holistic knowledge is the odd knowledge out, since it is created through establishing a focus rather than a boundary (represented by a star in Figure 8.1). Holistic thinking is insufficiently recognized as an explicit subculture of its own, except perhaps in the artistic segment of the community. Since it is constructed through identifying the essence of an issue or purpose, it is essential in planning the social change required for sustainability. 'Holistic' is used here in its original sense as employed by Smuts (1936): to mean the tendency of nature to form coherent systems of wholes. The focus itself can be created in many ways, such as an event (for example Environment Day) or a shared experience (for example bushfire or drought).

In working towards sustainable communities, learning is inserted into the existing structure of the planet's self-regulating life support systems. In any community, all five knowledges will need to be re-connected within a fresh holistic focus on sustainable environmental management practices if the social learning is to be complete and the change enduring. Within each stable com-munity, the knowledges will be strongly interconnected, forming as it were a self-contained island of whole-of-community knowledge, with its own inter-nalized version of reality. Any change coming from the outside will require connections to the inside through each of the decision making sectors.

We have discussed how whole-of-community social learning requires some combination of individual, local, specialized, strategic and holistic constructions of knowledge. In examining the Cool Communities Program, can we answer the following questions?

• Are there particular roles played by individuals in this particular whole-of-community learning process? (Individual knowledge)

- How do citizens establish the reliability and validity of their knowledge? How do they find a communal voice in whole-of-community decision making? (Common sense or local knowledge)
- Are all the specialists taking full account of the contribution of local knowledge? Have they established connections to each other? Is their contribution taking precedence over and masking other knowledges? (Specialized knowledge)
- Is there a whole-of-community strategic direction? Does this meet feasibility checks from citizens, specialists, government and industry? Can citizens, government and industry meet their internal goals as well as sharing a move towards sustainability? (Strategic knowledge)
- Is there a clear focus on the transition to sustainability and the need for greenhouse gas abatement in this community? Do individuals, citizens, experts and government strategists share the focus? Does this focus allow for synergy, that is, the generation of new knowledge and skills? (Holistic knowledge).

Nested knowledges and Cool Communities

These searching questions cannot be validly or reliably answered from external observation of any one community, or from the perspective of any one knowledge decision making sector alone. The Cool Communities Program, with its diversity of communities, and respect for multiple decision making channels, offers the opportunity to find some of the answers. The Australian Greenhouse Office programme was delivered in collaboration with environmental non-governmental organizations in every state and territory in Australia, with funding of AUS$5 million over three years. The programme supports householders in any community to take action to reduce their energy use, waste and car use. It was thoroughly documented and evaluated from both inside, and outside, for each of 22 communities over three years (see the list of Cool Communities Program documents at the end of this chapter).

The 22 diverse communities involved across Australia range from a football club in urban Melbourne to a remote indigenous community in the Northern Territory, a church parish in northern Australia to a timber and agricultural town in Western Australia, a workplace of scientists in the Australian Capital Territory and university students in Tasmania (see Table 8.1). Local communities joined with industry, governments and community groups to create their own Cool Communities and to help meet the challenge of whether the world can live sustainably. The Cool Communities Program moved beyond awareness raising and skills development to promoting changes in knowledge construction that can be matched to consequent behaviour and actual measurements of greenhouse gas abatement.

Strategically, programme facilitators were based in every state and territory to assist community steering committees help households take action. Programme facilitators provided information, support and financial assistance

Table 8.1 *Details of Cool Communities, May 2003*

Community	Project title	Number of households recruited	Community leader	Greenhouse abatement per household per year (tonnes)	Knowledge base
Australian Capital Territory					
CSIRO Gungahlin workplace		75	Staff member	0.6	Specialized
ANU Food Co-op		72	Coop coordinator	3.0	Local
Sullivan's Creek Catchment Group		65	Project manager	1.6	Local
Northern Territory					
Parap–Ludmilla Landcare Group		60	President	1.3	Specialized
Desert Knowledge Australia		140	Project officer	1.2	Strategic
Ikuntji – Haasts Bluff		30	Council clerk	0.32	Local
New South Wales					
University of New South Wales Ecoliving Centre	Ecoliving Cooperators	50	Coordinator	5.0	Specialized
Broken Hill Community Inc	Eco Link	107	Chairperson	1.2	Strategic
Leichhardt Municipal Council		70	Environment officer	1.0	Strategic
Queensland					
Maleny Credit Union	Earth Benefits Club/Cool Home Loans	100	Senior loans officer	1.0	Strategic
Catholic Justice and Peace Commission		90	Executive officer	1.2	Local

Table 8.1 (*continued*)

Community	Project title	Number of households recruited	Community leader	Greenhouse abatement per household per year (tonnes)	Knowledge base
South Australia					
Adelaide Cool Communities Program Councils	Save Water and Power	520	Cool Communities Program officer	0.4	Strategic
Campbelltown City Council		150	Engineering officer	0.4	Strategic
Bookmark Biosphere Trust, Berri Barmera Council		100	Secretary, Bookmark Biosphere Trust	0.9	Local
Tasmania					
Launceston Home Ideas/ Environment Centre	Energy Friendly Homes	61	Manager	0.15	Specialized
Taroona Community, and Tasmanian Bicycle Council	Cool Commuters	100	Council president	0.2	Local
University of Tasmania Student Association	Sustainable Student Living	51	Research officer	0	Local
Victoria					
Western Bulldogs Education Centre		104	Manager	0.8	Local
City of Port Phillip	Sustainable Living at Home	137	Environment officer	1.4	Strategic

Table 8.1 *(continued)*

Community	Project title	Number of households recruited	Community leader	Greenhouse abatement per household per year (tonnes)	Knowledge base
Western Australia					
Warren Renewable Energy Group		44	Chairperson	1.5	Specialized
Greenskills, Denmark and Albany		70	Manager, Greenskills	0.15	Specialized
Eastern Metropolitan Regional Council	Dr Cool It Home Energy Audits	44	CCP project	1.4	Strategic
Total		2240			

Source: Monitoring data from Cool Communities Project, 2003

for communities to implement their action plans. The search for a better understanding of whole-of-community learning involves not a single critique or evaluation, but a rich picture study of Cool Communities, one that respects both the diversity of the settings and the uniqueness of each community's individual synthesis of the knowledge cultures.

A synoptic framework to enable the construction of a rich picture of community change is borrowed from an anthropological study on how new cultures are absorbed into an established community. The jacket description of Greg Dening's *Islands and Beaches: Discourse on a Silent Land* transfers neatly to the study of Cool Communities. We can consider each community as a social island comprising the full set of knowledge cultures. The community is surrounded not by impenetrable knowledge boundaries, but by the unclaimed territories of beaches across which changes in knowledge can be negotiated:

> *Islands and Beaches is a metaphor for the different ways in which human beings construct their worlds and for the boundaries that they construct between them. It is a natural metaphor for the oceanic world of the Pacific where islands are everywhere and beaches must be crossed to enter them and leave them, to make them or change them. But the islands and beaches are cultural rather than physical. They are the islands men and women make by the reality they attribute to their categories, their roles, their institutions and the beaches they put around them with their definition of 'we' and 'they' (Dening, 1980, book jacket).*

Applying the same metaphor to the Cool Communities Program, each community is an 'island', that is, functioning as a whole-of-community knowledge system, when each project starts. A project aims to influence the island by introducing strangers bearing the different knowledge cultures, who must each negotiate with the islanders on the surrounding beach before they can proceed to influence the island community. Those who negotiate with the strangers may come from any of the knowledge cultures. They can be individual change agents, local community action groups, and specialized advisers using a transdisciplinary approach; or government agencies or local industries promoting the change. They can be holistic thinkers, possibly artists or writers, who offer the basis for a shared perspective.

Using the metaphor of a community as a self-contained island, with its own established set of interacting knowledge cultures, allows us to realize how all will need to be engaged for long-term change. Change agents from both the community itself and the change-initiating project management meet on the beach to negotiate across the neutral zone of the beach surrounds. The metaphor meets the twin criteria of respecting the integrity and the uniqueness of each community's constructions of knowledge, and at the same time helping to re-form the knowledge relationships of each community to improve environmental management.

In Dening's study, there were three principal sets of negotiations being played out across the beach – for cultural change (the missionaries), for a share of the island's physical resources (the voyagers) and for the ability to co-exist (the beachcombers). A detailed description of the programme will allow us to discover the possible relevance of these aspects of the metaphor, as well as the earlier criteria for interpreting change, compliance, identification and internalization suggested by Kelman (1975).

Cool Communities, diverse knowledges

The Cool Communities Program was launched in August 2001 by the then Minister for the Environment and Heritage with a public call for communities to participate. The 22 Cool Communities were selected from over 140 applications using the following criteria. Communities must:

*   be over 50 households in size
*   be household-focused rather than industry-focused
*   have a proven ability to undertake community-based social or environmental programmes
*   include established groups or organizations willing and able to coordinate Cool Communities project activities
*   demonstrate commitment to the programme and reducing greenhouse gas emissions at the householder level
*   show potential for behaviour change in areas targeted by a project
*   have the capacity to undertake 'greenhouse actions' with limited involvement of the project facilitator.

Priority was given to communities judged to have the best potential to develop partnerships with stakeholders across a wide range of sectors. The potential to integrate programme activities into long-term broader social and environmental objectives was also important. The ways in which the national strategy offered to support change in the islands of the Cool Communities are outlined in Table 8.2.

Establishing beachheads: Meeting the needs of Cool Communities

The Cool Communities Program convened focus groups in each potential community to identify needs, priorities and characteristics of the communities. The results are the source of the baseline knowledges of the communities described next.

Individual knowledge

The key characteristics of individuals volunteering for the necessary changes were:

*   the varying extent of their capacity to organize themselves and remain motivated
*   the desire to learn more about involvement in community cooperation

Table 8.2 *Tools for negotiating social change*

Recruitment	The Cool Communities Program built a positive national brand or identity to assist with household recruitment. It requires less effort to obtain interest and recruit at the local level if people have previously read or heard about Cool Communities in the media (strategic and holistic knowledge)
Knowledge development	Participants could learn about greenhouse action through workshops, theatre, audits, advisory services, demonstration homes and publications (specialized knowledge)
Facilitation	Programme facilitators were employed in each state and territory to work with participating Cool Communities and to help recruit other communities that want to take action. Community steering committees were established in each community to develop and implement approved action plans (strategic and local knowledge)
Recognition	Giving recognition certificates to participating households, community leaders and partners and promoting the programme and its participants and partners in the media increased motivation (strategic knowledge)
Funds	A barrier to implementing actions is often the cost. Providing discounted goods and services to counter these costs provided incentives to participants (strategic knowledge)
Part of a movement	People are more likely to act if they feel they can have an impact. The programme provided each individual with a broader action framework within which they could act (individual knowledge)

- that over 90 per cent believed they were already taking actions to conserve energy
- that only a minority were practising significant abatement actions, such as using solar hot water or alternatives to private cars.

Local knowledge

The concerns of each local community in negotiating change were regarded as paramount throughout the project. During the focus groups and interviews, community groups nominated their priority concerns for the Cool Communities support group as:

- dissipating resources over too many abatement actions and volunteer fatigue
- access to local tradespeople interested in undertaking energy-efficient retrofits or building energy-efficient housing
- the strain on the organizational capabilities of local environment centres and other supporting groups
- the ability to change technologies under current social conditions, for example people renting houses
- different community conditions, such as the efficient use of wood for home and hot water heating which produces relatively low emissions and so will not have as great a savings potential as other communities with a higher reliance on fossil fuels.

Specialized knowledge

Focus group members and interviewees nominated a need for specialist advice on the following particular issues:

- local abatement expertise, such as auditors and research
- technically sophisticated technical expertise
- alternative technologies for cooling that can be easily and quickly implemented
- alternative abatement advice available on results of home audits
- more information on abatement options, with some communities keen to obtain further information, some believing they knew what to do already, and others believing there was plenty of information 'out there' if they ever needed it.

Strategic knowledge

The strategic support system of the Cool Communities Program was one of its strongest features. A core group of a full-time administrator, facilitator and community development expert coordinated a regional facilitator based in each state and territory conservation council. In addition, each community nominated its own community leader, who was resourced along a range from full-time paid to full-time voluntary worker. There was thus a comprehensive network supporting the programme. Community groups outlined the need for the following strategic knowledge:

- how to save money
- how to save energy and help the environment
- how to maintain a high degree of community commitment
- how to deal with higher workloads for staff through time constraints, hierarchical organization, shift work and extent of management support
- how to implement and monitor when there are volunteer resource problems

- how the energy auditor could engage households and convince them to join the Cool Communities Program and buy abatement technologies.

Holistic knowledge

Exploration of community needs in the focus groups threw some light on the holistic knowledge of the community groups. The majority regarded the greenhouse issue (incorrectly) as not something that will significantly affect their generation or community but as having an impact on their children or grandchildren. Most had some idea of a central theme or core purpose, but generally lacked knowledge of what types of abatement actions would have the most impact. For example, recycling is a popular choice of abatement but has minimal impact. Using solar power is also a popular choice but is financially impractical for most households. To integrate knowledge across knowledge divides, it became a high priority to create a common language to be used in all project communications.

Achievements of Cool Communities

The aims of the Cool Communities Program were clearly stated, and monitoring events and measuring outcomes were constant throughout the three years of the programme. The achievements of Cool Communities, as of March 2003, are outlined next.

Greenhouse gas abatement. The potential was estimated at 150,000 tonnes of measurable greenhouse gas abatement over ten years; with a measured programme minimum of 23,500 tonnes over ten years. The average Cool Communities household achieved greenhouse gas reductions of over 1 tonne a year from actions, with some households achieving reductions of 5 tonnes.

Participation level. Some 2240 households have been recruited to the Cool Communities Program. A further 35,000 households have been directly contacted, with an outreach to over 200,000 households through direct mail and targeted education.

Partnerships have involved almost 200 direct partners who have taken a formal role in managing, implementing and resourcing programme initiatives. One-third of partners were drawn from community organizations, 20 per cent from industry, and 17 per cent from local government, with others from schools, academia, service clubs and state government agencies.

Media. The Cool Communities website received 3500 hits within two months of being launched. An audience of over 1.1 million was recorded for national and state radio and television through the public launch, and almost 200 positive media items.

Resources leveraged. Almost AUS$1 million in funds have been leveraged from community partners to date, including from water utilities, councils, regional organizations and community organizations such as Rotary. Volunteers are contributing approximately 355 hours of labour a week.

Community capacity. Community workshops and training programmes have resulted in over 150 trained greenhouse auditors across Australia. The auditors undertake greenhouse audits at participants' homes to identify actions to reduce greenhouse gas emissions.

Community recognition. The programme has strengthened relationships between different groups within Cool Communities, as evidenced by the following quotes from participants:

> '[Cool Communities] has definitely resulted in improved relationships – both internal and external... People are developing stronger friendships and making new friendships and are getting very excited by all of the activity.'

> 'The best part of the progress to date from a community perspective is the diversity of people getting involved, all members of the urban community are getting involved including the older generations, professionals, younger families, indigenous people, etc.'

On the beach

The outcomes described in the last section allow us to reflect on answers to the questions posed earlier in this chapter. We can now describe some of the traffic on the beach. Of the five knowledge cultures, a holistic focus was pre-determined for every community group by the identity of Cool Communities, with its catchy title, and a clear focus on greenhouse gas abatement. This focus, using language that linked a community positive sense (cool) with the scientific goal (lower temperature), was a strong influence on commitment to and perseverance in Cool Communities. Cases where a holistic direction lapsed were few. A lack of commitment of one appointed community leader and the focus becoming confused with other conservation goals in two projects caused the only failures to secure change.

While the figures in Table 8.3 cannot be generalized beyond the Cool Communities Program, even within that project, interesting observations arise. The figures suggest that projects based on local knowledge might have been assumed to have a more limited reach into households, and a weaker abatement effect than those based on the other knowledges. This is not the case. On both

Table 8.3 *Knowledge cultures and Cool Communities success criteria* (n = 22)

Project base (number of projects)	Number of households recruited	Tonnes of greenhouse gas abatement per household per year
Local knowledge (8)	611	5.02
Specialized knowledge (6)	361	4.55
Strategic knowledge (8)	768	8.01

these criteria, local knowledge-based projects recruited substantial results, intermediate between projects based on specialized and strategic knowledge. The clear leader in output measures is strategic knowledge, suggesting that capacity to negotiate change has had the strongest result.

Individual knowledge

Are there particular roles played by individuals in this particular whole-of-community learning process?

Individual facilitators in the core national group and in each state were identified as key to the success in reducing greenhouse gases. Facilitators negotiated with the conservation councils who were co-sponsors of the programme, with industry and councils in the several communities, and with state organizations and utilities. This required a particular set of personal skills in openness, dialogue and negotiation, and a firm grip on the holistic focus of the programme.

Issues for individuals were the different levels of commitment to the project among their co-workers in the community, and changing individuals in projects over time. It is worth noting that all the individuals involved in the core groups (national and state administrators and facilitators and community leaders) held a strong commitment to improving environmental management and achieving greater sustainability, a commitment they felt was part of their success.

Local community knowledge

How do citizens establish the reliability and validity of their knowledge? How do they find a communal voice in whole-of-community decision making?

There is a remarkable consistency of respect for the reliability and validity of the whole-of-community actions undertaken by each individual project. The extent to which local knowledge is, in turn, respected by the membership of each particular team can be inferred from this evidence (see Table 8.1). Consistent respect for the integrity of each community as a whole, and the ways in which each chose to design and deliver their own version of the programme, is apparent in all facets of the programme. How communities chose to operate was considered to be their own affair: their islands were not to be invaded. In only one case did the national team take over – because of a breakdown in internal leadership. For the rest, the project management group responded to the community programme needs as the community required, along the six explicit dimensions specified under project development earlier, namely:

- recognition for each individual project in a programme with a national identity
- open multidimensional learning processes
- expert facilitation at the disposal of community leaders

- funds and specialized assistance delivered according to community directions
- formal public recognition of individual community success
- sense of being part of an effective movement actually making a difference.

Specialized knowledge

Are the specialists taking full account of the contribution of local knowledge? Have they established connections to each other? Is their contribution taking precedence over and masking other knowledges?

A general criticism of many sustainability projects is that they cannot succeed because they continue to rely on the technological knowledge that led to the problem in the first place. There is some confirmation of this here, in that Cool Communities projects based on specialized knowledge recruited fewer households and made fewer abatement gains than those based on local or strategic knowledge.

On the other hand, technical expertise was not a limiting factor in any of the projects. Expert emissions audits, advice on abatement strategies and equipment, assessment of greenhouse gas reductions and ongoing monitoring of the effectiveness of different community choices were available to all participating communities. Thus projects using principally local or strategic knowledges were able to build on that specialist base.

Strategic knowledge

Is there a whole-of-community strategic direction? Does this meet feasibility checks from citizens, specialists, government and industry? Can citizens, government and industry meet their internal goals as well as sharing a move towards sustainability?

Overall, the Cool Communities Program is notable for both its planned and spontaneous use of strategic knowledge. The explicit focus on facilitation and negotiation as the mainstream process rather than efficient one-track administration is one of the hallmarks of the programme. The use of high-profile champions, various communication media and partnerships with existing organizations were all designed into the programme from the beginning. Programme organization maximized existing strategic strengths, such as using the conservation councils in each state and territory as the administrative base. Negotiation and agenda-setting at all policy levels, from changing state regulations to reversing a school's no-bikes policy, demonstrate the extent to which strategic knowledge was also spontaneously generated in many of the projects.

Communities basing their projects on a strategic knowledge culture made considerably greater gains in the stated aim of reducing greenhouse gas emissions than did those based on specialized or local knowledge. The projects continuing on their own resources after the external funding ceased were those with a strategic knowledge base. While under the umbrella of the Cool

Communities Program, the individual communities were free to pursue their own strategic direction under their own local label (see Table 8.1).

Holistic knowledge

Is there a clear focus on the transition to sustainability and the need for greenhouse gas abatement in this community? Do individuals, citizens, experts, and government strategists share the focus? Does this focus allow for synergy, that is, the generation of new knowledge and skills?

Before the project started, preliminary studies found the potential barriers to success were a lack of holistic focus and a mixed understanding of the issues. An outstanding feature of the Cool Communities Program has been the effort spent on finding and maintaining a focus. From the very beginning, the success in clearly defining and popularizing the goals of the programme had many positive effects. Individual projects have built on the jump-start that this shared identity provided in constructing a common language across the knowledges.

Conclusions

At the beginning of this chapter, we proposed that the Cool Communities Program be regarded as a social learning enterprise aimed at changing knowledge structure, rather than values and skills. The interaction between the five knowledge cultures of contemporary western society and the changes in whole-of-community knowledge were theorized through the metaphor of islands and beaches. Taking this metaphor further as the story of the social learning, we can draw some conclusions about the role of the five integrating strands of reflection, systems orientation, negotiation, integration and collaboration as aids in the interactions on the beach.

The community that is intending to learn is already an interconnected system, each island/project having its unique intellectual landscape of nested knowledges (see Figure 8.1). The driver of the knowledge changes, in this case the Cool Communities Program, has entered into the change negotiations from off the island, offering individual, specialized, strategic and holistic learning resources to link with those on the island. Short of a crude invasion, these negotiations required neutral ground, such as supplied by the beach.

The project managers could well have acted as missionaries (and tried to convert the islanders, redirecting their knowledges to their own purpose), or as invaders (re-assigning the islanders' knowledge resources for their own ends). In the event, they acted as beachcombers, accepting that they were there on sufferance from the community, and making use of any locally generated opportunity to advance their cause. The Cool Communities visitors had no expectation of taking up residence on the islands, but were prepared to remain on the beach for as long as they found it was furthering their strategic purpose.

Of the three stages of adoption of social learning proposed by Kelman (1975), there was little reward for islands/communities in stopping at compliance, since all support and rewards had been strategically related to sustainable advances in knowledge, values and skills. Negotiation began from there. The next stage, identification with the project, was also built into the negotiations from the start. Exceptions were where community leaders failed (two cases) and where specialized groups wished to own the process. The explicit aim of the Cool Communities Program was to reach the third stage, internalization of the sustainability ethic into each community, bridging all boundaries and linking sectors.

Successful internalization was confirmed by the outcomes that all but two of the 22 communities continued after the three-year support programme finished, using their own resources; and by the tonnes of greenhouse gases abated. The distinguishing factors appear to be the extent to which the programme addressed all five of the nested knowledges, through:

* the leading individuals at programme, regional and local scales incorporating all five knowledges in their own thinking
* the high level of respect for the autonomy and local knowledge of each client community
* the provision of the latest and most reliable specialized information, relevant to each community's needs
* the emphasis, not merely on process for its own sake, but on well-directed strategic knowledge
* the strong holistic focus constructed by the programme title and criteria.

To sum up, the Cool Communities Program is a remarkable example of the power of a whole-of-community and whole-of-knowledge basis for stimulating social learning for sustainability. The use of all five of the strands suggested as essential to social learning in Chapter 1 is very much in evidence. Reflection on every step of the programme, particularly by the networked system of facilitators, the acknowledgement of each community as an integrated whole, a systems orientation linking policy and practice, negotiation between the knowledges, and the over-riding ethic of partnership are all apparent. We have been able to review only a fraction of the information collected on the rich diversity of the 22 communities. We can only recommend to the reader to explore the documents further in relation to any particular aspect of social learning that may interest them.

Greg Dening (1980, pp31–32) should have the last word on beaches and social learning:

> *Islands and beaches, of course, are everywhere – in a jungle clearing, in an urban ghetto, within a social class. Everywhere where space and action are contained by boundaries which screen comings and goings, there is an island and a beach. Every islander has to cross a beach to construct a new society. Across those beaches every intrusive artefact, material and cultural, has to come... On the land, behind the beach, life is lived with some fullness and some establishment. Crossing beaches is always dramatic, from either side.*

References

Aslin, H. and Brown, V. A. (2003) *Terms of Engagement*, Murray–Darling Basin Commission, Canberra

Berger, P. and Luckmann, T. (1967) *The Social Construction of Reality: A Treatise in the Sociology of Knowledge*, Anchor, New York

Berlin, I. (1998) 'The hedgehog and the fox', in Hardy, H. and Hausheer, R. (eds) *The Proper Study of Mankind: An Anthology of Essays by Isaiah Berlin*, Chatto and Windus, London

Bohm, D. (1994) *Thought as a System*, Routledge, London

Brown, V. A. (2001a) 'Monitoring changing environments in environmental health', *Environmental Health*, vol 1, pp20–31

Brown, V. A. (2001b) 'Planners and the planet: Reshaping the people/planet relationship: Do planners have a role?' *Australian Planner*, vol 38, no 3, pp67–73

Costanza, R. and Jorgensen, S. (2002) *Understanding and Solving Environmental Problems in the 21st Century: Towards a New, Integrated, Hard Problem Science*, Elsevier, Oxford

Dening, G. (1980) *Islands and Beaches: Discourse on a Silent Land. A Case Study of the Marquesas 1774–1880*, University Press of Hawaii, Honolulu, book jacket and pp31–32

Douglas, M. (1973) 'Introduction', in Douglas, M. (ed) *Rules and Meanings*, Penguin, Harmondsworth, UK

Ife, J. (1995) *Community Development: Creating Community Alternatives – Vision, Analysis and Practice*, Longman, Melbourne

Kelman, D. (1975) *Dimensions of Social Change*, Routledge, New York

Kuhn, T. (1972) *The Structure of Scientific Revolutions*, Routledge and Kegan Paul, New York

Levi-Strauss, C. (1958) *Structural Anthropology*, Basic Books, New York

Ralston Saul, J. (1992) *Voltaire's Bastards: The Dictatorship of Reason in the West*, Viking, Toronto

Sahani, M. (2003) 'Separate realities: Community-based environmental management for health from the inside out and the outside in', unpublished PhD thesis, University of Western Sydney, Richmond

Smuts, J. C. (1936) *Holism and Evolution*, 3rd edn, Macmillan and Co, London

Toulmin, S. (1977) 'From form to function: The philosophy and history of science in the 1950s and now. Studies in contemporary scholarship', *Daedelus*, vol 106, no 3, pp143–162

Cool Communities Program material

The following documents from the Cool Communities Program (Australian Greenhouse Office, Environment Australia, Canberra) were also consulted.

Brochures (1999–2003)

Cool Communities (general programme information)
Cool Communities fact sheets (information on all 22 communities)
Understanding greenhouse science (FAQs)

Your home (good home design guide)
Shop smart: Buy green (consumer guide)
Guide to socially responsible investment (consumer guide)
Global warming: Cool it (hints for household action)
Cool news (quarterly newsletter)
Promotional materials (1999–2003)
Cool Communities thermometers (temperature measurement and information)
'Cool commuters aren't polluters' (reflective stickers for bikes and helmets)
Cool Communities fridge magnets (greenhouse gas reduction tips)
Cool Communities bags (reusable hessian shoulder bags)
Cool Communities 'cool solutions to global warming' (colour stickers)
Cool Communities poster (ten ways to reduce greenhouse gas emissions)

Public reports

Cool Communities greenhouse abatement actions (table of approximately 75 potential household abatement actions identifying greenhouse, energy and cost savings for each state and territory)
Cool Communities social research outcomes (summary of outcomes of social research with 401 householders across Australia and focus groups with Cool Communities to identify barriers, motivators, attitudes and behaviours in relation to greenhouse action)
Cool Communities media kit (a series of eight brochures providing generic greenhouse and specific Cool Communities information for media contacts)
Cool Communities greenhouse abatement measurement strategy (describes the approaches used to measure the greenhouse gas abatement resulting from the programme)
Motivating home energy action handbook and fact sheets (research report)
Cool Communities Program framework (outline of Round 1 Cool Communities Program design)
Cool Communities household energy audit manual (an energy audit manual designed primarily for people wanting to design and implement an energy audit programme)

Website

www.greenhouse.gov.au/coolcommunities

9

Changing Governments: Councils Embracing the Precautionary Principle

Victoria Critchley and Jennifer Scott

At a glance

- Government organizations are stereotyped as being tightly bound and conservative in their social structures, both vertically, locked into levels of authority, and horizontally, with strong walls between departments
- A sustainability strategy which incorporated social learning was launched by the environmental services department of a Sydney council, initially successfully recruiting personnel from throughout the council, that is, elected members, executive, strategic planning staff and specialized service departments
- Strategies implemented in council included staff development workshops, biodiversity mapping, state-of-the-environment reporting and a research project that developed an integrated sustainability assessment tool
- Strongly embedded boundaries between levels of authority and between service departments proved to be major barriers to social learning, but also offered opportunities for whole-of-council change. The precautionary principle and an integrated assessment tool provided the most useful boundary crossings.

Councils and urban development planning for sustainability

With a population of four million, the city of Sydney in New South Wales (NSW) is one of the so-called global cities. Caught between the World

Heritage Area of the Blue Mountains and the Pacific Ocean, Sydney offers a major challenge to both the planning and implementation of sustainability strategies. Recent expansion along Sydney's inland urban fringe has brought population growth, cultural shifts and a major transformation of the landscape (Bunker, 2002). As an example of the pace of development within this region, the current population of Sydney's western councils is set to increase by a third in 2020. For each council, this equates to at least 2000–4000 new lots created and approved each year, and an average of three new streets formed each week (WSROC, 2000).

Although constrained by the dictates of state government policy, Australian local government is the statutory body primarily responsible for jurisdictional urban planning decisions and shaping the future character of the local built and natural environments. Local governments are under tremendous pressure to meet the often conflicting demands of, on the one hand, landholders and developers eager to take full advantage of rising land prices and, on the other, residents increasingly concerned with the impact of development on the natural environment and the level of community resources.

In the past, councils in Australia met their responsibilities by providing basic waste, town planning, development control, infrastructure and community services, as demand required. Although local government is still expected to meet these primary functions, there has recently been an increasing expectation that councils will also demonstrate leadership and provide services that promote social wellbeing and ecological health, as well as fiscal responsibility. This expanding role reflects the growing community imperative, placed on all spheres of governments, to pursue a single bottom line approach that implicitly balances the social, environmental and economic impacts of decisions (Jacobs, 1995).

In addition, the NSW Local Government Amendment (ESD) Act 1997 specifically obliges local government to be guided by the ecologically sustainable development principles that take account of social, environmental and economic issues in planning decisions. Australia has added the term 'ecological' to the term 'sustainable development' commonly used elsewhere. Essentially, the phrases mean the same, both referring to the five principles of ensuring intergenerational and intragenerational equity, maintaining environmental integrity, valuing economic, social and environmental resources, and adopting the precautionary principle of acting cautiously in the face of serious risk.

There is general acceptance of the requirement that the ecologically sustainable development principles should define the framework for the overall planning system and that each strategy within that system should be consistent with these principles. Hence any failure to find these principles reflected in NSW on-ground urban policy and development practice would suggest a lack of government commitment to its own legislation. This is in fact the case. The State of New South Wales, although it has a democratic Labour government, has formally dropped the intragenerational equity principle. Moreover, the implementation of ecologically sustainable development principles is often neglected at the local government level, rather than used as a vehicle to improve local governance (Scott, 2004).

In spite of these disincentives, a number of councils in NSW, fuelled by community concerns and Local Agenda 21 commitments from the 2002 Rio Earth Summit, have formulated formal and informal internal sustainability management processes. Although these have been diversely articulated, there remains a common intention to establish sustainable planning and policy guidelines which realize community social and environmental values in guiding future growth and development. Members of this group, known locally as the Integrated Sustainability Action Forum, have instituted sustainable development processes in their councils, such as providing medium-density housing near transport and community nodes, mixed-use zoning and a broader focus on community environmental education (Brown, 2004). However, similar to local governments around the world, in the main Sydney councils still fail to significantly address the underlying social and environmental impacts of urban development (Lambert, 2002). This chapter explores a number of the reasons why this has been the case in one particular council.

In Australia, local governments have increasingly moved towards a corporate approach to governance, based on categorizing stakeholders as 'customers' and the council as a 'service provider'. This purchaser–provider framework has promoted the role of the applicant as client, disempowered broad community interests and maintained the dominance of financial over social and environmental accounting (Mercer and Jokowitz, 2000). Adopting this corporate model of functioning has also served to more firmly establish fixed administrative levels and service boundaries.

Within such a political and operational framework, the vehicles recommended worldwide for implementing sustainable development principles – tools such as environmental management plans, Local Agenda 21 programmes and community quality of life indicators – have been found to have limited overall corporate support and thus impact (Brown, 2004). Despite the difficulty of creating an open and balanced exchange of information and ideas within this corporatized environment, there has been some progress in constructing new modes of communication and learning. One innovative approach has been through research partnership projects such as that established between a broad-based project team of Green Valley Shire Council staff and a multidisciplinary action research team from the University of Western Sydney's Local Sustainability Project, the respective bases of the two authors of this chapter.

Through this project, tools have been developed to help engage traditionally opposing stakeholder interests within the Green Valley Shire Council, and establish new, inclusive models of input throughout the organization. In this case, the community of concern is the entire council, that is, it involves elected councillors, executive members, and specialized staff from the full range of departments. The proposition behind this strategy is that a combination of whole-of-organization support is needed to implement sustainable development principles, and so for localities to become sustainable.

As in most organizations, Green Valley Shire Council's management and political knowledge (which we call strategic knowledge) is stratified vertically.

Authority is vested in a well-established hierarchy from field staff, through project managers to programme managers, to heads of the three divisions of planning, infrastructure and administrative services. A fourth division, strategic planning, balances the other three. At the same time, technical and professional expertise (strategic knowledge) is divided horizontally, with tight boundaries separating the specialized service units that make up each division. Of all arms of government, the staff in the service units of a local council have the greatest access to the community knowledge in their area; and most staff live locally, so have direct individual knowledge of local conditions (Figure 9.1).

An interesting paradox is that, while the elected councillors are intended to be a representative sample of the community itself, they are often single-interest voices elected by strong lobby groups. Thus within a single council can be found a microcosm of the decision making system in the larger society. If these decisions are to enable sustainable management practices, we require synthesis of individual, local, specialized, strategic and holistic knowledges of the one shared place (the constructions of knowledge are further described in Chapter 8).

Issues facing a sustainability focus in the local government sector

In local government, sustainability advocates attempting to promote a stronger leadership role for councils face a wide range of impediments. These issues emerged during a unique intensive social learning workshop of national local government sustainability practitioners held in June 2002 at Green Valley Shire Council. Individual sustainability leaders from 25 councils identified the following reasons for their respective council's resistance to sustainability initiatives:

- fear of the unknown
- resistance to change
- slow pace of change
- ignorance of the need to change
- values-based conflicts with the new direction
- political imperatives that conflict with ecologically sustainable development
- redirecting available resources to something new and unfamiliar
- funding availability and priorities in a corporatized local government system with a single financial performance indicator
- lack of political understanding, and ownership, of sustainability issues
- lack of demonstrated community support
- level of frustration of those committed to ecologically sustainable development.

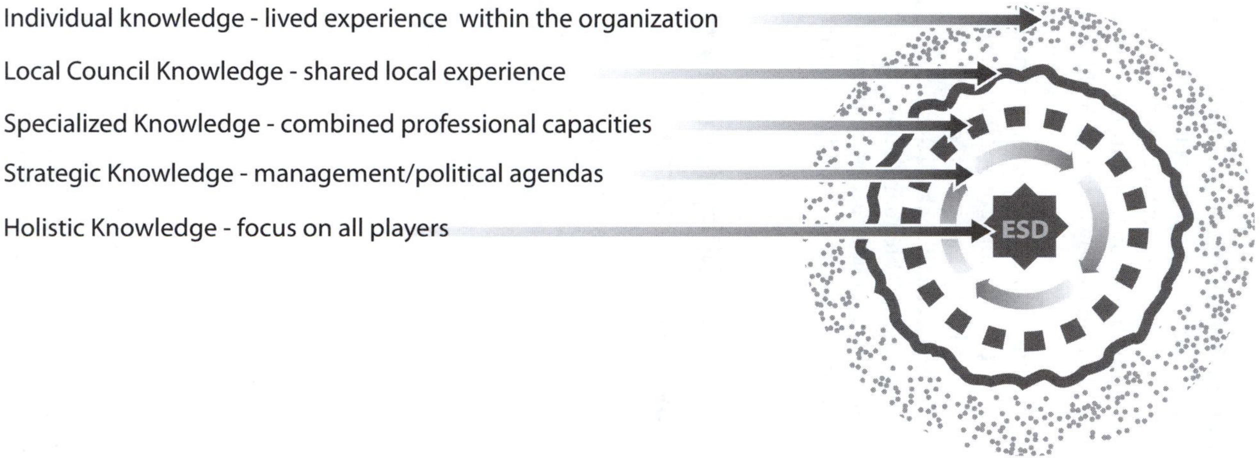

Individual knowledge - lived experience within the organization

Local Council Knowledge - shared local experience

Specialized Knowledge - combined professional capacities

Strategic Knowledge - management/political agendas

Holistic Knowledge - focus on all players

ESD

Source: Adapted from Brown et al (2001)

Figure 9.1 *Nested knowledge with a sustainable development focus*

It became clear during the workshop that the problems in Green Valley Shire Council, personally experienced by the authors, are commensurate with problems encountered elsewhere in the Australian local government sector. To overcome these deficiencies, Green Valley Shire Council devised a strategy to promote social learning throughout the council, integrating sustainability into the everyday work of all council officers and decision makers, the strategies of the executive and the policies of the elected council.

Pressure to urbanize (council's local knowledge)

One significant issue in determining the form and rate of residential expansion in the urban fringes of Sydney has been the fundamental political and economic drivers of urbanization. While national and state legislation commits governments at all levels to pursue a sustainable development agenda, reports both nationally and within NSW record the high costs that the country's rapid urbanization exert on social amenity and ecosystem function (Department of the Environment and Heritage, 2002; NSW EPA, 1997). Yet the economic and political pressure to release land for development is still superseding other considerations, such as providing adequate public infrastructure and enforcing environmental standards.

Western Sydney has one of the few available areas for urban expansion and has already borne a major share of Sydney's urban development programme. In December 2002, the State Government announced a new 15-year urban release programme to allow 89,000 new greenfield lots on the fringes of Western Sydney. This level of development is not only being pushed by developer or state government demand, but also by local government. State government development funds automatically accompany development approvals and local governments rely on the injection of capital from those funds, despite being offset by large shortfalls from the infrastructure costs as land prices rise (Mamouney, 2000). In addition, many costs external to the direct project costs of urban development remain hidden, unaccounted and unallocated, bequeathed to future generations to confront; thus subverting each of the ecologically sustainable development principles in the state legislation (Hundloe and McDonald,1997; Rees, 2000).

Politicization of policy development and decision making (strategic knowledge)

Councils have considerable latitude in interpreting planning instruments and assessing developments and therefore different approaches have evolved to determining applications. While this interpretive latitude allows for innovation and change, it may also encourage a perversion of the process by tempting elected councillors to manipulate the system for outcomes other than the public interest, for example prioritizing their personal political ambitions (Attorney-General's Department, 2002, p48; Environmental Defenders Office, 2001, p1). The Council of the City of Sydney concedes that 'many actions and inactions of local councils are "politically motivated" – that is, decisions are made or refused by reference to circumstances and events not authorized by law to be considered by councils' (Attorney-General's Department, 2002, p48).

Despite the occasional 'green development' exception, the vast majority of modern subdivisions fail to meet even the most basic tenets of sustainable urban design, testifying to the reluctance of governments to address accountability in urban form and function (Mant, 1995; Stilwell, 2000). In NSW, of five sustainable development principles generally accepted and approved by national policy, one has been eliminated (intragenerational equity); one is treated as largely outside the scope of a four-year election cycle (intergenerational equity); and one is regarded as the specialized concern of environmental services alone (environmental integrity and biodiversity). This leaves two principles as viable bases for social learning, both directly relating to a council's existing duty of care and statutory responsibilities. The first is unified social, ecological and economic state-of-the-urban-environment reporting. The other is the precautionary principle, understood as a willingness to act to safeguard the environment from harm, despite some degree of uncertainty that harm would occur (discussed more fully later in this chapter). There have already been major fines for breaches of the precautionary principle in NSW and at least one prison sentence resulting from polluted lakes and waterways (NSW Environmental Health Unit, 2002).

Trivialization of non-quantifiable outcomes (specialist knowledge)

Senior public servants in councils have considerable influence over policy development and application; but the value and belief systems driving the council agenda is securely embedded in resource efficiency gains (Mamouney, 2000). A current major goal for policy performance is the minimization of costs, incorporating a shift from community service to customer satisfaction, which, in turn, is thought to have a direct positive relationship with maximum efficiency (Foltin, 1999; Kline, 1997). It is unsurprising that sustainability objectives are considered ancillary, if not an impediment, to the development process if the key indicator for achievement is not the quality of a development, but whether it was assessed and approved in the required timeframe.

As can be read in every council's mandated annual strategic plan, local government performance outcomes are generally strictly quantified in terms of either time or money. Measuring performance using such a narrow interpretation of positive gain means many of the day-to-day issues directly relating to sustainability and quality of life fail to be considered. It is these issues that council officers are confronted with at the interface between the decision makers, commercial entities and the community.

Many NSW councils are key proponents of this shift from 'local government into local administration', as characterized by Mercer and Jokowitz (2000). Efficiency and quality control guidelines of a dominant administrative ethos have simply served to further isolate council sectors that are already divided into specialist service areas, with each area now independently responsible for specific performance objectives.

Therefore, even when progress is made in moving the sustainability dialogue forward in one specialized area, there is little flow on through the organization. For example, a number of NSW councils are integrating sustainability principles and standards within their mandatory development control plans, but are finding that placing guidelines on paper does not necessarily lead to control staff and management applying them appropriately in the assessment process (Lambert, 2002).

Knowledge boundaries rendered impermeable by lack of trust

One of the key dimensions that consistently arose in discussions of collaboration within government was the matter of trust. Trust between council staff and councillors, between levels of administration, between specialist departments, between the council as an institution and the community it serves, was continually called into question throughout the project. Some of these examples of absence of trust follow.

Lack of trust between council officers and elected councillors

Although councillors are usually better informed about the planning process than the general public, the Department of Local Government finds that '...Councillors mistrust the advice given to them by a Council's professional officer' and, further, that there is 'a failure of councillors to properly understand or appreciate planning issues' (Attorney-General's Department, 2002, p48). The lack of trust between elected members and their advisers in local government is compounded by the traditional divisions between professional entities and levels of administration. Lack of cohesion in vision and purpose is driving wedges into the decision making process and this allows gatekeepers of power with other agendas to intervene at every step.

Our personal observation has been that much of the reasoning in the decision making may remain hidden and gatekeepers of information and power are able to flourish under these circumstances. Justification for decisions may be quite contrary to the advice and research developed by council officers. Whether due to lack of trust in fellow officers, hidden rather than explicit political agendas, or competition within a hierarchical system, decision makers throughout local government appear to be able to act with a degree of impunity from scrutiny within the system. Variations in value and belief systems between professional paradigms, levels of administration and officers and councillors in local government confound attempts by those council officers acting as advocates for improved environmental management to promote sustainable outcomes. A high burnout rate in these sustainability advocates is the result (Griffith, 2003).

Lack of trust between the council organization and the community

'People don't trust institutions and leadership much anymore, I think that's a major problem in public life in Australia today, to cut corners and keep silent', states John Menadue, past head of the Department of the Prime Minister and Cabinet (*ABC Lateline*, 15 February 2002). Although governments commit to community participation in decision making, this is generally structured as a single-flow transference of information rather than as a collective learning endeavour. In addition to poor planning, a more fundamental issue may exist in the community consultation process, which is strongly related to the well-documented divergence in expert, government and public perceptions of risk (Health Council, 2002).

Moreover, recent state government attempts to encourage private competition for council services has led, in many minds, to a worsening of attitudes to neighbourhood design, and limits any sustainable focus to operational matters. Within the building application process, officers are encouraged to identify the developer or owner–builder as the primary focus for communication and negotiation (Lovegrove and Campbell, 1992). This sees concerns such as maintaining local community values and amenity reduced to secondary considerations at best.

Pressure on senior management to maintain income from customers (the development applicant) has led to a mindset that is not interested in regulation but simply in facilitating development interests. The strict hierarchical structure of a council's staffing framework and the fact that senior staffing contracts are tied to productivity gains precludes deviation from this position, regardless of personal or individual community concerns.

Lack of trust in sustainability decision making processes

Local government as a sector seems yet to come to terms with the pervasive and highly controversial nature of economic growth dominating other land use planning priorities. This was the experience unanimously reported by advocates at the Integrated Sustainability Action Forum. Implementation of strategic plans to balance economic imperatives with quality of life considerations such as biodiversity conservation remains limited.

Often unrecognized is that many ecosystems are fragile and do not necessarily have the luxury of surviving trial and error environmental management (Mamouney, 2000; Sattler, 1998). For example, in relation to Western Sydney's vast and unique Cumberland Plains woodland, a recent report by the Federal Government concluded that the threatened communities found there were inadequately reserved and under continued pressure, making it unlikely that biodiversity value would be recovered (Land and Water Australia, 2002). Of the councils bordering the area, one is as strongly committed to developing the land for housing as the other is to conserving it as a protected ecosystem.

According to Piper (2002, p20), sustainability assessment must ensure, as far as possible, that the full costs of development proposals are identified, mitigated, compensated or offset, consistent with maintaining natural resource functions of either 'source' or 'sink', and that cumulative effects are assessed.

That is, the objective or constraint of any development should be to work within the limitations of a region's ecosystem in order to promote a better than regulatory standard (Piper, 2002).

For local government coping with the fallout from rampant urban development, there is a long litany of concerns to be addressed. In addition to the list recorded from the sustainability leaders at the Integrated Sustainability Action Forum, the Green Valley Shire Council sustainability project identified two major structural barriers to integrated decision making as a whole: lack of trust between the decision making sectors, and lack of respect for each other's distinctive knowledge base. However, in spite of these considerable obstacles, there are also a number of examples of successful initiatives.

The Interactive Knowledge Management Research Project

One of the successes in progressing the sustainability agenda within local governments has been through the development of mutually beneficial learning partnerships with other agencies and academic institutions. Green Valley Shire Council has been a substantial beneficiary of such an approach with the establishment of a memorandum of understanding with the University of Western Sydney in 1997. One of the major outcomes of this agreement was the receipt of an Australian Research Council Strategic Partnerships with Industry – Research and Training (SPIRT) grant for three years to develop a framework for integrated local area decision making (see Box 9.1).

The local sustainability project team and Green Valley Shire Council senior staff took part in a futures planning exercise called Community 2000+: Designing the Future in Green Valley Shire. A major need identified in that exercise was the coordination of multidisciplinary information for strategic planning purposes. This need increased with a subsequent state decision to devolve planning and management responsibilities to local authorities; and the emerging emphasis on the holistic integration of ecologically sustainable development principles into council operations.

The council's strategic partnership with the University of Western Sydney was designed to develop social learning tools to enhance communication and assessment of sustainability principles. A set of existing planning projects that were key to council activities provided opportunities for enhanced information management and knowledge sharing. Each project was assessed to determine how closely or how far it varied from a perceived sustainability ideal (see Box 9.1).

Perceptions of sustainability varied markedly between council staff and councillors, between on-ground action researchers and specialized and research practitioners, and between service and strategic departments of council. It became apparent that the social learning approach to environmental management required sustainability to be presented in a framework that allows markedly different philosophical starting points, while allowing for collaboration on actions and outcomes.

Box 9. 1 Interactive information management in Green Valley Shire Council: Case study of a whole-of-council strategic approach to sustainable development

Resources

- Annual: AUS$20,000 from Green Valley Shire Council plus AUS$45,000 from the Australian Research Council
- Total: AUS$65,000 a year for 2000, 2001 and 2002.

Intended outcomes

- An interrelated system of council databases on sustainable development
- Optimum council internal communication on delivery of sustainable development strategies
- Optimum coordination of knowledge contributed by all five knowledge cultures.

Programme

- Develop sustainability goals for all council staff
- Review latest theories and practices of sustainable development in the local government sector, in relation to the five projects
- Develop and implement sustainability tools for each project.

Projects	Tools
– Environmental accounting	Economic and ecological accounting
– Rural land study	Integrated information management
– Natural asset audit	Integrated assessment tool
– Development approvals process	Integrated assessment tool
– State-of-the-environment report	Integrated website design

Source: SPIRT (1999)

Social learning process in council as it actually happens

The primary purpose of developing the social learning tools was to work towards creating a shared vision and understanding of local issues within council, and thereby establish joint ownership and implementation of environmental management solutions. One of the key tenets of social learning that the SPIRT project attempted to embed in the council's protocols was the facilitation of open and honest discourse and dialogue to encourage the most efficient use of knowledge and assets. With the understanding that the council's sustainability programme requires engaging a variety of stakeholder interests, the other imperative of the communication strategy has been to engage a range of voices and modes of participation.

A consensus reached among the council staff planning team involved in the SPIRT programme was the need to establish a process to break down entrenched barriers and develop a new corporate framework that moved away from the traditional hierarchical power structure. As a first step in achieving this objective, it was determined that a common vision identifying broad objectives and encompassing sustainable values should be established. Following the immediate exercise of analysing project areas, senior personnel met to determine a framework for a strategic plan that could achieve these objectives. The project goals, outcomes and timelines eventually gained approval from all levels of council (Figure 9.2).

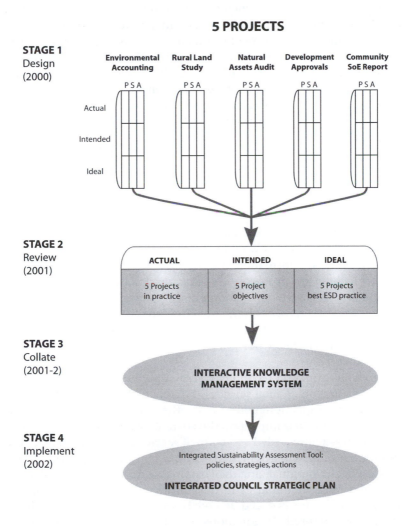

Figure 9.2 *Sustainable development in Green Valley Shire Council: Policy (P), strategy (S), action (A) and review*

In all councils, the most important person to engage and ensure ownership with in this collaborative process is the chief executive officer. This role has the most to lose corporately and politically from re-negotiating the focus of the organization, thus requiring some level of commitment to the process. All the documentation reveals that current management processes in Green Valley Shire Council at the time were top-down, linear and hierarchical, and strongly connected to the corporate governance ideology discussed earlier. Nevertheless, the chief executive officer approved the process.

Strategic planning staff, successfully recruited to the learning process, suggested that a necessary step was to develop the existing council strategic plan into a whole-of-council planning instrument, making the sustainability goals the linking thread between councillors' decision making, strategic planning and operational services. Although this is a major step in gaining acceptance of social learning in environmental management, it proved a difficult goal because of the firm borders between departmental responsibilities. Firm lines remained between the executive and councillors' sociopolitical engagement and the rest of the council's more pragmatic delivery of services.

For example, a series of collaborative workshops held by the SPIRT project group at each administrative level ended with positive and practical recommendations for strategic adoption of the sustainable development principles. At each level, the recommendations stalled for up to six months, dissipating the original commitment and delaying any support for implementation. Finally, the elected council approved the strategy outlined in Figure 9.2, and then postponed it until after the council elections one year later, to avoid introducing possibly controversial changes into council policy in an election year. By then, of course, there would be a new council and the whole social learning process would need to start all over again.

The major formal information link between departments was the council's information technology protocol. This was completed by every department and sent into a centralized information pool. However, individual departments could not access the central pool, and nor could the SPIRT research project, the reason given being that much of that content was commercial-in-confidence. Thus the very mechanism designed for integrating council information actually acted as a barrier.

Also in the information technology area, a public council website held extensive information on council services. The council's integrated state-of-the-environment report was designed to make the whole of council and the local community aware of their impact on the sustainable development parameters. However, this was not regarded as a council service and so had to be developed and paid for out of the environmental services budget, and provided only as a link, thus yet again marginalizing the sustainable development strategy.

In the end, these boundaries to developing a strategic planning process meant that it could not proceed as collaboratively or as dynamically as the main proponents desired. Negotiations with key actors under the status quo led eventually, in our opinion, to a badly compromised outcome that was not strongly supported by any party and unconnected to the original issues identified through the SPIRT project. The paths developed to whole-of-staff sustainability goals and integrated strategic planning remain in place, but with no strong champions other than the initiators.

On the other hand, the less ambitious sections of the process, such as whole-of-council social learning, the re-orientation of existing projects and development of tools for moving towards sustainable decision making, remain in place (see Box 9.1 and Figure 9.2). There is the potential to use both the experiential and analytical social learning tools delivered by the research project to create a coherent, integrated sustainability vision for the Green Valley Shire Council.

One of the key elements of whether such a process will be embedded in council processes is the presence and activation of key sustainability drivers within council. Therefore, the SPIRT research project also sought to raise the capacity of council officers to initiate alternative processes by encouraging the use of external expertise and collaborative learning environments in current council projects. A reluctance to operate outside of standard practice indicated a need to develop instruments that could make these innovations a part of standard management operations.

In order to challenge entrenched operational barriers to social learning experiences, an integrated sustainability assessment (ISA) tool, as detailed in the next subsection, was one of the instruments developed within the SPIRT project. The tool does not explicitly require the construction of a collaborative learning space, since it can be applied by an outside observer or a member of staff in a routine task. However, using it does demand the explicit integration of the user's knowledge and experience with the principles of sustainability, thus making it an individual learning process. Optimum utilization of the ISA tool requires a full commitment by management and the elected body to its use in the overall decision making processes. However, application of the tool demonstrated that, while still awaiting that commitment, it can also be successfully employed to drive change at the day-to-day decision making level.

ISA tool

Developing a tool to mobilize the application of ecologically sustainable development principles in council decision making required an understanding of simplified problem solving, systems modelling and the inquiry approach that underpins the social learning cycle. Although no tool can capture all relevant information, a tool designed to those specifications can highlight sustainability issues, encourage discussion and lead to negotiation of preferred outcomes.

The type of tool to be developed depends on the problems to be solved. The basis of a good tool is the ability to produce reasonably accurate predictions and be as straightforward as possible to use. It is all too easy for complex issues to become swamped with confusion that leads to a decrease in participants' confidence in the process. The tool developed in the Green Valley Shire

Council project allows for knowledge to be constructed from negotiation between the local reality of the context, and variations in the understanding, values and beliefs of the decision makers, industry and the community.

As discussed earlier, of the four sustainable development objectives in NSW legislation, the precautionary principle – the duty of care to ensure no harm to community or environment – was the only one with legislative teeth. This principle was therefore selected as the driving force behind the sustainability assessment process. The goal was to ensure that the full costs of a change in land use are identified, mitigated, compensated or offset, consistent with maintaining at least a better than regulatory standard. This approach diverts from a purely quantitative basis for decision making to a qualitative questioning: Does this decision advance or impede sustainability decision making?

This qualitative approach is in line with the Bellagio principles (Box 9.2) developed by international leaders in sustainability evaluation (Piper, 2002). Here the requirements are for the evaluation outcomes to be practical, to communicate and to influence the institution's decision making. In the case of Green Valley Shire Council, the institution had become aware of sustainability goals, but given only general and weak support to those goals while still maintaining strong boundaries between each of its service arms. A tool was therefore required that could be used within each of the council compartments, but could also be used to link between them.

Robert et al (2002) suggest that a systems approach consistent with the fundamental tenants of sustainability requires complementary tools. They find that when the tools are used outside the systems approach they begin to conflict with each other. They describe a systems planning framework as:

Box 9.2 The Bellagio principles

Principle   1: Guiding vision and goals
Principle   2: Holistic perspective
Principle   3: Essential elements
Principle   4: Adequate scope
Principle   5: Practical focus
Principle   6: Openness
Principle   7: Effective communication
Principle   8: Broad participation
Principle   9: Ongoing assessment
Principle 10: Institutional capacity

Source: Piper (2002, p21)

1   principles for their constitution of the system (ecological or social principles)
2   principles for a favourable outcome of planning within the system (principles of sustainability)
3   principles for the process to reach this outcome
4   actions, that is, concrete measures that comply with the principles for the process to reach a favourable outcome in the system.

The ISA tool assesses the level of risk to the ecologically sustainable development principles in planning and decision making documents, using a precautionary approach, the Bellagio principles and the recent work of Robert et al (2002). One aim is to build on the strengths of the existing tools used in the environmental/sustainability assessment areas of council. The ISA tool also seeks to expand the current use of a triple bottom line outcome to support the more holistic sustainability concept in order to:

*   provide better decision making information and act as an educational and training tool for decision makers and their advisers
*   inform not only policy development and planning instruments but also open up debate and change in operations and activities
*   be externally referenced, that is, directly linked to legislation requirements thereby allowing decisions to be based on acknowledged standards openly and transparently and not subverted by hidden (conflicting) agendas
*   be internally referenced to an organization's management plan and strategic development plans taking into context specifics and local issues
*   allow issues rather than people to be judged
*   be based on information familiar to decision makers and thus be simple and straightforward to use
*   motivate capacity building in governance and community for sustainability
*   integrate with current systems of practice to avoid a major process overhaul
*   provide consistency across all levels of decision making
*   provide a framework that is robust and able to accommodate internal and external changes over time
*   identify contra-indications to sustainability and facilitate policy review
*   make risk management and the ecologically sustainable development principles the basis of the tool.

The tool was designed in parallel with the events described earlier. The designer worked alongside council staff, observing their decision making processes. It became apparent that many crucial sustainability decisions were made by project staff at the public–council interface. Examples are development approvals, and the preparation of local environment plans and spatial zoning plans. This is a point at which guidelines are supposed to be followed, but there is little supervision of the actual decisions. Only when some planning disaster becomes obvious does the trend of the decisions become apparent to the wider public. One in ten development approvals for this project revealed consistent pro-development misinterpretation of the sustainability guidelines.

The ISA tool was designed to take account of this grounded end of the decision making process, although it can be used for any documented council decision making process. The sustainable development principles embedded in the legislation were translated into three categories of risk. Each statement in any relevant council document can be examined to establish whether there is an identifiable risk and if so, which risk category it represents. The risk may be relevant to intragenerational or intergenerational equity, biodiversity conservation or the valuation and pricing of environmental goods and services. Table 9.1 relates the three risk categories to sustainability and the symbol assigned to each statement in the plan as it is analysed.

Table 9.1 *The three risk categories and their relevance to sustainability*

ISA risk category	Definition	Symbol assigned to statement in plan	Rationale
Low	The risks are known, disclosed and controlled	√	Risks are evident from existing knowledge and are disclosed within the plan. Strategies and resources are identified within the plan to manage these risks
Medium	The risks are known, disclosed but uncontrolled	X	Risks are evident from existing knowledge and disclosed within the plan. However, there are no strategies nominated or resources identified to manage the risk
High	The risks are known but undisclosed and uncontrolled	?	Risks are evident from existing knowledge but the plan does not disclose the risk and subsequently does not nominate any controls to reduce the risk. Failure to disclose may relate to data on: • the proposed activity • the place • the risk management strategy.

Failure to take account of a known risk may occur for many reasons, including:

• the data are deliberately omitted as it is deemed too sensitive for public scrutiny
• the data indicate a constraint to 'business as usual'
• the information required is too expensive or too time-consuming to generate
• there is no understanding by the plan designer of the importance or relevance of the data.

There is a fourth position for decision makers, that is, where there is insufficient knowledge available about an issue to allow an estimate of the risk. These unknown factors cannot be included in the ISA tool because it is not possible to estimate whether the effect would be positive or negative. As the tool is applied in any one area, however, the use of the tool itself leads to the ignored element becoming apparent.

The precautionary principle, as defined in the Local Government Amendment (ESD) Act 1997, was used as the integrating theme for all the ecologically sustainable development principles, since it applies to all. In the ISA tool, precaution is based on the probability and degree of harm to the three companion principles that might occur as a consequence of some action. This judgement does not rely only on scientific facts but also on qualitative knowledge, including community values, opinions and aspirations. A set of criteria was developed to guide assessors in determining the presence of risk to each of the three ecologically sustainable development principles. The outcome is expressed as a ratio of the three risk categories. The number of times a plan scores a tick, cross or question mark is aggregated and expressed as a ratio.

The ISA tool can differentiate between magnitudes in consequence of risk. Where there are catastrophic consequences, an intrinsic weighting will occur because a cross or question mark will be recorded against each of the companion principles. Where the consequences are minor, the cross, if one is assigned, will likely be to only one ecologically sustainable development principle and therefore have less influence on the final ratio.

Analysis using the tool is based on an idealized decision making system. Under existing conditions, it is reasonable to expect a shortfall between the ideal and actual practice, with the tool acting as a mechanism for negotiating that gap.

Determining the presence and nature of the risk

A set of criteria was developed for each risk question to guide the user in determining which of the three risk positions it represents. The key questions come in two types:

- Type 1 questions relate to what is contained in the plan. They prompt an assessment of the link between sustainability and the information in the document and, as such, the link is a direct, first-order effect and can be described as explicit (definite, plain, clear)
- Type 2 questions analyse what should be in the document, either because it is required by legislation or by other administrative/cultural procedures, but is not included. The link between what should be and sustainability is indirect or a second-order effect and as such can be described as implicit (implied, suggested, hidden).

Both types of questions establish the presence of risk. The following tables provide the framework and the criteria to guide the strategic inquiry. The

Table 9.2 *Integrated sustainability analysis of a sample development control plan*

Ecologically sustainable development principle	Triple bottom line element	√	X	?
Precautionary principle	–	–	–	–
Biodiversity conservation	Ecology	6	8	9
Valuation and pricing	Economics	4	4	5
Intragenerational and intergenerational equity	Society	12	7	7
*******************	************	*******	*******	*******
Raw data trend		22	19	21

Bellagio principles as well as the concepts of Robert et al (2002) guided the development of these key questions.

Table 9.2 reports the outcome of the integrated sustainability analysis of a sample development control plan. The result is a ratio between controlled, uncontrolled and unknown risk to biodiversity conservation, intragenerational and intergenerational equity, and the true valuation and pricing of environmental goods and services.

The sample development control plan explicitly commits to conserving biodiversity and reducing indirect costs to the community, but provides little incentive to undertake a comprehensive cost–benefit analysis to verify the outcome. While committing to conservation in principle, there is very weak assurance for actions to conserve. The lack of clarity and strength in the demand for action, and deficiencies in language, allow the decision maker considerable latitude to waive compliance standards and provide any future proponent with considerable licence to appeal decisions.

Social learning context in local government

Social learning requires partnerships in data development, information management and decision making that bridge different disciplines, social divides and levels of bureaucracy. Integration of these groups currently occurs via both informal and formal networks, but the formal system contains deep divisions, mistrust and poor accountability. The informal system appears directed by political agendas, influential external players and considerations not authorized by law. The Bellagio principles incorporate strong social sustainability aspects and thus seemed ideal to use as the basis of an integrated assessment tool within an experiential and contested learning environment.

Table 9.3 summarizes our observations of the barriers to implementing the Bellagio principles in applying the ISA tool, matched to observations of actions that can overcome those barriers.

Table 9.3 *Social learning strategies potentially able to diminish sustainability barriers in local government*

Sustainability barrier	Social learning strategy
Extent of professional distrust	Create collective learning opportunities to build understanding between professional groups and feed back to decision making
	Support development of local assessment capacity across professional groups
	Develop an organizing framework linking common vision and goals to indicators and criteria
Dominance of political ambitions	Make judgements, assumptions and uncertainties explicit to all
	Ensure participation of decision makers to maintain a firm link between policies and actions
Informal networks of power and trust	Aim for a simple clear structure
	Consider all wider positive and negative consequences of human activity, in monetary and non-monetary terms
	Consider equity and disparity within the current population and between present and future generations
	Make methods and data accessible and transparent to all
Lack of dialogues, collective learning and genuine participation	Address the needs of the key actors
	Aim for simple structure and clear language
	Obtain broad representation of views to ensure recognition of diverse and changing values
	Be iterative, adaptive and responsive to change and uncertainty
	Provide institutional capacity for data collection, maintenance and documentation
Inappropriate reward structures, such as dollars or turn around times, used as measures of success	Standardize units for comparison purposes, use a time horizon covering the short term and future generations
	Adjust goals, frameworks and indicators as new insights are gained.
	Consider ecological condition on which life depends
	Consider economic development and other non-market activities that contribute to human–social wellbeing
Absence of a common vision between levels of government and departments	Develop a clear vision of sustainable development and goals that define that vision
	Ensure a firm link between policy and action

Table 9.3 *(continued)*

Sustainability barrier	Social learning strategy
	Clearly assign responsibilities and provide ongoing support in the decision making process
	Develop capacity for repeated measurement to determine trends
Dominance of values and beliefs incommensurable with sustainability principles underlying decision making processes	Consider the wellbeing of social, ecological and economic subsystems and interactions
	Consider the wider positive and negative consequences of human activity, in monetary and non-monetary terms
	Use a time horizon that covers the short term and future generations
	Obtain broad representation of views to ensure recognition of diverse and changing values

Conclusions

Local governments mirror a society in which environmental management and social cohesiveness are undervalued and where whole-of-organization goals are increasingly devalued by corporate imperatives. A single catalytic tool, no matter how valuable, cannot in itself embed sustainability within such a system. However the ISA tool can minimize the worst excesses of corporative environmental extravagance by facilitating iterative and open learning processes that work through a constantly evolving improvement cycle.

Many of the organizational barriers to using the tool experienced in Green Valley Shire Council are common throughout councils in Australia. From the output of the first national local government sustainability practitioners workshop (Brown, 2004), it is evident that even the most innovative council has ingrained resistance to moving from single-issue solutions with readily measurable results to multilayered transforming processes that have less quantifiable, if readily recognizable, benefits. Exacerbating this is the corp-oratization of council culture, which sees 'adequacy' as a perfectly acceptable level of service performance as long as it meets efficiency-based performance criteria, quantifiable in time or economic terms. Within this environment, a tool that seeks to achieve a richer, more qualitative standard of optimum performance and inverts established power relationships and challenges the dogma of economic growth can be deeply threatening.

However, any tool supporting improved environmental management requires social learning as a close partner and the establishment of collaborative, experiential learning processes can help overcome even the most entrenched disinclination to change. To become an accepted part of council practice requires the valuing of environmental expertise in collaboration with council staff, and between councillors and council staff. With the growing acceptance of the triple bottom line as a management approach in government circles and as part of a broad-based training of staff in some councils, there is growing support for environmental management skills. With this the opportunities to test the efficacy of tools that promote sustainability are also increasing.

What is required, however, is senior management and/or an elected body with sufficient understanding of, or commitment to, the principles of sustainability to overcome structural and political inertia to testing new and radical alternatives to accepted practice. Actively antagonistic or simply disengaged players in the process are one of the key impediments to progressing sustainability in local government. In many cases, these people are supported by a middle management who, either through job security concerns, ambitions, compromised interests or sheer disinterest, are unlikely to challenge the status quo. What is required is the presence of key sustainability drivers with the ability to motivate senior management and councillors to unlock the entrenched gates of power.

The council team behind the project intends to continue the social learning processes initiated in the initial research programme. As a first step, in a major review of the council's development control plans, staff have used the analysis generated by the ISA tool to incorporate sustainability objectives and standards. In addition, they intend to reapply the tool to the development control plans. This will not only illustrate council's progress towards sustainability, but also identify whether gaps originally identified have been covered. The latter identifies the need to reflect upon any learning process and seeks constant improvement – as knowledge improves and values change, the output from the analysis will evolve.

One of the more unexpected and pleasing products of the project was the enthusiasm of local government environmental management practitioners to expand upon the outcomes of the initial sustainability workshop held at Green Valley Shire Council. Like the internal council officers before them, local environmental managers felt the need to break down entrenched government barriers by promoting a cohesive vision of sustainability. In order to follow through on this goal, a number of local government environmental managers have agreed to work towards creating an open forum with the guiding brief being 'to advocate and catalyse genuine change in pursuit of sustainability'.

Thus, in one sense, the social learning process initiated through the project in Green Valley Shire Council with the University of Western Sydney has become a national venture.

References

Attorney-General's Department (2002) 'Auditor-General's report', report to parliament, vol 5, www.audit.nsw.gov.au/agrep02v5/Contents.htm/accessed 23 December 2004

Brown, V. (2004) 'Sustainability leadership in the local government sector: Working from the inside out', in Hargroves, C., Smith, M. and Moody, J., *The Natural Advantage of Nations*, Earthscan, London

Brown, V. A., Stephenson, P., Nicholson, R., Bennet, K.-J. and Smith, J. (2001) *Grass Roots and Common Ground: Community-based Environment and Health Action*, Department of Health and Aged Care, Canberra

Bunker, R. (2002) 'More than fringe benefits – the values, policies, issues and expectations embedded in Sydney's rural–urban fringe', *Australian Planner*, vol 39, no 2, pp66–71

Department of the Environment and Heritage (2002) *Australia State of the Environment (SoE) Report 2001*, Department of the Environment and Heritage, Canberra

Environmental Defenders Office (2001) 'Submission on PlanFirst – review of plan making in the NSW White Paper', a submission by the Environmental Defenders Office (NSW), National Parks and Wildlife Association (NSW), Nature Conservation Council of NSW, Total Environment Centre and World Wide Fund for Nature

Foltin, C. (1999) 'State and local government performance: It's time to measure up!', *The Government Accountants Journal*, vol 48, no 1, pp40–47

Griffith, R. (2003) 'How shall we live?', unpublished PhD thesis, University of Western Sydney, Richmond

Health Council (2002) *National Environmental Health Strategy*, Federal Department of Health and Ageing, Canberra

Hundloe, T. and McDonald, G. (1997) 'Ecological sustainable development and the Better Cities Program', *Australian Journal of Environmental Management*, vol 4, pp88–111

Jacobs, M. (1995) 'Sustainability and community: Environment, economic rationalism and the sense of place', *Australian Planner*, vol 32, no 2, pp109–115

Kline, J. J. (1997) 'Local government outcome based performance measures and customer service standards: Has their time come?', *The Government Accountants Journal*, vol 45, no 4, pp46–50

Lambert, J. (2002) 'Report on ISA Forum', unpublished report, Baulkham Hills Shire Council, Baulkham Hills

Land and Water Australia (2002) *National Land and Water Resources Audit*, Land and Water Australia, Canberra

Lovegrove, K. and Campbell, G. (1992) 'Private certification under the Model Building Act: Excluding local authorities from building control', *Local Government Management*, vol 26, no 1, pp5–6, 10–14

Mamouney, L. (2000) 'Should local government be responsible for biodiversity management? A critical review of local governments' ability to manage biodiversity loss in NSW through the development process', *Environment and Planning Law Journal*, vol 17, no 2, pp138–150

Mant, M. (1995) 'Form follows organization: Some suggestions for improving the quality of organisations and urban design', *Urban Futures* (Canberra), vol 17, pp9–12, February

Mercer, D. and Jokowitz, P. (2000) 'Local Agenda 21 and barriers to sustainability at the local government level in Victoria', *Australian Geographer*, vol 13, no 2, p163–181

NSW Environmental Health Unit (2002) *Report on Wallaroo Lakes*, NSW Government, Sydney

NSW EPA (1997) *State of the Environment 1997*, EPA, Sydney

Piper, J. M. (2002) 'CEA and sustainable development – evidence from UK case studies', *Environmental Impact Assessment Review*, vol 22, pp17–36

Rees, W. (2000) 'Ecological footprints', from the Sixth Biennial Meeting of the International Society for Ecological Economics, People and Nature: Operationalizing Ecological Economics, The Australian National University, Canberra, July

Robert, K.-H., Schmidt-Bleek, B., Aloisi de Larderel, J., Basile, G., Jansen, J. L., Kuehr, R., Price Thomas, P., Suzuki, M., Hawken, P. and Wackernagel, M. (2002) 'Strategic sustainable development – selection, design and synergies of applied tools', *Journal of Cleaner Production*, vol 10, pp197–214

Sattler, P. (1998) 'Management for ecological sustainability – introductory address', in *Management for Ecological Sustainability*, proceedings, The Centre for Conservation Biology, University of Queensland, pp10–13

Scott, J. (2004) 'Integrating sustainability provisions into contemporary decision making' unpublished PhD thesis, University of Western Sydney, Richmond

SPIRT (Strategic Partnerships with Industry Research Training) (1999) Grant application, Australian Research Council, Canberra

Stilwell, F. (2000) 'Towards sustainable cities', *Urban Policy and Research*, vol 18, no 2, pp205–217

WSROC (2000) *Regional State of the Environment Report 2000*, Western Sydney Regional Organization of Councils, Blacktown

10

Felt Knowing: A Foundation for Local Government Practice

Greg Walkerden

At a glance

- Managing the interplay of the social, economic and ecological to sustain societies and ecosystems is an evolving art
- Explicit knowledge (such as scientific insight, management models and legal reasoning) is not nearly as powerful as is often assumed. In many situations, tried and tested knowledge only covers a small part of the 'decision space'
- Modes of thinking that do not rely on explicit methods and theories play a central role in skilful professional practice; this is often not remarked on. In skilful practice in difficult circumstances, a holistic 'feeling' for what is at stake plays a pivotal role
- People can be trained to leverage their feeling of what is at stake in a situation more effectively, as has been demonstrated in psychotherapeutic practice. Skills in 'listening' to oneself play a central role
- When we make the role of felt knowing explicit, we describe professional practices in ways that make it much easier for practitioners to understand what good practice is.

Innovating and learning in ecosystem management

Sustaining ecosystems in the face of rapid population growth is extremely difficult. At Wyong, in the coastal zone on the northern edge of Sydney, we are not succeeding. But we are learning, and our practice is improving. This chapter explores how what we know implicitly about situations, but not at first explicitly, plays a central role in our learning.

Paying attention to what we 'feel' is at stake in a situation is fundamental to thinking creatively about it (Gendlin, 1997). 'Felt' knowing is our 'ground' for creativity and innovation. According to Kooiman (2003, p4), 'Creativity, intuition and experience are just as important as goal-directedness, criteria of efficiency and working "according to rules" ' in good governance.

Because we are generally not sustaining ecosystems at present, innovating is essential in ecosystem management. So listening to what we feel (sense, intuit, ...) is fundamental to good professional practice.

Uncertainty and ambiguity as givens

In ecosystem management, the adaptive management tradition has called for:

> *learn[ing] to see the world in a new perspective – a perspective that recognises adaptability and responsiveness [as the hallmarks of good practice] rather than prediction and tight control, and a perspective that actively views uncertainty as a fundamental facet of environmental life rather than as a distasteful transition to attainable certainty (Holling, 1978, p139).*

Whenever we explore how we should manage ecosystems, with a view to sustaining them and our communities, we find many uncertainties, many opportunities for learning, and no prospect of full and final knowledge. Experience in managing a catchment–lakes system at Wyong, north of Sydney, illustrates this. An adaptive management assessment carried out in 1995–1996 identified key uncertainties related to each of the following (see Table 3 in Gilmour et al, 1999):

- ecological processes operating on a much larger scale than the catchment–lakes system (future rainfall sequences)
- much larger-scale social processes playing out locally (in the speed and character of land use change)
- future managerial performance (the likely timing and effectiveness of catchment management policies)
- lake hydrodynamics (what a second channel connecting the ocean and the lakes would do)
- lake nutrient dynamics (the time it will take for the release of nutrients from sediments to the water column to ease off as catchment loads of nutrients decrease; the potential for sediment under main water bodies to become anoxic)
- lake plant dynamics (what determines macro-algae biomass; whether reducing sediment loads will trigger phytoplankton blooms)
- the power of scientific methods (the time it will take for the effects of, or ineffectiveness of, management decisions to become evident, given the 'noisiness' of monitoring data).

To this list of difficulties we can add sociopolitical uncertainties and funda-mental, difficult value judgements. An example of the former is: Will we be able to get further advances in the design of urban areas adopted as policy in the face of opposition from developers, who are strong supporters of many local politicians? An example of the latter is: Where should environmental needs sit in relation to social and economic needs when local and state governments are allocating their funds? In the Wyong region there are high rates of child abuse and youth suicide, serious decline in a lake system, and a local economy growing much more slowly than the local population.

This level of difficulty is usual in landscape-scale ecosystem manage-ment.

Making sense together

How do we go about 'making sense together' in difficult situations like these? Over the last few decades, workable alternatives to traditional technical solu-tions have multiplied (for example, Forester, 1989; Lee, 1993; Schön, 1983, 1987; Walters, 1986). Most of this work has focused on the social aspects of decision making processes. Walters uses multidisciplinary workshop-based systems analysis. Forester emphasizes the importance of listening, negotiation and correcting the distortions in communication that serve the more powerful interests. Lee has focused on integrating conflict resolution (a 'gyroscope') and adaptive management (a 'compass'). Schön has focused on what kinds of 'practicum' teach skills in working effectively amidst uncertainty and conflict, emphasizing learning by doing, and coaching rather than teaching.

There are many good reasons for being alert to the social character of ecosystem management:

1 Dialogue is fundamental to good decision making. For the most part, experts working within their own disciplines, or specialists in synthesis working alone, produce bad advice on how to manage (Holling, 1978)
2 Ecosystems bring together the interests and influences of many stakeholders. Cooperation is therefore essential to managing them sustainably
3 In practice, managerial decision making is often distorted by self-interest (Robbins, 1994, p159–161). With limited time and resources we 'satisfice' rather than 'optimize'. In the process, we commonly select visible problems that reflect our own interests and background; our self-interest is commonly an important de facto criterion in selecting from alternative courses of action; and commonly we measure performance only in ways that protect our self-interest. Given the risks that this creates for the common good, working collaboratively is highly desirable. It provides more transparency and constrains self-interest.

But decision making is also a personal process. When we make sense together, each of us engages in making sense of the situation for ourselves. Social learning and personal learning are the one process looked at from different perspectives. How we experience the meaning of situations – how we feel the meaning, and how we work with what we feel – plays a pivotal role in social learning. We can test the truth of this by considering what we actually do when we are making sense of problematic situations. Recently, a colleague and I were discussing how to manage an urbanizing landscape to protect the natural wetlands downstream. The range of frames that we heeded included ecology, engineering, planning, politics, management, interpersonal relations and intrapersonal relations (see Box 10.1). This list is not exhaustive. In principle it cannot be, as there is no absolute limit to the number of interests we might take in any *actual* instance (see Gendlin, 1997).

In situations like this, other edges to our decision making include ethics (anthropocentric versus ecocentric perspectives in public policy), community development opportunities (we are collaborating with community development workers in the new urban areas), economic development policy for the region (including the debate about the value of greenfield employment sites versus fostering growth in local small businesses) and demographics (including the potential to shift population growth into redeveloping town centres).

So how do we think about situations like this when the range of considerations we recognize are important is too exhausting to think through explicitly?

Technical rationality is stuck in situations like the one described in Box 10.1. Their complexity and openness are beyond its capacity. But *we* are only stuck if we rely on technical rationality to do something it was not designed to do. We have the capacity to think in ways that ideal types of deductive reasoning, mathematical calculation, categorization and the like do not describe.

A short experiential exercise will help bring some other facets of how we think into focus. Imagine you are going to explain to a colleague what's at stake in managing urban development to sustain the natural wetlands situation at Wyong (as per Box 10.1). Consider:

- If you were preparing to brief someone on this situation, what you would say?
- Where would you start? Where would you begin your explanation?
- What do you feel it is most important to explain?
- Is there more that wasn't said in Box 10.1 that you feel is important to bring out?

Allow your sense of what you would like to say to form, to take shape (without relying on re-reading to refresh your memory).

Now, consider what you are doing as you do this little exercise. Where do you go to find your answers? What are you listening to as you wait for words to come? What rhythms of pausing, waiting, and words coming do you notice? Is there a flood of words at first, and then a lot more waiting later, for example? And what is the quality of the pausing? Does it sometimes feel pregnant, rich with meaning? Is there sometimes a quality of wonder in the waiting? At other

Box 10.1 An example of complexity in ecosystem management situations

In a recent conversation with a colleague about managing a natural wetland in an urbanizing catchment, I had each of the following in mind:

- Our ecological understanding of how plants respond to wetting and drying cycles … which plants can tolerate getting wetter and which can't, how getting dryer is more tolerable than getting wetter for many of the trees… How, using our current understandings, we can't mimic pre-development flows very precisely, so long-term ecological change may follow anyway
- Our current understanding of the performance of engineering devices, for example what we know about our ability to spread flows at the edge of an urban area, as opposed to deliver channelized flows, as traditional engineering designs do. And whether it might be possible to sustain more sheet-like flow patterns throughout an urban subdivision, without negatively impacting amenity, flooding risk and so on
- Our understanding of current planning practice, for example what regulatory levers we have to draw on to shape current developments, and what changes in regulatory instruments are needed to strengthen our ability to make these urban developments more sustainable
- The current political context, for example the unwillingness of most developers to incur extra costs when they can find a way to avoid them; the partial dependence of some local politicians on developers for campaign funds; the fact that many developers are out of step with community sentiment, which provides some political leverage; the extent of tension between our community's aspirations for economic development and their aspirations for environmental conservation
- Our organizational capacity to develop a consensus, for example the play of support and conflict between people and between sections in our organization; the strengths and weaknesses of various manager–employee relationships; the extent to which different parts of the organization are aligned with different external stakeholders
- The substantial extent to which my colleague and I share a common value base and common aspirations, our past experiences of cooperation and conflict as they play into this particular task, our hopes for a mutually satisfying, ecologically effective collaboration here
- How I work with the ebbs and flows of my own relationship to these complications, for example the extent to which I do or do not feel frustrated by our ability to deliver the high-quality outcomes I aspire to; whether, feeling frustrated, I get reactive or return to being centred; what I do when I find I am feeling uneasy about something, whether, for example, I tend to shy away, or perhaps tend to probe vigorously, or perhaps to slow down and take my unease in.

times, does waiting have a kind of blank, frustrating quality? Are there other qualities, differences, differentiations that stand out?

Straight after reading a description of a situation like the one described in Box 10.1, most of us could not turn around and give a verbatim account of what we have just read, recapturing every detail. But we have a sense of what is at stake in this situation. And many of us have professional experience of other problems that are resonant of this one. In some respects then, what we each have to say is richer and broader than what was written. Having a *felt* sense of a situation is not having all the explicit details to hand. It is having a sense of the whole in a way that no amount of listing explicit details substitutes for.

For practical purposes, much of this richness is in play when I use my felt sense of the situation we are working in to guide me as I shape the action I take. We find there are many different ways in which we can speak from our experiencing to say what is and is not occurring, and what does and does not look promising. Felt dimensions of knowing differ from explicit (articulate) dimensions of knowing in that we can keep returning to what is felt to say more that is accurate and relevant (from where we sit).

What we see in an example like this is that in thinking in practice, quite a lot of the time we work directly from what Gendlin terms 'implicit meaning'. Implicit meaning is his term for meaning that has not yet been 'symbolized' (expressed in words, equations, pictures). Gendlin's take is that 'we employ explicit symbols for only very small portions of what we think' (1964, p64).

The possibility that felt meaning is functioning directly (as implicit meaning that we use in a variety of ways) is not even contemplated when technical rationality is put forward as an ideal for professional practice. As a result, it is not surprising that the tools of technical rationality cannot deal with many aspects of real world problems that we deal with effectively.

Feeling meaning is not a subject that usually comes up in discussions of ecosystem management. But it can surface when we pay detailed attention to how we are personally experiencing situations. When we talk about how we are puzzled, confused, inspired or excited, or about our inklings, intuitions, uncertainties or doubts, we are talking about aspects of how we personally experience our professional situations – what being ourselves in these settings involves. Intriguingly, in ecosystem management, these aspects of our experience are largely outside the bounds of professional discussion, even though they are very much inside the bounds of professional experience. When it occurs, conversation about such matters is usually informal. The lack of a professional discourse in this area marks ecosystem management out as a fairly unreflexive professional practice, compared with, say, community services or organizational development.

Feeling meaning is central to skilful practice

How much do skills in working with one's implicit understandings differ in practice? To get a sense of the upper bounds, we can ask: What do exceptional practitioners do when they're being effective? Schön (1987, p13) comments:

> *outstanding practitioners are not said to have more professional knowledge than others but more 'wisdom', 'talent', 'intuition', or 'artistry'.*

Somehow they are using what is known more effectively. Their way of being professional, their process, is different.

Schön (1987, p13) goes on to remark:

> *Unfortunately, such terms as these ['wisdom', 'talent', 'intuition', 'artistry'] serve not to open up enquiry but to close it off. They are used as junk categories, attaching names to phenomena that elude conventional strategies of explanation.*

But this is not necessarily the case. We use these terms to point to something that we recognize but (commonly) do not know how to describe. We use them because we have a felt appreciation of what is at stake, but no theory yet. From our felt appreciations, new theory can be built.

Can we say more about how what exceptionally skilful practitioners do is different? Describing his life as a thinker, Einstein remarks (2002, p24):

> *I have no doubt that our thinking goes on for the most part without the use of signs (words)... For how, otherwise, should it happen that sometimes we wonder quite spontaneously about some experience? This wondering appears to occur when an experience comes into conflict with a world of concepts already sufficiently fixed within us. Whenever such a conflict is experienced sharply and intensively it reacts back upon our world of thought in a decisive way. The development of this world of thought is in a certain sense a continuous flight from wonder.*

What Einstein is describing here is having an 'experience' that does not fit the 'concepts' that he usually accepts as true. And he is describing 'thinking about' what might be said next without using words, signs or symbols. He is 'wondering'. Wondering is, for him, feeling a 'knowing' that has not yet found words or symbols, and allowing new concepts to come out of this process.

We can see in Einstein's practice a central gestalt flip: for him, wordless thinking is primary, and what is said is derivative. Implicit meaning (meaning that is felt) is the place from which fresh insight comes. He listened to his inarticulate knowings for a long time, with great patience, allowing them to unfold. He describes, for example, reflecting for ten years on what kind of universal principle could take a central place in physics, given that neither mechanics nor electrodynamics (as he found them) provided what was needed. Out of this process came rejecting absolute simultaneity – a presupposition ordinarily taken for granted – and the special theory of relativity (Einstein, 2002, p42).

But Einstein is exceptional. Should these lessons from his practice be broadly applied?

Schön provides some more mundane examples that show how feeling what to do – feeling what kind of action makes sense – is fundamental to skilful practice:

> *When good jazz musicians improvise together, they similarly display reflection-in-action smoothly integrated into ongoing performance. Listening to one another, listening to themselves, they 'feel' where the music is going and adjust their playing accordingly... As the musicians feel the direction in which the music is developing, they make new sense of it. They reflect-in-action on the music they are collectively making – though not, of course, in the medium of words (Schön, 1987, p30).*

And:

> *A tennis teacher of my acquaintance writes, for example, that he always begins by trying to help his students get the feeling of 'hitting the ball right'. Once they recognise this feeling, like it, and learn to distinguish it from the various feelings associated with 'hitting the ball wrong', they begin to be able to correct and detect their own errors. But they usually cannot, and need not, describe what the feeling is like or by what means they produce it (Schön, 1987, p24).*

Feeling what to do, and allowing action to arise from this, is a foundation for skilful practice.

Working from felt meaning makes innovating easier

The shift from taking technical rationality as the heart of professional practice to acknowledging, affirming, and embracing 'the *primacy* of the functioning of experienced meaning and the *relativity* of all formulations and schemes with respect to it' (Gendlin, 1997, p207; my emphasis) is very empowering. This is evident if we explore how it affects innovation in ecosystem management.

Professional practices are often conveyed through recipes, templates for action. In my milieu over the last two decades, the mainstream approach to urban drainage system design has had four main phases:

1   A period when flooding was the dominant consideration, so respected recipes moved water from urban areas to receiving water bodies as quickly as possible
2   A period in which managing litter and sediments was also a central consideration, so the design recipe set included gross pollutant traps
3   A period in which nutrient management also became a central issue, so the recipe set included constructed wetlands, and the assumption that quicker was better than slower was abandoned; water quality management was largely an end-of-pipe issue, however
4   The current period in which trying to mimic the pre-development water cycle (both quality and quantity) in urban areas is becoming a dominant paradigm: the recipe set that is taking shape includes rainwater tanks, purpose-designed swales, infiltration and evaporation beds, retaining natural creek lines, and the like; water is consciously managed at multiple scales: lot level, subdivision level, subcatchment level, and whole-of-catchment level.

One can observe deepening insight into sustainability in the changes in prevailing recipes. Innovation has clearly been occurring. Practitioners' relations to it have varied, however. What happens if (as some of my colleagues have done at times) we assume that the *explicit* concepts, the *explicit* methods, are the heart of what ecosystem management is? If ecologically responsible drainage design *is* managing flooding, litter, sediments and nutrients, all our work comes from this conceptual model. But if we approach professional practice like this, when a paradigm we are relying on is not working, we suffer, because we adapt more slowly. We have felt the effects of this at Wyong. There is a legacy of drainage infrastructure developed under earlier drainage paradigms that could have been smaller.

From the period when flooding was the dominant consideration there is a footprint of forest dieback and weed invasion. Pre-development sheet flows were channelized. Some trees received much more water than they did before, so many of these have died. Nutrients were not managed, so weeds have invaded the wetland down new drainage lines.

From the period when managing nutrients to protect the lakes down-stream became a central issue, there is a large constructed wetland programme designed to maintain water quality as urban development proceeds. However, the intricacies of managing wetting and drying cycles (how often a bushland area gets wet, and for how long) to sustain natural wetland dynamics were not considered when it was designed. Developer contributions, which are funding the constructed wetland programme, were based on the original designs. Drainage systems that do a reasonable job of protecting the lakes downstream, but a poor job of protecting the natural wetlands nearby, are being built.

When our designs are failing, defining good professional practice as using the tools of technical rationality correctly is distracting. It is harder to take in that the designs *are* failing, and that a quite different approach, perhaps one not yet invented, should actually be used.

Of course it is possible to say that good professional practice *is* using established technical methods and models correctly. An engineer reviewing the set of paradigm shifts that I have just described might say: 'These failures are not engineering failures, as engineers we have simply done what was asked of us; we have been asked to do different things at different times.' But the fundamental engineering design question is: Have we changed the way water moves in this landscape responsibly? Where that is not a live engineering question, professional practice is clearly stunted. Taking responsibility for outcomes *is* good professional practice.

If we have a *felt* sense of the design task self-consciously at the centre of our designing, we are profoundly more open to innovations in process and practice. Our feel for what is needed is holistic in a way that mass balance equations and related drainage design rules are not. If we check a possible design concept against our feel for what is needed, and we do this knowingly, that is, more slowly, unexpected aspects of a situation may come to our attention. Inklings and uneases can segue into insights.

To manage adaptively, we need to understand the practice of ecosystem management as a change process: as a process of adapting when we need to, and being open to adaptation as a matter of course. This is fundamental to managing ecosystems effectively (Holling, 1978, p36). If we place the pulsation of (1) feeling implicit meaning that we can't articulate yet, and (2) explicating felt meaning, allowing words (actions, ...) to come, at the heart of our understanding of good professional practice, we build a conception of ecosystem management in which adaptation is central. We provide practitioners with a conception of their practice that evokes exploration of what action best fits each new situation.

Working from felt meaning makes collaborating easier

We each have a personal sense of what is at stake in a given ecosystem management situation. How holistic this is will vary. It depends on our experience and sensitivities. Making felt meaning primary simply ensures that what we say and do will express all we experience as relevant. Making sense together – embracing learning within a social context, and specifically embracing dialogue – is important because we each embody personal and disciplinary limitations.

Taking felt meaning as fundamental, and concepts and models as derivative, opens us up for interdisciplinary dialogue and collaboration. When we work from felt meaning, we are drawn to whatever is relevant. When we work from explicit concepts, we tend to limit our exploration to logically related considerations.

When we assume that explicit paradigms, methods and theories define a professional tradition, we assume that a specific set of parts and processes is fundamental. When we think about managing a natural wetland in an urbanizing catchment, it is obvious how problematic this is (see Box 10.1). Any actual situation can be helpfully explicated in many different ways. It is nonetheless commonplace to talk as if the legal were one domain, the ecological another, the interpersonal another and the intrapersonal another. If we take any discipline as fundamental, then we put its kind of 'objects' at the heart of our exploration: chunks of legal reasoning, statistically defensible assertions about ecological dynamics, engineering design considerations, and so on. But actual situations are not put together from legal parts, or kinds of parts canonized by any other discipline. When we make referencing felt meaning the heart of good professional practice, we work with a way of understanding that is radically open to the characterizations of all disciplines. Collaborating across our disciplinary boundaries is much easier.

Working from felt meaning makes radical flexibility and appropriateness possible

The process of redefining good professional practice as profoundly expressing 'the primacy of the functioning of experienced meaning and the relativity of all formulations and schemes with respect to it' (Gendlin, 1997, p207) can be carried much further. This shift opens the way to a fluidity and openness in thinking that is unimaginable in the canons of technical rationality. Professional practice can become radically adaptive.

We can appreciate some of the possibilities through the model of professional practice that Gendlin provides for philosophy. His method is equally relevant to ecosystem managers thinking into practical situations. Key principles he lays out are (Gendlin, 1997, pp208–219):

1   Every experience (situation, occurrence, ...) can be symbolized, described, articulated and explicated in countless possible ways
2   But what can be said is not arbitrary. Our sense of what is at stake in a situation demands a precision
3   Because there isn't a single true description of a situation, we are free to describe it in any of the countless possible ways that we find helpful. We have huge flexibility in what can truthfully be said. What fits our felt sense of what's at stake in a situation is what we can truthfully say. But we can look at situations from many different perspectives
4   All terms are relative to felt meaning. All the terms in all the theories are relative to how felt meaning can be explicated accurately, faithfully and genuinely. No basic term is actually fundamental in a way that gives it priority over felt meaning: it is always derivative and relative
5   Terms come to acquire a certain independence from experiencing, because we use each specific term to explicate many experiences. Their meaning keeps shifting because it is always relative to felt experiencing, but each term evokes a feeling of how it has been used and can be used in situations. It is the experience of likeness between situations that this involves that underlies concepts having 'logical implications': we come to expect patterns to be repeated in new situations. Logical implications help us explicate situations: they make thinking more efficient because they signal descriptive possibilities that we may find relevant and helpful. But we always have far more flexibility than any one set of logical implications offers, and no logical implication warrants rejecting a *felt* meaning.

This is a compressed account. I hope it evokes your curiosity. Thinking can be approached in a very unusual way that is profoundly empowering (Levin, 1997, p42). We can make listening to how the whole of a situation feels basic to all our work. We can say and do only what makes sense when the whole of a situation is taken into account, through our felt sense of what it is. We can take explicit meanings (theories, schemas, models...) as always derivative from, and relative to, and only one of many explications of, our felt sense of what is at stake. To do this is to embrace a flexibility and openness that is profoundly adaptive, but not usually sanctioned.

Skills in feeling meaning can be taught

How can we develop ourselves professionally so that we embrace this gestalt shift to working primarily from how situations feel, rather than primarily from what our conceptual models say they are?

Many people assume that skills in feeling the meaning of situations cannot be taught. Schön claims they can be, but only indirectly: by coaching rather than teaching. He has focused on the design of 'reflective practicums': practice arenas that we can create in which students can learn by doing. Some of their design elements are (Schön, 1987):

- kinds of coaching, for example 'joint experimentation' and 'follow me' (p212)
- the mediums in which coach and student dialogues occur – 'the drawing/talking language of designing, the playing/talking language of musical performance' (p209)
- the use of 'virtual worlds' like the architect's sketchpad, orchestral rehearsal or computer simulations (p77)
- processes that make use of 'inner and outer views of action – action as felt and action as observed', for example in psychoanalytic training 'doing to the student as the student might do with her patient or client' (p254).

But we can teach skills in feeling the meaning of situations more explicitly than this (Hendricks, 2001). By teaching people skills in how to work with their feeling for what a situation involves as they are trying out professional skills in a practicum, we deepen their process of learning by doing.

A way to underline that skills in feeling meaning can be formalized sufficiently to be taught is to show how two research traditions have independently discovered analogous procedures for thinking effectively from felt meaning. Gendlin's work goes back to the late 1950s and his collaboration with Carl Rogers. Table 10.1 includes a short form of the steps used to train people in 'focusing' – Gendlin's term for his method of listening to oneself. Petitmengin-Peugeot (1999) worked independently, using 'intuition' as her orienting term. She has developed a generic process model (with many variations articulated) of what people do when they think, intentionally, in an intuitive way.

If you compare the structure of the procedures that Gendlin and Petitmengin-Peugeot have delineated (see Table 10.1), it is clear that his 'heeding felt knowing' and her 'intuition' are in the same movement genre and that the sequences of movements they have observed are closely aligned. It is not a genre for which there is a well-established, widely used vocabulary, so their terminology is quite different. Their process descriptions can be used as reusable, teachable procedures for listening to ourselves (Gendlin, 1981, 1996; Hendricks, 2001).

Table 10.1 *Two schemas for listening to ourselves*

Gendlin (1996, pp71–75)	Petitmengin-Peugeot (1999, p59)
Clearing a space	Letting go
Begin by taking a minute to just rest and be friendly with yourself inside. See what stands between you and feeling fine. Each one of us carries several problems at a time and it is usually a mix of these. It helps to sort them out in the following way...	The gesture of letting go, of deep-rooting, of interior self-collecting, and of the slowing down of the mental activity, which makes it possible to reach a particular state of consciousness, the 'intuitive state'
A felt sense	Connection
Pick one of those concerns you found. Whatever you may know about the concern you have chosen, since it is a problem it also has an unresolved edge, a felt sense of unease, unresolvedness, or implicit richness that is more than you can fully comprehend. To find this unclear edge do the following...	The gesture of connection, which makes it possible to enter into contact with the object of the intuitive knowledge (a human being, an abstract problem, a situation...)
Getting a handle on it	
Try to find one word, a phrase, or an image to capture exactly the quality of that felt sense	
Resonating the handle	
If the word, phrase, or image really fits ... there should be a little relief, a bodily signal, that says 'yes (breathes) that's it all right'	
Asking	Listening
Now, just as if you did not know anything about it, ask in your body, ask the felt sense itself, what it is. Most people find quick answers coming in from what is already known or can be surmised. Let all thoughts just go by if the felt sense does not stir in response to it. Asking the felt sense takes more time. Before there is any effect there might need to be a whole minute of tapping the unclear felt sense, touching it, perhaps backing off, and then touching it again	The gesture of listening, with an attention that is at the same time panoramic and very discriminating, focused on the subtle signs announcing the intuition
Receiving	Intuition
Whatever comes with a little stirring in the felt sense, please welcome it. To 'receive' in our sense means to let the step be, give it a space to be in, not to reject it, however odd or wrong it may seem in itself. It comes with a little bit of bodily felt release, a breath, breath, a bodily sense that something is right about it, and that is what you want	The intuition itself, of which certain of the subjects have acquired (or acquire during the interview) a sufficiently discriminating consciousness to point out three distinct moments: the moment preceding the intuition, the intuition, the moment following the intuition

Note: All the contents of the table are direct quotes. There is some compression to facilitate comparison

Getting used to slowing down and listening to ourselves

How can we weave this shift to make referring directly to felt meanings fundamental in thinking into the everyday texture of our lives?

In my experience, working from felt knowing in practice in professional life is centrally a matter of:

- slowing down in the midst of conversations, thinking, writing, experimenting and observing
- taking in a layer of knowing that it is easy to feel in a background way without heeding.

It is a matter of taking time to take in what we are experiencing … what we know in a felt way, but have not yet said… There are a number of movements like those described by Gendlin and Petitmengin-Peugeot that I rely on greatly in a kind of conversation with myself. I describe some of these in the following subsections.

It may help to understand my descriptions if you slow down your reading, and read more ruminatively than usual. I suggest self-consciously taking in what I describe myself doing, and checking if it reminds you of things you have done yourself. As you check, you will probably notice that how I 'move' is not exactly the same as how you move. I invite you to be very sensitive to the details of how your own experiencing works, so that as you read you are exploring how you 'companion yourself'…

Heeding uneases, inklings…

Uneases, inklings, intimations are important resources for us as practitioners. If we take time with them, slow down, and gently let them unfold and become clear, we allow something that we felt was important but at first didn't know how to articulate fully, clearly, to become explicit. In meetings, for example, I often sit with something that doesn't feel comfortable – companioning my unease in a gentle, patient, curious way – until it becomes clear to me what I am unresolved about, and *then* I raise it for discussion. Taking time to get clear is a better use of everyone's time, and far better practice than shying away from a difficulty.

Allowing space and stillness to arise…

It is easy to grow impatient with anxieties and uneases, and rush to address them in a way that doesn't keep faith with what we implicitly know. Personally, I create space for stillness, letting things come in, allowing things in and taking them in. Sometimes this occurs in response to some difficulty … at other times it is a kind of pausing and taking stock. One of my own processes for reviewing how my team and I are progressing in our ecosystem management work is to sit, with a notebook to hand, and allow issues to come in their own time, writing them down in a pattern that reflects how the issues have given rise to each other: placing a central issue (concern, potential, context, …) in the middle of the page, then around it, linked by threads that grow longer and longer, the issues that come out of it. My way of writing is an adaptation of Gabriel Lusser Rico's 'clustering' (Lusser Rico, 1983) (see Figure 10.1).

Feeling for fresh edges...

When I am in situations where I know we need to do more … to innovate, to find a creative way forward … I quite self-consciously feel for the fresh edge of something. For example, when I was considering the long-term conservation needs of a threatened tree species (which has a lifetime of at least 250 years) I sat with how action now could help it. From this came an explicit emphasis on increasing the 'ecological permeability' of our urban and agricultural landscapes: providing more rather than less support for gene flow through these landscapes. This has led to an increased emphasis on backyard planting of native plants, ecological restoration of drainage lines and enhancing the conservation values of urban bushland.

Asking our felt knowing questions...

Sometimes I explicitly ask my felt knowing questions. This is like asking: What have I forgotten – my wallet, some papers? when one has something on the tip of one's tongue. When trying to remember we often rush our felt knowing and try to push it to reveal its answers. If we are spacious and allowing, we give what we know, but can't yet say, a better chance of crystallizing, explicating.

In ecosystem management I often find it helpful to ask myself the following questions about a possible course of action:

- Does this make political sense? (That is, will it work when we include our community and our politicians in the picture?)
- How will this sit with our professional colleagues and our managers? (Does my sense of what we should do shift in some way when I include them in the picture?)
- Is there anything technical that I am vague about, or uneasy about, that I should check out?

Political, managerial, technical. In each case I put my question to my felt sense of the situation and I listen. I allow my felt knowing lots of time to respond with what it knows.

I find this set of questions particularly helpful because when talking to a professional colleague, thinking together in a technical frame, I find we sometimes neglect the political or institutional contexts. Similarly when talking with our local politicians, we sometimes miss technical intricacies that shift a 'decision space' profoundly, and so on.

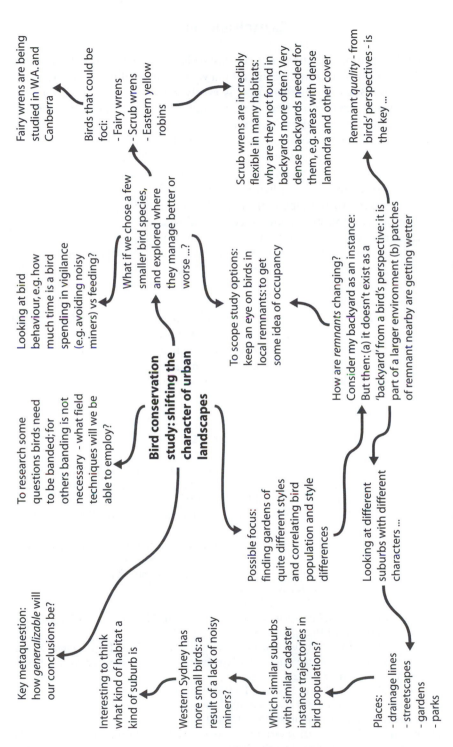

Figure 10.1 *Scoping a project using Gabriel Lusser Rico's clustering*

Key metaquestion: how *generalizable* will our conclusions be?

Interesting to think what kind of habitat a kind of suburb is

Western Sydney has more small birds: a result of a lack of noisy miners?

Which similar suburbs with similar cadaster instance trajectories in bird populations?

Places:
- drainage lines
- streetscapes
- gardens
- parks

To research some questions birds need to be banded; for others banding is not necessary – what field techniques will we be able to employ?

Bird conservation study: shifting the character of urban landscapes

Possible focus: finding gardens of quite different styles and correlating bird population and style differences

Looking at different suburbs with different characters ...

Looking at bird behaviour, e.g. how much time is a bird spending in vigilance (e.g. avoiding noisy miners) vs feeding?

What if we chose a few smaller bird species, and explored where they manage better or worse ...?

To scope study options: keep an eye on birds in local remnants: to get some idea of occupancy

How are *remnants* changing?

Consider my backyard as an instance:
But then: (a) it doesn't exist as a 'backyard' from a bird's perspective: it is part of a larger environment (b) patches of remnant nearby are getting wetter

Fairy wrens are being studied in W.A. and Canberra

Birds that could be foci:
- Fairy wrens
- Scrub wrens
- Eastern yellow robins

Scrub wrens are incredibly flexible in many habitats: why are they not found in backyards more often? Very dense backyards needed for them, e.g. areas with dense lamandra and other cover

Remnant *quality* – from birds' perspectives - is the key ...

Conclusions

Heeding felt meaning is a subterranean skill. It is a foundation for skilful practice in all disciplines, and in interdisciplinary, cross-disciplinary and transdisciplinary work. But our reliance on it is rarely articulated. I am advocating that professional ecosystem managers acknowledge, embrace and develop their skills in leveraging feelings of what is at stake. We always know more than we have said; and we always know more than we have worked out how to say. We can learn to do more with what we know but can't yet say (for example, using Flanagan, 1998; Gendlin, 1981; or Weiser Cornell, 1996). Developing our skills in explicating felt, implicit understanding is at least as vital to skilful practice in ecosystem management as traditional competencies in business administration, environmental law or ecological science.

In western intellectual traditions we are commonly taught to value logical reasoning, but not taught to value felt meaning. This book has been written because it is debilitating to restrict the kinds of knowing we use like this. The more we draw on different ways of knowing, the richer both our professional practice and our personal lives are.

When we allow our felt sense of what's appropriate to reshape, and reshape, and reshape what we are doing, we keep our action appropriate to our changing circumstances. When we let felt understanding play a pivotal role, our professional practice becomes sharper, more creative and more influential. The art of sustaining societies and ecosystems evolves. We need it to.

References

Einstein, A. (2002) 'All concepts are freely chosen posits', in Steele, D. (ed) *Genius: In Their Own Words: The Intellectual Journeys of Seven Great 20th-century Thinkers*, Open Court, Chicago (originally published 1949)

Flanagan, K. (1998) *Everyday Genius: Focusing on Your Emotional Intelligence*, Marino, Dublin

Forester, J. (1989) *Planning in the Face of Power*, University of California Press, Berkeley

Gendlin, E. (1964) 'A theory of personality change', in Worchel, P. and Byrne, D. (eds) *Personality Change*, John Wiley & Sons, New York

Gendlin, E. (1981) *Focusing*, Bantam, New York

Gendlin, E. (1996) *Focusing-oriented Psychotherapy: A Manual of the Experiential Method*, The Guildford Press, London

Gendlin, E. (1997) *Experiencing and the Creation of Meaning: A Philosophical and Psychological Approach to the Subjective*, Northwestern University Press, Evanston, IL (originally published 1962)

Gilmour, A., Walkerden, G. and Scandol, J. (1999) 'Adaptive management of the water cycle on the urban fringe: Three Australian case studies', *Conservation Ecology*, vol 3, no 1, p11, www.consecol.org/vol3/iss1/art11

Hendricks, M. (2001) 'Focusing-oriented/experiential psychotherapy', in Cain, D. and Seeman, J. (eds) *Humanistic Psychotherapy: Handbook of Research and Practice*,

American Psychological Association, New York, www.focusing.org/research_basis. html

Holling, C. (ed) (1978) *Adaptive Environmental Assessment and Management*, John Wiley & Sons, Chichester, UK

Kooiman, J. (2003) *Governing as Governance*, Sage Publications, London

Lee, K. (1993) *Compass and Gyroscope: Integrating Science and Politics for the Environment*, Island Press, Washington, DC

Levin, D. (1997) 'Gendlin's use of language: Historical connections, contemporary implications', in Levin, D. (ed) *Language Beyond Postmodernism: Saying and Thinking in Gendlin's Philosophy*, Northwestern University Press, Evanston, IL

Lusser Rico, G. (1983) *Writing the Natural Way*, JP Tarcher, Los Angeles

Petitmengin-Peugeot, C. (1999) 'The intuitive experience', in Varela, F. and Shear, J. (eds) *The View from Within: First-person Approaches to the Study of Consciousness*, Imprint Academic, Exeter, UK

Robbins, S. (1994) *Management*, Prentice Hall International, London

Schön, D. (1983) *The Reflective Practitioner: How Professionals Think in Action*, Basic Books, New York

Schön, D. (1987) *Educating the Reflective Practitioner*, Jossey-Bass, San Francisco

Walters, C. (1986) *Adaptive Management of Renewable Resources*, Macmillan Publishing Co, New York

Weiser Cornell, A. (1996) *The Power of Focusing: A Practical Guide to Emotional Self-healing*, New Harbinger, Oakland, California

Section 4

Personal and Professional Learning

11

The Ethics of Social Engagement: Learning to Live and Living to Learn

John Harris and Peter Deane

At a glance

- There is a need to open up questioning and thinking on the ethical dimensions of social learning in environmental management
- The concept of sustainability in environmental management suggests a new ethic in our relations with each other and the planet. In this, sustainability can serve as a platform through which the consequences of our actions on the world can be discussed, reflected on and perhaps acted upon anew
- A case study of university field-based learning in an environmental management course reveals some of the complexity behind encouraging ethical reflection. It also shows the importance of being immersed in the world in order to see, and resist, modern societies' abstract representation of the relationship of nature and self
- Both in and beyond the university, immersion in place has the power to allow people to potentially engage with profound questions of 'what is gained and what is lost' when we act on the world and each other
- We all have a role to play in asking what is gained and what is lost in the choices we are all making for our future, but of most importance is the vital role the young have to play in this.

The price of domination

Consistently we have difficulty in accepting the human as an integral part of the Earth community. We see ourselves as a transcendent mode of being. We don't really belong here. But if we are here by some strange destiny then we are the source of all rights and values. All other earthly beings are instruments to

> *be used or resources to be exploited for human benefit. Now, after centuries of plundering the Earth for our own advantage, we begin to reflect on who we are and what has happened both to the planet and ourselves. A sudden reversal is taking place even while our bright, new, antiseptic, mechanical world is finding its fulfilment in the global range of its activities. The inescapable question arises: what is gained and what is lost? (Berry, 1999, pp104–105).*

Over the last 500 or so years, humanity has largely replaced a holistic and socially meaningful interrelationship of nature and self with a mechanistic and socially confusing relationship between nature and self (Franklin, 2002; Merchant, 1980). Among the many drivers of this change, one of the most important is the idea that only people have moral worth. This idea has had a fundamental effect on the decisions we make and the actions we take in the world (Hamilton, 2002).

There is little doubt that shifts in the way we understand nature (or more adequately 'socio-nature' – the co-construction of culture and the material world; Castree and Braun, 1998; Sayer, 2000) have been accompanied by great changes in many aspects of human endeavour. Unfortunately, the attendant price has been a broad-ranging blindness to the costs of externalizing nature to self and society. We show little sign of seeking new ways out of the impasse in which we find ourselves. Nature remains an objectified other, stripped of rich meaning and passively available to be worked on. We operate on nature as though it were dead, a mechanical thing 'out there', with which the individual is empowered to do as they please (Plumwood, 2002). This has significantly complicated our cultural interrelationship with nature, thereby helping to conceal the consequences of our growing domination and appropriation of the material world. Michael Redclift (1987, p204) summed this up well when he wrote:

> *...through the use of methodologies developed in the natural sciences nature has been divested of social control. We are losing control both of the destruction of nature and its recreation.*

As domination is predicated on this false duality between ourselves and nature, we have really only managed to dominate ourselves in new and alarming ways. These are manifested in consistent structural inequalities across society and the simplification of our understanding of significant parts of the material world (Bookchin, 1990; Fitzsimmons, 1989). Revealing the outcomes of dominion over nature (the aim of this chapter) is no easy task; although sustainability as a global ethic and a central concept in environmental management may offer the potential to do so in its re-tooling of the ethics of economic and environmental development ideology and practice.

Revealing domination

In this chapter, morals are taken as relating to what ought to be in light of what is good, right or just; ethics are '...disciplined reflection by persons in all walks of life on moral ideas and ideals' (Engel, 1990, p6). At the personal level this comes down to asking: What should I or we do? Such a question may be informed by ethical theories (see Singer, 1991) that set out principles in order to make sense of action and behaviour. But for most of us, our underlying morals are implicit in our actions or emerge explicitly within the freefall of conversation and thoughtful reflection. Morals embody the fundamental values of society and are transmitted across time, reflecting and reinforcing the dominant structures of society. Most of us grow up tacitly understanding what is generally good, right or just within our particular cultures. Thus much of what we consider to be good about our interrelationship with nature today (especially in the west) remains implicit and may not often get to see the light of day (Hattingh, 1999). However, unlike factual claims, which are descriptive and largely testable within particular logics, moral and ethical claims prescribe and are open to evaluation and contestation (Preston, 1997; Tomsons, 2001). This opening of our morality to reflection, evaluation and contestation is an important step in assessing how we might deal with the challenges thrown up by the interrelationship between ourselves and nature (Elliot, 1991; Minteer and Manning, 1999).

Implicitly, sustainability suggests a new ethic in our relations with each other and with the planet, not just technical or managerial prescriptions for overcoming difficulties with economic development (Kothari, 1990). But what this ethic is remains contested in the environmental management field amidst confusion and disagreement over the meaning of 'sustainability', whether literal, social, ecological or economic (Lélé, 1991). This has a great deal to do with the history of sustainable development, in which sustainability is articulated, and has strong links to the very development processes that are implicated in dominion over nature.

From the 1960s, sustainable development emerged in the context of longstanding pressure from those who were environmentally sensitive. Development-centred organizations responded to these pressures in terms relevant to their own activities. The pivotal moment was the Brundtland report (1987), which is widely credited with popularizing the concept across the globe. Compromises between existing development imperatives and a wide range of philosophical and evidential standpoints on environmental crises contributed to sustainable development becoming a theoretically thin and reformist modification of development ideology and practice (Adams, 1990).

Little wonder then that sustainable development can accommodate within its conceptual boundaries a wide range of differing and at times disparate ideas about environmental management and development (Buchdahl and Raper, 1998). For example, at the level of everyday discussion, this difference can move between thinking (and action) that incorporates the environment into socioeconomic systems and, on the other hand, thinking that has humanity as part of and within natural systems (Hay, 2002). Any social learning approaches in environmental management will have to deal with the consequences of this and other such tensions. As already stated, sustainability involves a new ethic that suggests a different interrelationship between nature and society than the one prevailing in the recent past (Hay, 2002; Nash, 1990).

In this chapter we point towards an understanding of sustainability (and sustainable development) in environmental management that engages with and seeks to rectify the blindness to dominion. The application of sustainability in environmental management we would like to recognize is one that reinforces:

> *...the kind of human activity that nourishes and perpetuates the historical fulfillment of the whole community of life on Earth (Engel, 1990, pp10–11).*

Further, in terms of western societies, this form of sustainability is likely to require circumscribing those social structures associated with unfettered capital and the degrading of those power relations that require some form of dominion for their reproduction (Drummond and Marsden, 1999). These positions though, as we discuss further later in this chapter, are just one way of working through some of the consequences about 'what is gained and what is lost' when we try to 'manage' the environment.

This brings us to our central question: How do we, as individuals and as a society, go about engaging in widespread reflection on what is gained and what is lost in our decision making about environmental management and the consequences our decisions may have for life on earth? This question does not suggest any answer to how environmental management should unfold. Rather, it focuses on opening up learning places and revealing the extent to which we are blind to our dominion in society that broadly constitutes and reproduces an implicit ethic that '...we are the source of all rights and values' (Berry, 1999, p104). Asking this question allows entry to the complex task of designing diverse new pathways into the future that can then be reflected upon, discussed and potentially reasoned through more adequately.

At the end of the day, how people work through and deal with the ethical side of sustainable environmental management needs to be left open. What matters is to take on board the message about the death of nature suggested here, rather than simply take on the need to engage with the moral value of '...what is gained and what is lost' (Berry, 1999, p105). We would like to take this thought a step further and briefly take Berry's quote out of context to give this chapter two voices: one on domination over nature and a second of not knowing in what way to approach living. In relation to the second point, we reflect on the thought that humanity's very existence brings environmental as well as social consequences – with effectively no correct resolution. Among all the questions we are confronted with, this is the one that is with us for the foreseeable future as an '...indispensable part of human life on Earth' (Kirkman, 2002, p153). This is a place of humbleness alongside struggle and, in the end, of hope, which we will discuss later. We can return now to our life-centred ethics, and pick up how all this might be considered as a pivotal part of the Great Work of humanity into the future.

The Great Work: Dealing with domination

According to Berry (1999, p1), the Great Work of a people is one of:

> *...those overarching moments that gives shape and meaning to life by relating the human venture to the larger destinies of the universe.*

Our Great Work is arguably equal to the most challenging Great Work ever to have confronted humanity. It involves overseeing the shift from a period in which we largely achieved ascendancy over our environment (but at the cost of the global degradation of nature and aspects of our social life) to a period in which we find some comfortable and mutually enhancing place on earth, with perhaps a sustainability ethic lighting the way. This is an especially poignant issue for the young of this era who, by and large, are excluded from participating in the Great Work. For these individuals, the current problematic path of humanity is presented as the only way forward. This is a pathway the young may very well have to live out in the future, to their cost.

The case study presented here shows one way we can frame the terrible complexities surrounding our interrelations with nature. The case study is located within a university – one of the primary organizational systems that should be engaging with those complexities but is struggling to do so. Sadly, universities are deeply implicated in the dominion over nature (Berry, 1999). For example, university students are often taught outside the settings in which their knowledge will be used, and much knowledge is divorced from the fuller context of life (not surprising in a culture where mechanistic, dualized and externalized relations dominate). Purposely, the case study charts a story from within a university on the re-enchantment of wisdom and of reflection. The students' voices express their experiences of the consequences of taking seriously moral and ethical thinking surrounding an emergent ecological sensitivity.

The case study involves students and staff who journey off campus on field trips to engage directly with the consequences of their day-to-day lives in context with the broader realities and challenges represented in environmental issues. It shows what can occur in drawing young people into conversations over the Great Work and the unconfined, largely positive outcomes that can result. Outcomes that suggest these journeys can be real spaces for inspiration, creativity, connectivity, purpose and renewal.

The study involved interviewing former undergraduate students who took field courses in the Applied Science programme at the University of Canberra in the last quarter of the 20th century. It details the conversations between university graduates and their lecturer, John Harris, who regarded his role as a facilitator and co-learner. The study covers a significant period of the life of the students, with some recalling experiences that occurred 20 or more years ago. At the time of the fieldwork, most of the students were aged in their 20s and their questing presence opened up the curriculum far further than initially envisioned by the academic staff, to general benefit. Moreover, the study serves as an example of social learning as:

> *the process of collective action and reflection among different actors directed toward improving the management of human and environmental interrelations (Ison, Chapter 2, p37).*

This case study can be read for the specific purpose of opening up fieldwork experiences or spaces for socio-nature immersion (for any co-learner and student), not necessarily linked to environmental management or dominion per se. It can also be read to help clarify some of those aspects of journeying that assist self-learning about socio-nature situations. Finally, it can be read for ways to engage people in questioning the high price we pay in the west, and increasingly everywhere else, for a culture that has turned abstraction in learning into an art form.

Entwined stories: Reflections on field-based learning experiences

Passing on knowledge and skill, like any human exchange, involves some kind of interaction between a teacher and a learner. Bruner (1996) calls this the interactional tenet of education. In this case study, we focus on 'a subcommunity in interaction' that specializes in co-learning, where people help each other to learn, including lecturers as facilitators and co-learners.

Bruner (1996, p20) suggests that the western teaching tradition hardly does justice to the importance of inter-subjectivity in transmitting culture. By inter-subjectivity he means:

> *The human ability to understand the minds of others, whether through language, gesture or other means. It is not just words that make this possible, but our capacity to grasp the role of the settings in which words, acts, and gestures occur... It is this talent that permits us to negotiate meanings when words go astray.*

Teaching usually focuses exclusively on words. It is often fitted into a mould in which a teacher explicitly tells or shows students something they presumably know nothing about. Yet only a small part of learning takes place on such a one-way street.

Gaining competence in a subject requires that learners not only acquire knowledge, but that they also gain good judgement and sharpened intuitions, become more self-reliant and able to work with each other. Such competencies do not flourish under a one-way transmission regime. They are learned best through interaction in a context where people learn from each other. Knowledge is most useful to students when they discover or construct it first hand, because it is then related to, and used in reference to, what they already know and can build on or reconstruct. And it is fundamentally a social process, as explained by the following interview participant:

> *'On all the field-trips you were reminded that there was a real world out there and that's what we had to connect with. That connectedness is important because if you can connect with the environment you can then connect with other people because you realize the interdependence and interconnectedness of everything. I think that's got to be better for us all.'*

Bruffee (1993) and Keen and Mahanty (Chapter 7) call this kind of learning 'collaborative learning', which assumes that knowledge is generated by a consensus process among the members of a community of knowledgeable peers; something people construct by talking together and reaching agreement. It is the way environmental science students can be enabled to cross the disciplinary boundaries of science, as well as share their subjective experiences of nature. Acknowledging such a position also helps to pull the sciences back from their privileged position as the most important form of knowledge (within universities) and allows other ways of knowing some reasonable legitimacy (Lal, 2002; see also Chapter 8).

Addressing real problems in small groups on and off campus creates a social dynamic or interaction that facilitates learning, provided that the participants come to the problem with an openness and interest in each other's knowledge and perspective. The role of the teacher and co-learner is to create such suitable contexts for learning and to inspire, facilitate or guide students to learn through their own efforts. Bruffee (1993) refers to research that suggests university teachers have their greatest influence indirectly, when they establish learning contexts in which students can spend a good deal of time together, preferably without a strong sense of constraint. In these contexts, students jointly create shared norms relating to their common interests and thereby influence one another in a process of social learning, as the following interviewee recalled:

> *'There was a great attitude towards the trips and they set up a great bonding amongst us such that the whole social values became more permeated within the group. The things that were important to change, the attitudes and values that we had to change in order to do something significant for the environment.'*

These small groups become transition communities providing the support that students need as they go through the risky business of becoming new members of knowledge communities. Students vest authority and trust tentatively and for brief periods in other members of their group. Then, as they gain greater confidence, they vest authority and trust in the larger community that comprises the class as a whole. And finally, they come to accept their own authority and trust themselves as individuals who have internalized the language, values and mores of the community of knowledgeable peers that the teacher (and co-learner) represents, and that they have been striving to join.

Another interviewee recalled how staff encouraged students to have greater confidence in their own thinking ability, including the encouragement and space to be reflective about the world:

> *'What comes to mind, and it's not necessarily the most important aspect, is the phrase "go away and think about it". It made me realize that not only do I have the capacity to work things out but that I should be doing it. "You can do it!" It not only forced one to think but also gave that extra confidence in oneself, which was a really important thing.'*

In one sense this student was building the professional capacity to know, and to allow one's own intuition to guide that process of coming to know (see Chapter 10). When the interviewee talks about going away and thinking about it, we are being privy to the potential capacity of one person's experience of their own reflectivity: reflecting upon their reflections. While reflection is a concept difficult to teach or practise (Holland, 1999; Lynch, 2000; Pels, 2000), we can use Thomashow's (1995, p173) understanding of the term:

> *Reflection involves mindfulness, introspection, and deliberation – thinking carefully about the personal meaning of knowledge, considering the wider ramifications of personal and collective action, and using information and relationship to attend the moment, the direct experience of the here-and-now, the direct experience of nature ... [leading to] ... the integrating capacity to make knowledge whole.*

Reflective thinking is likely to require (free) time and some kind of quiet space. Since it is not necessarily a given that it can occur, reflection does require sensitivity to appropriate contexts and an environment that supports students and teachers on their reflective journey (Teekman, 2000). Reflective thinking can also include a capacity for critique, in that it may be driven into spaces that emphasize the undermining of the taken-for-granted knowledge a person has developed during their life (Willis, 1995). The capacity of reflection to activate and enhance one's immersion in the world and, over time, to become recognized as implicit in self is important in developing a sensitivity to dominion. It allows us to build up confidence to morally deliberate about what is gained and what is lost. Reflection is enhanced through interpersonal communication, all of which can expand 'knowing'.

Learning through interpersonal communications and interactions fits with the idea that each student has a zone of proximal development (Vygotsky, cited in Bruffee, 1993, p39). This is understanding that lies just beyond a person's current knowledge and ability, or that we cannot learn on our own at the moment but can learn with a little help from our friends. A fieldclass is made up of a heterogeneous group of students and staff that includes diverse experience, talent and ability with overlapping zones of proximal development. As a result, each student may be ready to understand a good deal more as a member of a field group than they would on their own. It is in such situations that students can experience the joy of learning and of feeling competent, as illustrated in the following recollection:

> '*The enthusiasm was infectious. If you're surrounded by a very enthusiastic bunch of people you can pick up on that and can take a lot of it on board. It brings things out that you don't know you have. You're not just doing it on your own. You're doing it as part of a group and I found that important. It sticks in my mind.*'

During field trips students developed a new group solidarity, which helped to build a sense of community so essential for mutual learning. And, just as importantly, the collaborative teamwork and division of labour helped to produce a dynamic learning environment connected with practice and the development of self-confidence.

Almost without exception, interviewees recalled strong positive memories of the practical nature of their undergraduate course:

> '*I had come with an experience of being lectured at. An arts and history degree involves going and sitting in a lecture theatre, being lectured at, and then going to a tutorial. Your books are your field trip, so for me the big difference, the thing that I loved about doing the Applied Science degree was how practical it was – and the fact that it was hands on. You actually got into the laboratories and did things, or you got out in the field and did things... I think that over time I got more inventive at [putting into practice what we were learning], and taking those opportunities to do more creative things.*'

All interview participants talked enthusiastically about their fieldwork experiences and how they lived and worked together with fellow students in achieving common goals. They thought it was relevant for them to be working on real environmental problems in preparation for contributing towards a better world. If staff showed trust in their students' abilities to work together on real issues, an enormous amount of energy and creativity was released in students. In the process, everyone was imbued with fellowship for each other and the fieldwork. For a time, at least, it was possible to overcome what Gardner (1964) saw as one of the most difficult problems of education – to make it possible for young people to participate in the tasks and issues of importance to their time.

Students on field trips developed a strong sense of fellowship and goodwill towards each other and staff, especially on long trips to remote locations in the Australian bush that were new to the students. Fellowship develops when fellow travellers come together as companions to share mutual interests or activities. Students and staff can be pitched out of their ordinary everyday world to experience it, and each other, anew. Accompanying this shared experience is an overwhelming feeling of one's common quest for knowledge and understanding of their world. This powers social learning and personal growth:

'The field trips made a big impression. The experience of being miles away from your normal environment and the chance to have other limitations disappear as you went away – the camaraderie is a big aspect of it. Once you get out in a vehicle and go out into a natural area, particularly if you're a long, long way away from other things that shaped your life, you lose a lot of the associated trappings. You're no longer a person with a name and a role, you're just you. You're out there and much closer to the environment and you take things in and react to them and the other sort of smaller details of life just slip away.'

Part of what disappears is the stark division of learner and teacher, which is so strongly apparent on campus, where formal institutional arrangements reinforce academics as experts and students as in need of training. In the field there is usually a more equal relationship between staff and students, especially when staff acknowledge that some students know more about, for instance, specific aspects of the local plants and animals than they do, or have first-hand experience of local history. In this situation the on-campus power relationships between students and staff can melt away, allowing members of a mutual learning community to experience the joy of learning in a convivial and interesting environment. These changed relationships can be carried back to formal classes.

Field classes at their best can create this fellowship feeling, which at times extends beyond the fellowship of people to include all life forms and, potentially, that which is not living (for example, landscape, stones and water). Only a handful of interviewees spoke of this fellowship towards the non-human world, although this should not detract from the extent to which such connectivity may occur. One interviewee recalled:

'I often thought about the balance between science and the spiritual. I suppose the way indigenous people talk about the spirit of the land. For me that's the essence, that's probably the underlying reason I have such an interest in the environment. I find it beautiful and I find it interesting. It just has such a wonderful spirit about it, which you cannot find anywhere else except in natural places.'

Ecological identity and ecological intuition refer to the way some people feel themselves to be interconnected with all life forms on the planet (Thomashow, 1995). It is an expanded form of identity. Another two interviewees recalled:

'Of course, what came out on the natural environment side [of the course] was the extraordinariness – the whole sense of respect and awe. This was something that also came from the course and I think that's what the field trips really helped people come to grips with.'

'The things that have stayed with me are the ecological principles, the interrelationships between things, the dynamic nature of the environment and how one thing affects all other things.'

Cautious encouragement, in the field, towards expressing and reflecting on the interconnectivity between ourselves and nature can help create powerful and confronting contexts for people to draw out moral ideas, and this also pays subtle acknowledgment to the importance of our decisions about ourselves and nature (Hay, 2002). In the words of Milton (2002, p50):

> *Human beings cannot survive without engaging with their environment, and relational epistemology [that is, the recognizable interrelatedness of all life] is an inevitable consequence of this fact. Nature does not just do things, it does things to us.*

These relational aspects affect both abstracted thinking and the consciousness that is not readily incorporated into 'how we know we know' (Gallagher and Marcel, 1999), what we might call the unconscious or fully embodied biological experience of living. In this, nature is not just something we act upon. Rather, it acts upon us in ways we are not always aware of, though ways that have a significant impact on who we might want to be and how we might want the world to be. This broad point about the relational interconnectedness of life is of fundamental importance in understanding the real strength of fieldwork.

Out in the field, face to face with socionatural dilemmas, the duality between nature and society can break down, thereby revealing the extent to which non-human actions and events might affect us. This can allow us to more adequately deal with the consequences of our sociotechnological power and what is gained and what is lost when we act. In the field:

> *...nature 'pushes back' with its own vitality which is manifest in specific material processes ... [and in] ... this way, agents of nature are now seen as palpably active, not only in terms of their own biological constitution, but also relationally when bound up in the construction of ecological, social, economic, cultural, political and material formations (Jones and Cloke, 2002, pp6–7).*

Thus, in the end, establishing the opportunity to interact in field contexts can help students to reflect on and potentially clarify the problematic extent to which nature is falsely externalized from our culture as an 'it'.

A potential example of a person going through this relational experience follows. What can be noted in this example is how trees, undergoing conversion (from one state to another) within a particular sociotechnological context (a woodchip mill), trigger in the (involved) observer a relational interconnectivity that leads to a particular moral claim about how the world ought to be. The following interviewee recalled her field trip in the 1970s to study the environmental impacts of the woodchip industry on forests in southeast New South Wales (NSW):

> 'The visit to the Eden Woodchip mill and the whole exposure to what was actually happening down there was one of those horrendously memorable

experiences. Going to the actual mill and seeing those logs gobbled up in seven seconds really symbolized the power of how Homo sapiens destroys. This tree had been growing for a hundred years say and was extraordinarily complex in what it was able to do and how it could be used in the forest ecosystem. That log could be used for something that would last another 100 years too. You could turn it into something that was beautiful and useful but what we chose to do was chomp it into bits, turn it into paper and sell it off for landfill all within a year probably. I mean that's very symbolic of what we seem to be doing to the natural world. What was so horrifying about it was that we could not respect it. You couldn't say, "That was the mill" [doing it] because that's us, that's our culture. And that's a horrible thing to be facing up to. That was confronting but very good.'

Here, our power to act leads to the 'death' of the trees (in the mill). This reinforces the point that our existence on this planet brings consequences and we need to focus far more closely on the range of actions we engage in, especially regarding the flow of consequences generated by those actions in terms of what is altered or destroyed.

There is a final aspect of a good field trip that is very important to mention because it helps to explain their almost universal popularity with the interview participants in the case study. Each field trip is a journey. There is a beginning, a period of travelling to new places and the return home. It tells a story. Each student will personalize a field trip in the form of a personal narrative and this is what they will remember over the years. The stories of interviewees are of travelling through real environments, learning through 'on-the-skin experiences' and dealing with real environmental issues, all of which makes it more likely for students to grasp the meaning of academic concepts relating to the environment and society. As staff, we err by divorcing (environmental) science from the narrative of culture (Bruner, 1996, p42). It is in the narrative mode that students, and staff, can construct their identity and find a creative way to contribute to society.

Drawing the case study to an end and in connection with our effort to use many differing voices in this experiential pathway, we reproduce the words of Cheetham (1993, p246), who neatly summarizes many of the points made herein:

The role of imagination in the salvation of individual lives is suggested by the liberating experience that true education can be for those who are open to it. We must begin to actively reinsert ourselves in the world of day to day activities, and consciously fight the abstractive effects of contemporary culture ... sustainable human cultures can only be enacted through a reimagination of ourselves and a recreation of our world which celebrate the diversity and plurality which characterize the living.

Conclusions

Emerging from this discussion is a picture of one of the real challenges of environmental management: how the complex moral and ethical issues arising from our interrelationship with nature can be seen more clearly and, ultimately, acted upon. At the start of this chapter, we posed the question:

> *How do we, as individuals and as a society, go about engaging in widespread reflection on what is gained and what is lost in our decision making about environmental management and the consequences our decisions may have for life on earth?*

What steps then might you, the reader, take in engaging with the question of what is gained and what is lost?

We encourage you to become more involved with thinking about and discussing what is gained and what is lost in terms of (environmental) ethics, through imagining and creating your own place in the Great Work (of course, you may already be doing so). Teaching yourself about ethics is an important and powerful way to nurture a number of capacities, including the growth of self-awareness; reflective powers; sensitivity to ethical dimensions; recognizing consequences; justificatory reasoning; empathy; sensitivity to rights and responsibilities; and envisioning alternatives (Preston, 1997). But the study of ethics will not necessarily or inevitably lead us to becoming better (more ethical) persons, nor do any of these capacities necessarily require the study of ethics; however, it may help.

How useful the concept of sustainability might be in the end is rightfully under question (Jamieson, 2002; Pretes, 1997). But at the bottom line, widespread understanding of some of the primary writings and thought on (environmental) ethics may give a better appreciation of some of the relevant issues. Gaining a widespread understanding is no simple task, not the least because intense and broad-ranging debate continues within philosophy on questions of (environmental) ethics (Light, 2002). There is no one act, no one thought, no special key or simple answer to what an individual can do, either in opening up reflection on our interrelationship with nature or in making apparent some of the problems invested in the social structures we live in tension with. The attendant struggle and doubt, though, can be embraced and made to work in positive and unique ways.

In this chapter we have concentrated on participation and engagement in the context of the university, because of the pivotal and often failing role it plays in reproducing knowledge in modern society and, specifically, on the process of 'in-field experience'. But can you do your own version of social learning in the field?

Our answer here is simple – yes – although the conceptual step required is not at all simple. Such a step involves fostering a certain way of thinking of the world, which might open other potential pathways into the future. When we discuss in-field experience we are essentially using it as shorthand for practices of journeying that involve leaving behind the desk and classroom (a polite way of saying the decontextualized and the abstract) and moving out into the world. While such places may involve obvious socionatural dilemmas, perhaps what is more important is the very fact that our moral and ethical reflection is grounded in our own 'place' and this can be any place. The slow, incremental and at times painful building of this understanding, perhaps in part through learning about ethics, can allow us to:

> *...become increasingly aware of the tensions, contradictions, and distractions that pervade our lives. [In this we] are no longer satisfied to live in forgetfulness and denial. We realize the necessity of balancing hope and despair, liberation and suffering, reflection and engagement. We learn how to find nature everywhere – how to see the ecological, political, and spiritual significance of everyday life. We will continue to be challenged by the shifting terrain of our cultural milieu. There is no escape from this. It is the reality of our times, the landscape of our lives (Thomashow, 1995, p205).*

Finding nature everywhere is not easy, but to find this space in our own place will be to see more clearly, to know more comfortably what it is we as a species have constructed as our world and hence to see where it is failing, and perhaps herein determine what your part might be in the Great Work.

There is a real need to inspire people, especially the young, to reflect on moral ideas about their interrelationship with nature, to discuss these ideas and to engage in spirited evaluation and further reflection with others about them. Although only one of a large variety of challenges facing humanity, the question of encouraging moral and ethical reflection remains one of the more important challenges. Such a process may produce groups of individuals who are more adequately equipped to deal with the great tasks of our time.

We have suggested one way that we might engage with such an issue is through the lens of domination of nature. In our everyday lives as relational beings of nature, ethics are a constant and we need the creativity and imagination to embrace more fully the consequences of the continuing struggle of our existence on earth. It is likely to be, after all, in the gritty day-to-day revelation of our responsibilities in the complex interlace of people and nature that any real idea and practice of sustainability may be found. The role of imagination and creativity alongside the practice of reflectivity may spur the crafting of new or reworked ethical ideas in which all of us, especially the young, can play a part.

Acknowledgements

The University of Canberra supported the research for the case study. We are deeply indebted to the former students of the environmental science programme for the material on which we have reflected.

References

Adams, W. (1990) *Green Development: Environment and Sustainability in the Third World*, Routledge, London

Berry, T. (1999) *The Great Work: Our Way into the Future*, Bell Tower, New York

Bookchin, M. (1990) *Remaking Society: Pathways to a Green Future*, South End, Boston

Bruffee, K. A. (1993) *Collaborative Learning: Higher Education, Independence, and the Authority of Knowledge*, Johns Hopkins University, Baltimore

Brundtland, G. H. (1987) *Our Common Future*, World Commission on Environment and Development, Oxford University Press, Oxford

Bruner, J. (1996) *The Culture of Education*, Harvard University Press, Cambridge, MA

Buchdahl, J. and Raper, D. (1998) 'Environmental ethics and sustainable development', *Sustainable Development*, vol 6, pp92–98

Castree, N. and Braun, B. (1998) 'The construction of nature and the nature of construction: Analytical and political tools for building survivable futures', in Braun, B. and Castree, N. (eds) *Remaking Reality: Nature at the Millennium*, Routledge, London

Cheetham, T. (1993) 'Shifting ground: Imagination and the diversity of worlds', in Lehotay, D. (ed) *The Relationship of Man and Nature in the Modern Age: Dominion Over the Earth*, essays from the Basic Issues Forum, New York, Edwin Mellen Press, Lewiston, NY

Drummond, I. and Marsden, T. (1999) *The Condition of Sustainability*, Routledge, London

Elliot, R. (1991) 'Environmental ethics', in Singer, P. (ed) *A Companion to Ethics*, Blackwell, Oxford

Engel, G. (1990) 'Introduction: The ethics of sustainable development', in Engel, R. and Engel, G. (eds) *Ethics of Environment and Development: Global Challenge and International Response*, Belhaven, London

Fitzsimmons, M. (1989) 'The matter of nature', *Antipode*, vol 21, pp106–120

Franklin, A. (2002) *Nature and Social Theory*, Sage, Thousand Oaks, CA

Gallagher, S. and Marcel, A. (1999) 'The self in contextualised action', *Journal of Consciousness Studies*, vol 6, no 4, pp4–30

Gardner, J. W. (1964) *Self-renewal: The Individual and the Innovative Society*, Harper & Row, New York

Hamilton, C. (2002) 'Dualism and sustainability', *Ecological Economics*, vol 42, pp89–99

Hattingh, J. (1999) *Are We There Yet? Taking Stock of Three Decades of Environmental Ethics*, proceedings of the Annual Conference and Workshops of the Environmental Education Association of South Africa (EEASA), University of Rhodes, Grahamstown, 6–10 September, pp50–78

Hay, P. (2002) *Main Currents in Western Environmental Thought*, University of New South Wales, Sydney

Holland, R. (1999) 'Reflexivity', *Human Relations*, vol 52, no 4, pp463–484

Jamieson, D. (2002) *Morality's Progress: Essays on Humans, Other Animals, and the Rest of Nature*, Oxford University Press, Oxford

Jones, O. and Cloke, P. (2002) *Tree Cultures: The Place of Trees and Trees in their Place*, Berg, Oxford

Kirkman, R. (2002) *Skeptical Environmentalism: The Limits of Philosophy and Science*, Indiana University, Bloomington, IN

Kothari, R. (1990) 'Environment, technology, and ethics', in Engel, R. and Engel, G. (eds) *Ethics of Environment and Development: Global Challenge and International Response*, Belhaven, London

Lal, V. (2002) 'Unhitching the disciplines: History and the social sciences in the new millennium', *Futures*, vol 34, pp1–14

Lélé, S. (1991) 'Sustainable development: A critical review', *World Development*, vol 19, no 6, pp607–621

Light, A. (2002) 'Contemporary environmental ethics from metaethics to public philosophy', *Metaphilosophy*, vol 33, no 4, pp426–449

Lynch, M. (2000) 'Against reflexivity as an academic virtue and source of privileged knowledge', *Theory, Culture & Society*, vol 17, no 3, pp26–54

Merchant, C. (1980) *The Death of Nature: Women, Ecology and the Scientific Revolution*, Harper & Row, New York

Milton, K. (2002) *Loving Nature: Towards an Ecology of Emotion*, Routledge, London

Minteer, B. and Manning, R. (1999) 'Pragmatism in environmental ethics: Democracy, pluralism, and the management of nature', *Environmental Ethics*, vol 21, pp191–207

Nash, R. (1990) *The Rights of Nature: A History of Environmental Ethics*, Primavera, Leichhardt, Australia

Pels, D. (2000) 'Reflexivity: One step up', *Theory, Culture & Society*, vol 17, no 3, pp1–25

Plumwood, V. (2002) *Environmental Culture: The Ecological Crises of Reason*, Routledge, London

Preston, N. (1997) *Understanding Ethics*, Federation Press, Leichhardt, Australia

Pretes, M. (1997) 'Development and infinity', *World Development*, vol 25, no 9, pp1421–1430

Redclift, M. (1987) *Sustainable Development: Exploring the Contradictions*, Routledge, London

Sayer, A. (2000) *Realism and Social Science*, Sage, Thousand Oaks, CA

Singer, P. (1991) *A Companion to Ethics*, Blackwell, Oxford

Teekman, B. (2000) 'Exploring reflective thinking in nursing practice', *Journal of Advanced Nursing*, vol 31, no 5, pp1125–1135

Thomashow, M. (1995) *Ecological Identity: Becoming a Reflective Environmentalist*, MIT Press, Cambridge, MA

Tomsons, S. (2001) 'Western ethics and resource management: A glance at history', *The Forestry Chronicle*, vol 77, no 3, pp431–437

Willis, E. (1995) *The Sociological Quest: An Introduction to the Study of Social Life*, 2nd edn, Allen & Unwin, St Leonards, Australia

12

Science Communication for Scientists: Reshaping a Culture

Sue Stocklmayer, Mike Gore and Chris Bryant

At a glance

- Some scientists communicate effectively, but as a group they tend to be reluctant public communicators, believing that the practice of science is its own justification
- Widespread concern about the failure of science communication in environmental management and more widely has been growing, and there are increasing demands for more effective communication in every area of science
- In particular, communication in environmental management requires a close interaction between scientists and the public
- The authors of this chapter, all of whom have been successful scientists, have been running communication workshops for scientists for five years. Workshop participants often do not understand that what they find obvious is based on years of training, nor how difficult it is to make their work accessible to their audience
- The culture of Western science is pervasive, often transcending international differences. Cultural change is required to alter scientists' perceptions about their traditional approaches to communication.

Communicating science

Scientists generally are poor communicators. While some individual scientists communicate with clarity and charisma, as a group they tend to be inward looking, cleaving to the belief that the practice of science is its own justification. Unfortunately, the community has other ideas. When it comes to communicating issues that are important to environmental management, the gulf between what scientists believe to be important and the perceptions of the 'public' concerned with those issues may be very great. In Australia, the debate over whether to use embryonic stem cells became heated following some controversial comments by an eminent scientist. This was a failure in science communication because the scientist underestimated the capacity of his audience to find out the facts.

Much of this book deals with the interactions between learning, generating knowledge and changing behaviour. In this chapter, however, we seek to describe some reactions of research scientists to the challenges these ideas represent, and suggest some steps that might be taken to make the whole process a little less painful. The scientists in this study were those with whom we have conducted workshops in communicating science with the public. They number over 200 across Australia, with a few internationally. The research culture from which they come does not incorporate such communication as a matter of course so, in many cases, their learning curve is steep and difficult.

Much has been written about the culture of science, especially western science. We will simply summarize here those characteristics we believe to be relevant to the problems of communicating outside that culture, with the general public. Western science grew out of a superstitious and mysterious alchemic tradition, through the efforts of the embryonic Royal Society which, in many respects, was equally mysterious but which placed objectivity and scientific method high on its list of virtues (see, for example, Jardine, 1999).

Today the characteristics of science are often debated, but are generally agreed to incorporate something about process and a great deal about impartiality, hypothesis, prediction and so on (Prelli, 1989). Learning about science is a linear process, from the earliest 'fun' activities of primary school to the final accolade of a fellowship of a learned society. Western science is compartmentalized knowledge and takes on an increasingly narrow focus until one becomes a specialist in a very limited field. Such specialization helps to provide deep insights into environmental systems, but can also create a barrier between communicating information across disciplinary divides, the very divides environmental managers need to bridge.

The so-called scientific method is one that, in our view, is seldom actually employed by practising scientists, yet it is one to which all scientists subscribe. They all have to publish within their peer culture, according to well understood and prescribed forms. These dictate not only the structure of a journal publication, but that of conference presentations, the judgements made about the value of the science and the public front which scientists believe must be presented to preserve the validity and respectability of the research.

Small wonder, then, that scientists, in general, find other forms of public communication so confronting. Yet, increasingly, they are not only being asked to communicate their research, its intentions, its methods and its findings, but are being required to do so as part of their funding conditions and in the face of increasing public concern and involvement. They are being asked to share and to respect other forms of knowledge, including local and cross-cultural understandings.

Concern about the failure of science communication has been growing in recent years (Stocklmayer, 2003). In the developing world, much time and effort is being expended on science communication, particularly in studies relating to the environment and its management (Keen and Stocklmayer, 1999a, 1999b).

The United Nations Educational, Scientific and Cultural Organization (UNESCO) World Conference on Science ended its six-day meeting in 1999 by adopting a declaration on science and the use of scientific knowledge. Part of this declaration was a political commitment to wide-ranging principles for promoting and carrying out science and technology in the long term and states:

> *The Framework for Action aims to sensitize stakeholders in science to the crucial roles of science education and communication about science in promoting both understanding and participation of issues that increasingly affect us all... It also calls for more and better facilities for training journalists and communicators, on the one hand, while including science communication training as part of a scientist's education, on the other (UNESCO, 1999).*

Even more recently, the political establishment has been concerned to distinguish between the 'public understanding' and the 'public awareness' of science. In 2000, the British House of Lords published the findings of a Select Committee on Science and Society. The overall findings of the committee focused on the imperative for science communicators to build bridges between science and the public, citing recent developments in biotechnology and the mad cow disease disaster as eroding public confidence and creating public unease. Echoing the UNESCO document, the committee recommended that all scientists should have training in communication and should understand the social context of their research. The connotations of 'knowledge' and 'comprehension of facts' implicit in the public understanding of science is, according to the committee, problematic. Consider these two sections:

> *3.9. Despite all this activity and commitment, we have been told from several quarters that the expression 'public understanding of science' may not be the most appropriate label. Sir Robert May called it a 'rather backward-looking vision'... It is argued that the words imply a condescending assumption that any difficulties in the relationship between science and society are due entirely to ignorance and misunderstanding on the part of the public; and that, with enough public-understanding activity, the public can be brought to greater knowledge, whereupon all will be well. This approach ... is felt by many of our witnesses to be inadequate; the British Council went so far as to call it 'outmoded and potentially disastrous'.*

> *3.11. It is therefore increasingly important that non-experts should be able to understand aspects of science and technology which touch their lives. It is also increasingly important that scientists should seek to understand the impact of their work and its possible applications on society and public opinion (UK Parliament, 2000).*

So, where did it all go wrong? We believe the problem has its roots in a failure to understand the difference between the 'public understanding' of science and the 'public awareness' of science. It is further compounded by scientists who fail to understand the processes of communication, who fail to realize that each person builds their own view of the world. Too frequently, scientists think that the facts speak for themselves. They do not understand that what is obvious to them is based on years of training, nor that they must take great pains to render their work into language and metaphor that are accessible to and make sense for their audience. These are among the issues that are frequently encountered and confronted, sometimes with considerable discomfort to the scientists concerned, in our workshops.

Communication as a process

Science communication processes, if they are to be successful, require ideas to be shared. Ideally, there will be mutual meaning-making, resulting in mutual understanding. Unfortunately, this is not the mode by which scientists are accustomed to learn or, indeed, to communicate. Consider, for example, that the scientific conference centres around the research paper, in which is enshrined the 'transmission mode' (Garvey, 1979). The lecture theatre, also a one-way communication, is often regarded as the academic ideal.

The transmission mode of communication is a simple one of sender, message and receiver. In order to send a message that we would like understood, we 'encode' the message in a form we believe to be suited to the receiver. Shannon and Weaver (1963, p98) imagined the transmitted message as similar to a telecommunication signal. This enabled them to incorporate the notion of 'noise' into the transmission model, where noise represents anything that distorts the message. This might mean physical noise in which the message is blurred, more complex semantic noise (confusions about meaning of the message or the words) or psychological noise (a resistance to receiving the message itself).

The success of this essentially one-way process depends entirely on how the receiver 'decodes' the message. The decoding is influenced by past experience, present understandings, and the 'remindings' evoked by the message (Stocklmayer and Gilbert, 2002). Each of us frames the information 'depending on our disciplinary backgrounds, organizational roles, past histories, interests, and political/economic perspectives' (Schön, 1987, p4). This may result in a very different interpretation from that intended by the sender (see, for example, Day, 1975; Mohan et al, 1992). More recently, however, the constructivist view of learning has led to the promotion of the 'transaction model' of communication. Rather than a linear process, this involves mutual feedback to negotiate meaning. Interpretation, rather than information-giving, is the goal of the process. Individual understandings therefore become critical to the communication method itself.

That this mode is alien to the training of a research scientist has been evident for many years. After reviewing environmental management projects and their communication of research science in Australia, Keen and Stocklmayer (1999a, p198) concluded that:

> *Better communications to effect better understandings require a shift in the modus operandi [of the researcher] from a linear model of information transfer to an interactive one characterized by multilateral feedback and reflection.*

They further note that:

> *Science communication by its very nature means crossing divides – divides between disciplines (such as that of the scientists, journalists and social scientists) ... and between ways of knowing (such as community and scientific)... Thus science communication is not just about packaging information in easy to understand language, it is also about understanding the social, professional, and institutional contexts in which the communication occurs.*

It was this need for understanding that led to the introduction of the workshops for scientists. Many of the scientists who attend the workshops are actively working on science that makes a positive contribution to achieving sustainability, for example vertebrate pest management, land and water research, including salinity and agricultural research.

Origins of the workshops

The authors of this chapter have all been practising scientists. Stocklmayer graduated in physics and chemistry and has worked in industry and education. Gore is a physicist and has carried out research and lectured in the physics department at The Australian National University (ANU). In later years he developed and ran Questacon – The National Science and Technology Centre. Bryant is a biologist, a former dean of science, with more than 100 research publications and several books to his name. We established the first Australian Graduate Program in Science Communication and The National Centre for the Public Awareness of Science, of which Stocklmayer is now Director.

This statement is not meant to be idle self-aggrandizement. It explains much of the genesis of the communication workshops for scientists and their very high acceptance, by junior and senior scientists across Australia. We have credibility in the scientific world as communicators because we are part of the science culture and have personal experience and understanding of the pressures and demands that are placed on scientists. We have applied for grants and have struggled to meet deadlines for applications; we have laboured into the night writing lectures; we have fought with editors of learned journals and administrators; we have battled with recalcitrant equipment and suppliers and have felt the sheer, unalloyed pleasure of a successful experiment – 'Ah, so that's how it works!'

Like most scientists, we never received formal training in the art of communication, whether lecturing to undergraduates, presenting papers to our peers or talking to Rotary or Lions clubs. Anything we have learned we have gained through many years of practice. Between us, we developed a range of knowledge and skills that Stocklmayer was anxious to make available to a much wider audience than our own students and colleagues. So the idea of the workshops was born. They would combine theory and practice of communication with associated topics such as the history of science communication, its present world context, the image of science and gender issues, public speaking and writing.

Format of the workshops

Workshop participants are all practising researchers. The least experienced are those just starting their PhDs, through to postdoctoral fellows. The more experienced hold academic positions in universities, or positions in government instrumentalities. They include the most junior scientific appointments and deans and directors. Generally, we find greater receptivity to the need for science communication among the junior ranks. This is understandable. Senior people have devoted a career to science and along the way they have acquired experience of attempting to communicate with a wide range of audiences and have developed a style with which they are comfortable. Unfortunately, the younger workshop participants are often much less comfortable – even critical of this traditional style. To many of the senior scientists, this comes as a surprise.

We have now given many workshops, both in Australia and overseas, and have tried several different formats. By a process of trial and error we have arrived at our current format (see Box 12.1), which has proved very acceptable to Australian scientists. We can vary this format if agencies have special requirements, but have found that major departure from the well-tried formula detracts from the participants' experience. A typical workshop lasts two and a half days; it is a very intense period of work and people frequently underestimate the amount of effort it requires. There is homework on both evenings and, by midday on the third day, presenters and participants are exhausted.

When we started the workshops about five years ago, the general reaction was one of resentment and frustration. 'I'm not trained for this and I don't see why I should have to do it' was a typical response. This view has softened somewhat as scientists recognize that they have to communicate with the general public. Further, for those working on environmental management issues, it is almost a prerequisite for funding and for ensuring that practitioners will use the scientific findings.

Box 12.1 A typical workshop programme

Day 1: Introduction to scientific communication

- Why should scientists communicate? An introductory discussion
- Elementary presentation skills. An interactive session during which participants first stand up and talk for one minute
- Considering your audience. Perspectives on understanding. This session gently introduces the importance of listening as well as speaking and the importance of clear language, cultural considerations and thinking about the audience
- Writing for an audience and the media. A workshop session
- Homework. Participants are asked to come with a short written summary of some aspect of their own work. They are now asked to use this is as a basis for preparing a four-minute talk and a short written piece (not more than two to three hundred words) that might be published on the features page of a newspaper. They also practise a short talk on a general topic.

Day 2: Communication strategies

- Talking to other scientists and talking to the public; the image of science. An interactive session that looks at the cultural norms of science, what we know about the public and what the public knows about science
- More about presentation skills. An interactive session, during which participants present a prepared short talk on a general topic
- More on writing and 'translating' the science for a general audience. Participants are taken through more aspects of the demands of writing for a newspaper
- Homework. Participants revise their previous assignments in light of the day's experience.

Day 3: Synthesis

- Written assignment. Final discussion and revision
- Talking with confidence. Participants present their own science for a general public audience
- Reflection, evaluation and close.

A walk through a workshop

The opening session, 'Why should scientists communicate?', is an important one. It has two purposes. The first is to get the scientists talking to us and among themselves. The second is to allow us to gauge the mood of the scientists so we can fine-tune our presentations. It is in this session that we begin to detect those who are hostile to the workshop, having been wrenched away from their benches by their director; those who can't (or won't) see the point of the exercise; those who are garrulous and those who are the shrinking violets. This session, quite independently of the formal evaluations, gives us a sense of the affective changes that might have taken place in individual participants by the end of the workshop. It is absolutely critical that we understand our audience, so that we can start with their current understandings and work from there.

A number of attitudes commonly surface in this opening session. Firstly, less commonly now than when we started, is: 'I'm a scientist. It's what I do best. Let other people do the communicating.' This view has been current in research establishments for years. It has led to the emergence of the extension officer, whose task it is to get the science of the institution 'out there'. Unfortunately, extension officers often flounder as they are put in the invidious position of trying to explain both the science and the behaviour of the scientist, which often seem to take no account of the sensibilities of potential consumers.

Many scientists are disconcerted when they are asked to explain their work in simple language. They make the mistake of trying to find synonyms for abstruse terms like 'mitochondrion' or 'entropy', when a descriptive sentence or two is what is required. This leads them into the frequently voiced fallacy: 'People wouldn't understand what I'm doing.' The hardliners extrapolate from this to: 'People don't need to know about science. They should just let us get on with the job.' Nobody, however, has ever actually said: 'Trust me, I'm a scientist'!

A very commonly expressed view is: 'If only people knew how exciting science was, they'd give us more money.' This is pronounced with great eagerness, but if you ask why people should pay them to have fun there is no answer. And finally, it is with some reluctance that they come to the view that: 'If people knew what we are really up to, they might stop us'. They are slow to concede this, even in the face of science communication disasters like genetic manipulation, mad cow disease and 'Frankenstein foods'.

After this icebreaker, the workshop pursues three intricately braided themes of speaking, writing and communicating. We follow each theme through the whole workshop in turn. To ensure that the themes are seen to be interlinked, each of us is present during all the presentations and is free to interact and interject as appropriate. A team rapport has grown up so that we usually know when we are required to contribute without being asked.

Stocklmayer, as the instigator of the workshop and the person with an extensive background in the field, ranges widely across communication theory and science communication in particular. Her role is to provide the theoretical underpinning upon which sound science communication is based. These sessions are concerned with communication techniques, the distinction between the public understanding and public awareness of science, with the conscious inclusion in the discourse of all groups in the community, gender issues and the public perception of science and scientists. Many scientists are unaware that there are other models for the communication process than the simple conduit (source, transmission, sink) metaphor. The constructivist argument often comes as a revelation to them.

In particular, Stocklmayer challenges the commonly held view that 'the masses' are indeed 'them asses'. This shibboleth is attacked on three fronts. The first is the presentation of visual evidence that even highly educated people retain misconceptions long after they have been exposed to the true state of affairs. Secondly, she sets the participants a famous test (Durant et al, 1989) purporting to assess 'public understanding of science'. To the consternation of the participants, they find that their own results in the test are not significantly different from those of the general public and that even in their areas of expertise they give 'wrong' answers – not because they know too little but because they know too much. In the light of this experience, they are invited to consider how the general public – whatever that means – might have responded to the test. To emphasize this point further, Stocklmayer asks participants to work in small groups to create explanations, with visual aids, of simple phenomena such as surface tension, transpiration and the phases of the moon. Participants are confronted by the inadequacy of their own knowledge and, consequently, the difficulty of creating convincing explanations.

Gore opens the public speaking strand with elementary presentation skills. He starts with an anecdote: 'Newspapers on both sides of the Atlantic have run surveys of what people fear most and have determined that fear of public speaking ranks higher than fear of flying or fear of death. This means that people would rather be in the coffin than speaking the eulogy.' This strikes a responsive chord in the audience, many of whom apparently envy the corpse! We have had relatively senior people running away from the workshop rather than stand up and speak and other, braver souls, for whom it is a great trial, go through it and then sit down visibly shaking. The first session is a distillation of Gore's extensive experience of public speaking. Each participant must then stand up and talk about him or herself for one minute. At the end of the session each participant draws out of a black bag a card with a general topic printed on it.

The following day participants are required to speak on their topic for two minutes. In that friendly, supportive environment, the scientists do so with considerable wit and charm. We each criticize the performance in detail, concentrating on things like stance, audibility, verbal flow and distractions, but not content. They are then informed that on the last day they are to prepare a four-minute talk about their science. On this occasion, as well as comment from the team, one of the participants is also asked to comment. When they come to the session on the last day, they discover that they will be filmed, but that they will be the only ones to see the video. Often we find that someone who spoke with humour and vivacity on the previous day turns into a zombie-like creature mouthing lifeless words. This outcome was at first astonishing to us, but we later discovered it to be commonplace. Wit and lightness are often thrown aside. Many participants drone through their four minutes using detailed overheads (despite advice to the contrary), abandoning the first person for the passive voice. Many of the offerings can only be described as dreary. Science is obviously a serious business. Yet many of the science stories that emerge are fascinating, potentially full of interest. It is clear that there is considerable resistance to making them entertaining. The culture of science, we find, seems to inhibit joy and levity when discussing one's research.

Participants are thus asked to speak three times. As the workshop progresses, most people's nervousness disappears. There are a few, however, who never conquer their nerves but persevere, and a very few who feel so threatened they cannot complete the workshop.

Humour is important and the workshops, though demanding, are conducted in a fairly light-hearted vein. Use of humour contributes to the easy atmosphere and disarms would-be critics, heightening the level of acceptance. This has made us expert at identifying cartoons and documents that encapsulate the spirit of what we are attempting to do.

Do we model an ideal presentation? Yes. At the end of the first day, Gore demonstrates how it can be done in a session entitled 'Science to inform and entertain'. For about 20 minutes he holds the participants enthralled as he presents some elementary but counter-intuitive concepts about measurement, rotational mechanics, topology and macromolecular behaviour.

The writing strand commences with an interactive session entitled 'Plain English' in which issues such as vocabulary, style, sentence structure, punctuation, use of jargon, colloquialisms and acronym are discussed. These issues are also canvassed during the public speaking and the theoretical sessions, so that participants clearly see that there is a relationship between the spoken and the written word and the theory of how to reach the public. The remainder of the session is devoted to writing for the media, taking, as a 'case history', an actual press release (see Box 12.2) that later went through five iterations before being deemed satisfactory to be understood by a member of the public.

This detailed dissection is the model that the group will use in their own writings. The participants are asked to edit their own work that evening, in light of the day's experience. The following day they are divided into four groups of about five people to undertake the detailed analysis. That night, further editing takes place in preparation for the final critique (Box 12.2).

We point out the importance of simplicity, structure, acronym-free vocabulary and immediacy for the reader. In spite of this, most first attempts are riddled with jargon. Jargon certainly has a place in conversations between scientists but talking about energy transduction in mitochondria conveys little to a lay audience. A real problem that scientists have is failing to understand that even words that are commonplace to them may be totally without meaning to anyone, other scientists included, who lacks the necessary background. Scientists also have a tendency to replace one jargon word with another until, in simplifying something they have written, they are stretched out on a rack of progressive simplification. Hence, the remark: 'But I had no idea that you had to simplify it that much!'

It is a mistake, however, to assume that the scientific ideas must be purged from the document in order for it to be understood by the thinking adult population who are not scientists. Many scientists assume at first that

Box 12.2 Sample writing exercise

The following piece is a 154-word extract from a press release that was 425 words long. Note that names have been changed to preserve anonymity and there is no intent to disparage the excellent scientists involved in the research:

> *'Plants grow mainly by expanding their cells rather than producing lots of cells',* Dr Smith said. *'A great deal of pressure is generated within the cells during this process and plants use a molecular framework to maintain the integrity of the cells and also to determine the direction of growth.' The MOR-1 gene is involved in this process, and the next step is to discover how it works. Dr Smith and his team were intrigued to find that a closely related gene was recently found in cancer cells in humans.*
>
> *Genes are usually discovered by studying what happens to an organism when a particular gene has a spelling mistake. Usually these spelling mistakes render the code useless. However, this method does not lend itself easily to the discovery of genes that are vital.*
>
> *Professor Brown, Director, said, 'this is a very exciting discovery, and all the more so because an innovative approach was required'.*

After criticizing four versions in detail, workshop participants finally agreed on the following version. This is the whole document, rewritten in 256 words:

> *Animals grow because their cells continually divide. They get bigger as the number of their cells increases. Plants grow in a different way. Most of the cells of a plant are formed in the embryo – a leaf inside a bud often has all the cells it is ever going to have. During growth, the cells don't divide, they expand.*
>
> *The key to plant growth lies in millions of very tiny tubes, known as microtubules, which are found in the cells. 40,000 of them side by side would measure one millimetre. They act like scaffolding that builds itself into organized patterns that dictate the shape of the plant.*
>
> *In order to find out more about how plants grow, scientists often use a tiny plant, Arabidopsis thaliana. It is distantly related to the cabbage and grows very quickly. By studying how growth of this plant changes under different circumstances, Dr Smith and his colleagues have discovered a gene that controls the way the microtubules are assembled in its cells. The work involved huge effort. Samples from more than 10,000 plants were examined under the microscope but only two provided the necessary information. The gene has been named MOR, short for 'Microtubule Organisation'.*
>
> *Scientists expect that this knowledge will enable them to control microtubule formation experimentally and to change the mechanical properties of plant cell walls. Because plant cell walls have a lot in common with composite polymers like fibreglass, an intriguing aspect of this work is that it may well lead to the development of useful new materials.*

simplification implies condescension. That this is not so is perhaps the hardest lesson for them to learn.

Constructing the piece also proves difficult as scientists have a great need to 'tell everything'. They find it difficult to let go of material that is relevant to their own understanding and simply concentrate on the basic message. Many feel uncomfortable in simplifying, almost as if they were giving away in five minutes something that had taken them ten years to master. They confess to feelings of insecurity in some cases, as if by explaining their work they are somehow demeaning both it and themselves. Given their long period of training in science, this is perfectly understandable.

By the end of the workshop, many recognize that change has occurred but more needs to be done. The need for further work is often recognized with self-deprecating humour and honesty:

> *Me written skills is much betterer!*

> *I am absolutely exhausted! But I can see that time is necessary to consolidate and improve practical skills.*

> *[I am surprised at] how much I know I will be able to improve now.*

Cross-cultural issues are dealt with, in part, through an exercise in which groups of participants rate a selection of texts as 'science' on a scale of one to five. Often there is dissension, within and between groups, with subjects such as acupuncture provoking lively debate. We point out that if a relatively homogeneous set of scientists cannot agree on what constitutes valid science, how much less will the public be able to form an opinion. Taking the high ground about one's own views may lead to misunderstandings, especially with people from non-western cultures.

The workshops have been influential in changing practice. How relevant, however, are these issues of science communication in a completely different culture? The next section outlines a rather different workshop held in Samoa, which revealed the universality of the problems.

Science communication in the Pacific

The structure of workshops is culturally dependent. The happy-go-lucky confrontational style that Australians enjoy fails miserably with the people of Thailand, for example, who set much greater store on courtesy and form. In the Pacific region the nations are not homogeneous; there are many languages and many cultures. A successful science communication workshop involving these different cultures must depend on forms with which the delegates themselves feel comfortable. They cannot be imposed from outside. In order to address communication problems, it is therefore important to know how much commonality exists between scientists from these cultures.

In 2001 The National Centre for the Public Awareness of Science and UNESCO, Apia, jointly sponsored a three-day workshop, a forum on science communication in cultural contexts, in which practising research scientists from eight Pacific countries came together to discuss common science communication issues and difficulties. The invited participants were asked to present papers on issues of science communication in their own countries. The breadth of topics was wide, from hydrology to conservation, but each case history exhibited common communication problems. The delegates' most important task at the workshop was to start to develop a strategy, facilitated by members of The National Centre for the Public Awareness of Science, to promote science awareness appropriate to developing countries and engender a feeling of common cause.

The first day and a half of the workshop was taken up by delegates presenting scientific papers. The process involved was familiar to them and was carried out in an environment in which they could feel confident and relaxed. Paper presentation was, at least in part, a device for creating a comfortable ambience for the small group sessions, which involved more demanding participation.

The delegates were then divided into small groups representing a mix of Pacific states. Members of The National Centre for the Public Awareness of Science were distributed between the groups, not to guide the discussion, but to assist by asking questions and perhaps commenting on similar problems encountered in Australia. It was also their task to emphasize that all of the issues raised were endemic in every country, developed or developing. To set the scene, the following two questions were asked:

1   If you could have the perfect communication situation, regardless of resources (human or physical), how would you describe it?
2   What one very small but achievable step would be possible in your country (assuming money was not the problem)? Just saying 'more money' isn't enough. How would it be used?

These questions were intended to lead to some specific examples of the kinds of behavioural change the delegates would like to effect. They led further to the question of what issues in their regions, other than those addressed in their papers, would benefit from better science communication. The delegates were then invited to consider how these issues were similar (or not) to the ones they presented in the scientific part of the proceedings, and to those presented by others. In subsequent deliberations, delegates were asked to develop generic solutions to those issues and to identify the individuals and groups with an interest in resolving the issues (stakeholders). In particular, they were asked if it were possible to define who had the responsibility in any particular community to identify, analyse and explore ways to change and communicate the results to all interested parties.

Finally, delegates were asked to identify the specific barriers to and vehicles for effectively communicating science in their regions, especially with reference to the specific issues they listed. For example, they were invited to consider science and scientists in their regions, and address the following questions: What are the public perceptions of scientists? What are scientists' perceptions of the various publics? What are people's perceptions of science itself? It was hoped that this would permit the exploration of notions of who were considered to be credible communicators and whether scientists were the best people for the job.

A further hope was that the delegates would be able to suggest solutions to many of the problems arising from poor science communication and identify whether those problems needed to be addressed by external funds (long-term solutions), or whether there were sufficient internal resources available (short-term solutions).

In the small group discussions, there was continual reference to the issues arising from the papers presented earlier, as well as to issues that were identified as the debate progressed. There was a strong appreciation of the gulf that existed between themselves, as scientists, and the people they were trying to influence. At they same time, they recognized that, although deriving from several different cultures themselves, their scientific culture was something they held in common. This scientific culture emerged also as a communication barrier, just as it does for the Australian group.

In response to the first question: 'If you could have the perfect communication situation, regardless of resources (human or physical), how would you describe it?' there were many answers, all illuminating different aspects of a common theme. High on the 'wish list' was cooperative effort directed at goals that everyone identified as desirable. Thus one group gave the highest priority to working together to improve the lifestyles of all communities. In particular, the issue of sustainable management of local resources was seen as very important. Over-exploitation (as in the live reef fish trade) is very widespread. As the local communities depend on the income from such trade to maintain their lifestyles, only by making the scientific argument against exploitation one of extreme personal relevance to every member of the community is there a chance of success. Finding this relevance was as difficult for this group as for scientists anywhere.

The quest to use environmentally appropriate technology must sometimes involve a change in local culture. This is extremely difficult. In Tonga, scientific and local cultures clashed over composting toilets that were being introduced to reduce groundwater contamination by the septic tanks. Encouraging the community to use composting toilets failed, in spite of royal intervention, because of the greater convenience of flush toilets in houses and the cultural taboo on using human waste for fertilizing. Change of behaviour takes more than a royal fiat.

The second question, defining the 'one very small but achievable step' towards the desirable outcomes, elicited a unanimous appeal for greater awareness of scientific solutions. There was a strong feeling that environmentally appropriate technologies should be promoted to change community behaviours that are detrimental to local environments. The extent to which local scientists themselves can effect change is very limited. Public perceptions of scientists are not high unless they are seen to achieve practical outcomes. As one delegate remarked:

'...if they can identify you in association with your experience and what practical solutions you have to offer, then you will gain the respect accordingly.'

Government scientists, however, may be viewed with suspicion because of the failure of governments to respond to community expressions of need. Several of the scientists had hair-raising stories of threats of personal violence when in the field. Too often, 'the work stays on the shelf' remarked one scientist. Another problem was that governments change, destroying continuity of environmental policy.

Much more needs to be done in the field of public awareness of science to make even the first easy steps possible to achieve. This is compounded by the fact that many of the Pacific nations have several languages before English. As English is the international standard language of science in the 21st century, this issue must be urgently addressed, as far as science communication is concerned.

It was clear, from the evidence of the submitted papers, that there is a lack of communication between national agencies and between communities and the agents of international bodies. This is compounded by the geographic isolation of the various Pacific states. Travel is both expensive (air) and dangerous (boat); at best it is tedious, and at the worst, tortuous. It is a real disincentive to sharing knowledge.

The lack of face-to-face contact is a huge barrier to sharing knowledge in all cultures. Personal contact as an element of communication protocol is absolutely essential for developing relationships of trust in Australia, no less than in and among Pacific societies. Partly as a result of the lack of this humanizing contact there is, generally, a marked lack of recognition by scientists of local ownership of knowledge.

All of these barriers are made more complex by an understandable resistance, in every culture, to change. In the Pacific, anything that threatens village autonomy is viewed with justifiable suspicion. As government scientists are likely to be the spearhead of government initiatives, this mistrust will be focused on them. Finally, in many societies there is an enormous issue that must be addressed by others, the mostly incorrect public perception that science and religion are opposing forces.

Conclusions

At the end of all the workshops, participants are invited to fill out evaluation forms. They have been very willing to do so, with a total of 204 in a sample of 217 (94 per cent) handing in completed forms. An overwhelming percentage (99 per cent) agreed that the content of the programme addressed their needs and that the mixture of topics and presenters were excellent or good. The relevance of the workshop to their own situations was considered either excellent (strongly agree, 41 per cent) or good (agree, 59 per cent). It contributed to their understanding (strongly agree, 34 per cent; agree, 60 per cent). An overwhelming majority believed (strongly agree, 49 per cent; agree, 50 per cent) that the skills acquired in the workshop would allow them to improve their communication practice.

A remark by a PhD student that the workshop was 'Very timely and relevant in helping to develop material on my research' illustrates the urgency that young scientists feel about acquiring the skills for public communication. In our experience, no such urgency was felt by PhD students ten years ago. It is a measure of the impact that scientific administrators are beginning to attach to communication. Whether this urgency is felt by some of their more senior scientific colleagues is open to question.

We are at pains to point out that the only way to improve communication skills is to do more of it. After the first, fraught morning, when people are getting over their natural reticence to expose their shortcomings to others, the group usually settles down into a friendly, mutually supportive team. We are careful to nurture this attitude because we want it to continue beyond the workshop. By the end of the workshop the participants understand that it is a 'safe' environment in which to improve their skills and that criticism is constructive and not a personal attack. As participants often come from the same institution, we try to encourage the notion that they have colleagues who have participated in the same process, to whom they can turn for advice without fear of ridicule.

After the workshops it is not uncommon for the scientists to share stories of communication triumphs with us. These range from perceptions that they presented well to some group (such as the Thai researcher who wrote that she had given a talk to farmers on many occasions but had now been told that it was, for the first time, understandable) to their asking us to assist with articles, talks or posters. The process of learning continues – and we, in our turn, learn from them, especially about the exciting and important endeavours in which they are engaged.

The problems that these scientists experience are not trivial and should not be underestimated. Just as acceptance of new scientific ideas requires the public to change – even, as in the Pacific case, the culture itself to change quite dramatically – so those responsible for initiating that change undergo cultural confrontation. No one should expect these understandings on the part of scientific researchers to be universally intuitive. They are counter to all the training we give through our science education process. Until specific training in scientific communication, knowledge sharing skills and appreciation of 'other' knowledge is part of every university science course, we must appreciate the degree to which current communication demands are confronting and threatening.

There is little else to say in conclusion, so we will let the participants have the last words. One of the workshops comprised mainly young biologists.

They were asked what most surprised them about communication. Here are some of their answers:

Simple is good!

How long the writing assignments took to simplify.

and, most poignantly:

Our own ignorance of the importance of science communication!

References

Day, S. B. (1975) *The Communication of Scientific Information*, Basel-Karger, New York

Durant, J. R., Evans, G. A. and Thomas, G. P. (1989) 'The public understanding of science', *Nature*, vol 340, pp11–14

Garvey, W. D. (1979) *Communication: The Essence of Science*, Pergamon Press, Oxford

Jardine, L. (1999) *Ingenious Pursuits*, Little, Brown and Company, London

Keen, M. and Stocklmayer, S. (1999a) 'Science communication: The evolving role of rural industry research and development corporations', *Australian Journal of Environmental Management*, vol 6, pp196–206

Keen, M. and Stocklmayer, S. (1999b) *Communicating Research: An Overview of Communication Efforts of Rural Industry Research Funding Bodies*, Rural Industry Research and Development Corporation, Canberra

Mohan, T., McGregor, H. and Strano, Z. (1992) *Communicating Theory and Practice*, 3rd edn, Harcourt Brace & Company, Sydney, Australia

Prelli, L. J. (1989) *A Rhetoric of Science*, University of South Carolina Press, Columbia

Schön, D. (1987) *Educating the Reflective Practitioner*, Jossey-Bass, San Francisco

Shannon, C. and Weaver, W. (1963) *The Mathematical Theory of Communication*, University of Illinois, Champaign, IL

Stocklmayer, S. M. (2003) 'What makes a successful outreach program? An outline of the Shell Questacon Science Circus', *International Journal of Technology Management*, vol 25, pp405–412

Stocklmayer, S. M. and Gilbert, J. K. (2002) 'New experiences and old knowledge: Towards a model for the public awareness of science', *International Journal of Science Education*, vol 24, pp835–858

UK Parliament (2000) 'Science and technology, third report', The Stationery Office, London, www.parliament.the-stationery-office.co.uk/pa/ld199900/ldselect/ldsctech/38/3801.htm

UNESCO (1999) 'World conference adopts declaration and plan of action for science', UNESCO Press, Paris, www.unesco.org/bpi/eng/unescopress/99-150e.htm

13

The Reflective Practitioner: Practising What We Preach

Valerie A. Brown, Rob Dyball, Meg Keen, Judy Lambert and Nicki Mazur

At a glance

- This chapter has been written by the members of the group responsible for organizing the social learning workshops that contributed to the development of the book
- The five members reflect on their own small group learning, particularly the marked differences between traditional and open social learning programmes
- The personal learning of the organizing group is explored through reflexivity and negotiation, enabled by tools that could help other small collaborating groups with three essential elements of social learning:
  - integration: to identify and build on their individual differences in designs for social learning
  - negotiation: to clarify individual contributions to the team planning processes in an open dialogue with each other
  - partnership: to be prepared to take into account the varying experiences arising from one's own small group.

Social learning in practice: Challenges for the practitioner

In many forms of inquiry, the person doing the inquiring acts as an observer, mentally standing outside the process in order to describe it objectively, and thus more accurately, according to traditional science. Here we are assuming that a subjective, individual experience, such as social learning, can be described more validly and accurately through the people involved reflecting on their experiences (van Manen, 1990). In this chapter, the five members of the organizing group for this book reflect, individually and together, on the dimensions of social learning involved in preparing the book.

In *The Reflective Practitioner*, Schön (1983) argues that it is necessary for all practitioners to reflect on their work. This is necessary for both ethical and practical reasons, that is, to take professional responsibility for their actions and improve their performance. More recently, other scholars have also pleaded for more critical and subjective reflection on our professional practices, and on the contexts affecting these practices (Flyvbjerg, 2001; Wenger, 1998). The dominance of the scientific model of objectivity can make this particularly difficult for academically trained theorists and researchers. This was certainly true of the environmental scientists and social theorists who made up the organizing group. In developing this book, the group had agreed to try and move beyond a narrow stereotype of objectivity and its prescribed learning structures to create a learning cycle that supported mutual participatory and collaborative approaches (see Figure 13.1).

Being a member of any team responsible for adult learning and social change brings with it the challenge to practise what we preach. This presents a double challenge for those working with social learning in environmental management. We must practise what we preach and follow the reflexive learning process we advocate. In addition, the processes of social learning for social change require us to move outside the more formal learning process that has informed our professional understanding.

As part of professional education and experience, we are trained to internalize the boundaries of our field of practice and accept the ethical and social constraints of our roles (Bordieu and Wacquant, 1992). For those designing and delivering social learning for sustainable environmental management, the goal is the opposite. Rather than working within disciplinary boundaries, they have to find ways to transcend them, or at least to build bridges across the disciplinary and social divides.

Social learning in environmental management will thus involve opening up boundaries and combining practices. Basic changes to the existing social learning frameworks of practitioners in most fields include moving from short-term to long-term decisions, and from purely technological to include integrated social solutions. As practitioners we are being asked to bring change not only to our clients, but to ourselves and our profession.

This multiple layered learning (see Figure 1.5) means that it is all the more important for designers of social learning in environmental management processes to become reflexive practitioners, in the sense recommended by Schön (1983). In accepting that challenge, in this chapter we share our experiences in designing and delivering a six-month social learning process. Our small group included experience in environmental management as researchers, educators, administrators and consultants, all holding multiple roles. Separately and together, as members of the organizing group, we reflect here on the events as they unfolded within our group, and between the group and the diversely skilled participants.

Participants in the overall social learning process came from backgrounds as varied as ecology, economics, human ecology, sociology, education, physics and biology. Their professional experience included environmental management, teaching, policy development, local government and administration. The participants and organizing group members were striving to bring their wide range of knowledge, skills and experience together in a transdisciplinary process, at the same time as they were bringing together their ideas on social learning in environmental management. The organizing group expected the transdisciplinary process to spontaneously and smoothly generate a synthesis of existing knowledge and practice, an expectation that proved too optimistic. Transdisciplinarity was interpreted variously among members of the group, as working either within or beyond the academic disciplines. Expectations of outcomes varied widely.

As well as taking part in the social learning planned for the participants, another layer of social learning was in progress among the small organizing

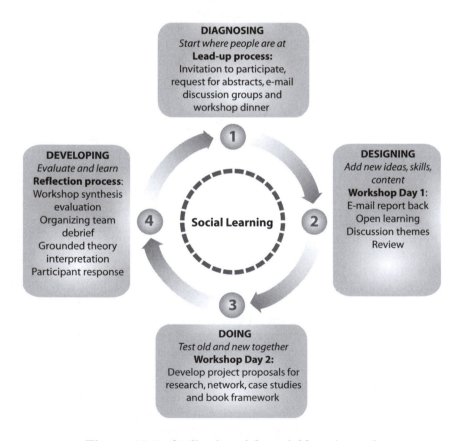

Figure 13.1 *Application of the social learning cycle*

group itself. The original research backgrounds of our five members were social ecology, environmental education, human ecology, biology and social science. All had developed further interests in group facilitation, become interested in fostering social learning and had varied experiences in working with the transition to sustainability in environmental management. In addition to learning from sharing the larger group's social learning experience, we found that we had to reconcile their own varied disciplinary bases and negotiate diverse understandings of social learning in environmental management within our small organizing group.

Planning for social learning

The organizing group agreed to design the workshop on the basis of the seminal ideas of Malcolm Knowles's classic framework for adult learning, extended through David Kolb's work on problem solving and experiential learning (Knowles, 1980; Knowles et al, 1998; Kolb, 1983). We followed the findings of these authors that the designers of any learning process should offer conditions where adult learners collaborate, learn from each other and remain responsible for their own learning. Knowles gives us the important sequence of starting where the learner is at, then introducing new material, testing and evaluating that material in practice and reviewing the whole before the process can be called learning. We followed Kolb in recognizing the matching stages of the experiential learning sequence of reflection and observation, abstract conceptualization, concrete experience, and evaluation and review (see Figure 1.3). Our challenge was to establish those ideal conditions in practice.

This challenge required that the learning cycle be reflected in the social learning design, including recruitment of participants, the use of online dialogues, a two-day social learning workshop and its follow-up writing workshop. While the cycle in Figure 13.1 is depicted as a single cycle, we accepted that it is in practice a continuing spiral, and the learning an iterative process. This was particularly so for the organizing group, with multiple loops occurring as we organized, acted, reflected and re-negotiated the learning process among ourselves, and between ourselves and the participants. The iterative and adaptive approach to social learning provided many unexpected challenges as we sought to ensure that all participants shared a common understanding of the process and outcomes.

These social learning approaches do not stand alone. They complement a new range of learning techniques in management practice, based on confidence in the capacity of the participants in any process to learn together, given appropriate support. For example, in action learning each participant in a learning group draws on their own learning from sharing reflections on their individual experiences. Participatory action research involves a team of people drawing collective learning from a collective experience (Parkes and Panelli, 2001; Whyte, 1991). Experiential learning, whether from life events or events designed for the occasion, underlies the learning approach in each case (Creswell, 1997; Knowles et al, 1998; Kolb et al, 1995).

In the first stage of the book planning process, the organizing group held an interactive session with a number of potential participants to consider possible approaches to the workshop and the writing of the book. After this session the larger group accepted the challenge of designing a 'practise what you preach' process. This led to a round of invitations proposing that the social learning spiral of Figure 13.1 and David Bohm's rules of dialogue in Box 13.1 be the basis for all communications. Bohm holds that social learning arises from recognizing the differences between positions, not in reducing or resolving them. Exploring a paradox, he suggests, is the opportunity to advance knowledge, not a trivial difference that should be argued or swept away.

Box 13.1 Rules of dialogue

Throughout the dialogue:

1   Commit yourself to the process
2   Listen and speak without judgement
3   Identify your own and others' assumptions
4   Acknowledge the other speaker and their ideas
5   Respect other speakers and value their opinions
6   Balance inquiry and advocacy
7   Relax your need for any particular outcome
8   Listen to yourself and speak when moved to
9   Take it easy – go with the flow – enjoy.

Sources: Bohm (1996); Gang and Morgan (2002)

In the planning meetings, it quickly became apparent that two sets of ideas were competing for the design. One was for an adaptation of a traditional conference-style workshop, with keynote speakers and pre-arranged paper presentations, but longer-than-usual group discussion and plenary sessions. In this model, the organizing group would determine the themes and timetable. The other idea was to take advantage of the growing use of the 'open space learning' concept, maximizing dialogue, with participants coming together to determine the agenda, themes and outcomes (Bambridge, 2002). If papers were to be written as a product of the workshop, these would be determined through mutual discussions by participants, not by individuals before the collaborative learning process. The open space process offers a democratic learning process that has worked well when participants have an interest in the topic and a commitment to share their learning.

The rules for managing the open space process include accepting the learning of the people on the spot, encouraging opportunities for emergent knowledge and permitting the law of two feet. The first two points are achieved by allowing participants to structure the learning agenda together at the beginning of each day, facilitate their own discussion groups and summarize the core learning from these discussions through informal sessions reporting back to the whole group. The law of two feet holds that if you are neither gaining from, nor contributing to, the learning process where you are, explain why to the group and move on to somewhere more fruitful. For traditional conference organizers, having no previously set agenda and participants free to move whenever they wanted would be expected to create anarchy rather than mutual learning. For those experienced with and committed to the process, the structure allows self-directed learning and an exchange of ideas less constrained by predetermined boundaries.

At their two extremes, combining a traditional formal conference and an unmodified open learning workshop would clearly be administratively and intellectually incompatible. The two forms of planned learning differ in terms of the learning unit, knowledge content and status, key skills, role of speakers, role of the organizing committee and criteria for success (see Table 13.1). As there were members of our group that leaned towards each end of the continuum, we agreed on a mix of the two, which brought its own problems of consistency of design and unresolved tensions. It gradually became apparent that we held a range of differing perspectives on the construction of knowledge, educational values and practical organization, that is, on each of the three pillars of individual or social learning (Bruner, 1999). For example, some members of the organizing group were wary that the model placed too much emphasis on process at the expense of content and that this could diminish the importance of the social learning in environmental management theme and the task of advancing intellectual ideas for this book. In addition, they feared that the language and structure of the open space model could alienate some participants and thus narrow the range of disciplines and practitioners participating. Conversely, others had experienced regular and highly successful outcomes from the open learning approach, which they

Table 13.1 *Traditional and open designs for adult learning*

Learning component	Traditional conference	Open learning process
Learning unit	Single event	Cumulative process
Knowledge content	Pre-existing	Emerging during events
Knowledge status	Expert-evaluated	Group-generated
Sources of knowledge	Leaders in the field	Exploring potential
Organizers' role	Managers	Facilitators
Process	Analysis and debate	Synthesis and dialogue
Key goal	Efficient, productive	Responsive, productive

believed could not have occurred using a traditional approach. They argued that the more traditional approach was, by its very nature, incompatible with social learning – that is, it imposed a pre-set, formal, single-focus framework on a dynamic and emergent process of collective action and reflection linking a range of very different perspectives.

The programme design was eventually agreed upon, partly through dialogue and partly through compromise. The outcome was a design for six months of interactions between the invited participants, with opportunities to reflect on and redirect the process as it was happening. As the process unfolded, practical matters of time constraints and distance between group members resulted in a failure to explore some of our assumptions on key matters of task management, group decision making processes and the concepts and values driving the planning process itself. This is a key step in applying Bohm's rules of dialogue that proved to need much more emphasis than we had realized.

On reflection, next time we would build in times for our own shared reflection throughout the planning process. However, we also learned that in trialling any new and innovative processes, there is an inevitable cycle of learning-by-doing, when mistakes will be made and it becomes important for lessons to be learned. In advance, all one can do is agree on how those learning processes will be handled constructively and fed back as quickly as possible into the process.

The sequence of events

The agreed learning programme of 26 interconnected events is outlined in Box 13.2, the A–Z of a social learning process. This represented an open-ended social learning process, but not the full open space process. To generate

---

Box 13.2 A social learning programme from A–Z

Establishment

a   Invitation letters to 80 colleagues with interests in social learning. 'Open call' through formal and informal channels

b   Abstracts of 300 words from each of 45 participants: abstract themes form the basis for email discussion

c   Four email discussion groups of nine members pursue a theme for three weeks

d   Weekly questions and answers on the theme collated and circulated

e   Group dinner the evening before a two-day workshop

Development: Workshop – Day 1

f   Registration, refreshments and join email theme tables

g   Welcome by workshop sponsors and organizing group

h   Email discussion groups report back to full group on themes arising from their discussions

i   Open learning process for members to develop themes for Day 1

j   Five parallel sessions on selected themes, report back sheets posted on wall

k   Brainstorm session on subject matter for the proposed book, drawing on the day's discussions

l   Affinity groups (researchers, practitioners, postgraduates) review the day

m   Working dinner to plan Day 2

Progression: Workshop – Day 2

n   Organizing group presents possible publication structure for redesign based on brainstorm session

o   Critical review of book design by whole group

p   Other desirable projects that could emerge from the workshop are negotiated by whole group and project groups formed to discuss these – learning networks, case studies, research grants

q   Reporting back to plenary. Further discussion of book and projects with whole group

Review

r   Synthesis panel of three (from each sector group) reflect on workshop; facilitator reflects on workshop

s   Facilitated plenary review of outcomes and panel reflections

t   Debrief and evaluations

Follow-up

u   Debriefing workshops and organizing group meetings

v   Organizing group advised participants of four projects arising from the workshop

w   Book project set up: authors' instructions, sample table of contents and timetable

x   One-day synthesis forum for integrating chapters and preparing final draft

y   Final chapters submitted and edited

z   Book scheduled for publisher in 2004.

The dialogues that commenced in the email discussions (c) were extended during an informal dinner the evening before the workshop (e). Discussion topics and seating arrangements were used to help establish the workshop as a social learning process that went beyond the constraints of commonly constructed disciplinary boundaries, and the social and knowledge divides between academia and community. Over a third of the participants were practitioners, mainly from the local government sector, the remainder were academics and private consultants.

a shared knowledge base and set of skills, participants were asked to provide abstracts of their possible contributions or areas of interest. Based on these abstracts, the organizers grouped participants according to common interest areas. Members of these email discussion groups then exchanged ideas and insights on a series of questions for three weeks before the workshop. Each group established its own distinctive pattern of social interaction and knowledge management during the email discussions. This reinforces the view that learning and knowledge management can be driven by small groups committed to a learning process, and that people will develop a process best suited to their needs, when left to their own devices. One group kept a running summary of their responses to each question, another group recorded each individual's responses separately and a third group did not answer the questions at all. Drawing on the rule of two feet, this last group was not pressured to participate in this particular learning process.

The evaluation comments revealed different expectations of the process, with some feeling it was not open enough and others finding it too structured. Some found a lack of depth in the initial discussions as people unfamiliar with each other explored ways to effectively share ideas and experiences. Others recorded a reluctance to move beyond familiar disciplinary or professional boundaries. A number of participants felt the open learning process and its rationale (which was new to many) needed to be explained more fully by the organizing group at the beginning of the workshop. This diverse response to a largely unfamiliar process highlighted the importance of briefing participants about the design of social learning processes before participation. Participants are then in a better position to negotiate any aspects of the process early on, or to suggest adaptations to better suit their needs.

As part of the learning process, on the last afternoon a synthesis group of a practitioner, a researcher, a student and an organizing group member reflected on the personal experiences of the workshop. The collected view was that the workshop held great promise and aroused great expectations. The outcome had exceeded expectations for some, but for others it did not deliver the benefits they expected. For the record, and to provide the context for our own group reflections, the results of the participants' workshop evaluation are shown in Box 13.3.

It was two weeks before the organizing group managed to meet again and share the reflections reported in the next section. These reflections led to a re-energized group, the development of a book design, collaborative writing of book chapters and, finally, a one-day writing workshop in which authors critiqued each others' chapters and agreed on the final format of the book. The learning from the debriefing meetings of the organizing group is discussed next.

Reflection on events

The experiences of organizing group members of a social learning process must, by definition, differ from those of other participants, no matter how

---

Box 13.3 Evaluation of social learning for sustainability workshop (*n* = 24)

Ratings summary (on a scale from 1 to 5, where 1 = very unsatisfied, 5 = very satisfied)

Administration
Pre-workshop dinner (4.8)
Venue (4.5)
Expectations (from email discussion)
Expanded experience (4.0)
Personal boundaries expanded (3.8)
Solutions to barriers (3.1)
Integration across disciplines (3.1)

Email discussion groups
Information flow (3.0)
Usefulness (2.7)

Forum/workshop
Theme discussion sessions (4.2)
Synthesis session (3.9)
Facilitation (3.8)
Agenda-setting (3.1)
Book chapter sessions (2.9)

Group dynamics
Supportive climate (4.1)
Equal participation (3.8)
Cohesion (3.8)

---

open and collaborative the process. The organizing group experienced at least three dimensions of learning:

- learning from being part of the full group and following the planned programme ourselves
- learning from feedback from the experience of others in the full group
- learning from the organizing group's internal processes of reflection.

On reflection, we realized that traditional meeting programmes have built-in conflict management systems, or perhaps conflict minimization or suppression. The ordered rows of chairs, the rostrum, the chairperson, the plenary hour,

15-minute presentation times and limited discussion times can be regarded as a form of crowd control. The programme is generated from existing work by a small committee, usually well acquainted with one another as colleagues, with control of the agenda through such means as refereeing proposed papers from known contributors. There is limited interaction on informal, optional and non-essential matters. Yet the ordered process does set out tight expectations and take care of many unresolved tensions.

The members of the organizing group agreed that in facilitating social learning we needed to become familiar with and sensitive to all the interest groups that make up our potential social learning population. There are no fixed rules that dictate how they should be brought together, nor what will happen once they are brought together. This dimension of uncertainty was particularly acute in this case since one of the few things we thought that we knew for certain about social learning is that it is responsive, adaptable and context-dependent; and about environmental management that it is complex and open-ended (Chapter 1).

The record shows that the post-workshop debrief produced a very rich dialogue and considerable learning. More difficult was interpreting our learning. The process we had been through was difficult to interpret in terms of the implications for social learning – even for ourselves, even more so to share with others. The solution we chose was to take the approach of grounded theory, the classic inquiry method of Glaser and Strauss (1967), the grounded data being our own interpretation of events. One member of the organizing group suggested two theoretical lenses through which we could share our learning experiences in practice:

- personal construct theory, developed by Kelly in 1963 and expanded by Bannister and FranSella (1986)
- a local adaptation of the Johari window, which allows for parallel perspectives to be expressed (Luft and Ingham, 1955).

The organizing group's individual perspectives on the social learning process: Personal construct theory

George Kelly's personal construct theory suggests that individuals establish their reality as a negotiation between opposite poles, each pair of opposites establishing the dimension of the reality being considered (Kelly, 1955; Bannister and FranSella, 1986). Each idea has many possible opposites, and the opposite that someone chooses indicates the way they are personally constructing the situation. For instance, the opposite of learning might be forgetting, rejecting, instruction, stupidity or ignorance. Which opposite one chooses changes the dimension being constructed. In the dialogue here, we have been constructing social learning as a dynamic process, the opposite of instruction. In applying personal construct theory as a reflective tool, as part of the debrief, each of us in the organizing group generated our own key words, firstly for how we perceived the process from our own point of view

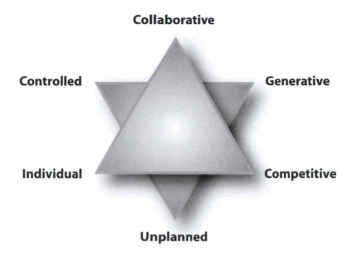

Figure 13.2 *Representation of Kelly's personal construction theory, showing two possible constructions of the same social learning process*

and then from our understanding of the participants' point of view. We then identified two opposite descriptors for each key word.

Figure 13.2 shows two possible constructions of the same social learning process. The upper triangle represents an individual's personal perspective of the learning process and its polar opposites, and the lower triangle represents that same person's understanding of the perspectives held by the workshop participants. Together it demonstrates the multiple understandings that may need accommodating if social learning is to be enhanced.

Using Kelly's personal construct theory helped to reveal both how different, and in other ways how alike, our individual constructions of the process were. The purpose was not to decide who got it right, but to look at the patterns made between them as a mirror of our social learning from the process. By expressing our perceptions more clearly, everyone could understand more fully some of the unspoken assumptions and meanings each individual held. For example, one group member described the process as 'unstructured' while another referred to it as 'structured', but did they understand these terms in exactly opposite ways? Apparently not, by using polar opposites to clarify meaning it became apparent that for one person the lack of structure related to concerns about a need for processes to build trust and constrain unproductive exchanges (such as violations of Bohm's rules of dialogue); while the person referring to the process as 'structured' was concerned that alternative open learning processes could have been more fully used to guide our learning objectives.

As predicted by Kelly, our five experiences of the planned social learning process were construed in five different ways, each providing a window into the individual's experience and judgements. Each person's description of the success or failure of the workshop as a learning process as they experienced it is coupled with their description of the opposite process that could have reversed that experience. The five descriptions of the workshop were:

- Collaborative: By constructively working together and engaging change processes, as opposed to diverging on to individual pathways, collaboration had been achieved
- Unstructured: By failing to build trust and provide strong frameworks for transdisciplinary dialogues the workshop exhibited a lack of structure. This could have been reversed through structured processes that could generate high levels of trust and help to resolve tensions arising from crossing disciplinary and professional boundaries
- Creative: By accepting the inevitable challenges in generating a third way the workshop had been creative. The opposite of this would have been to use structures that would have stifled creative thought
- Guided: A guiding structure had helped to facilitate the building of bridges between new and old thinking through open learning, rather than using structure to control proceedings and the range of ideas discussed
- Clear: Engaging in dialogue to resolve ambiguous and changing ground and find a firm basis for collaboration helped achieve clarity. The opposite to this would have been to have ignored conflict and tensions between ideas.

We had been using similar words that had very different personal meanings. Finding methods like Kelly's personal construct theory helps to address the ambiguity of language – a common challenge in social learning – and to find mutually acceptable pathways on which to move forward.

The organizing group's perspectives on social learning process: The Johari window

Having explored our personal constructs of our planned social learning process, the next question was: How did we interpret the experience of working with others? One way to consider events from several perspectives at once is to use the Johari window (Luft and Ingham, 1955). Reflection on our experience of events suggested that there were four concurrent windows on the social learning process outlined earlier: one's own learning, one's own group's learning, the learning from observing other groups, and the learning from discussion within the full group of participants (see Figure 13.3).

The lessons drawn from the experiences of each member of the organizing group are summarized next. This summary draws on the Johari windows completed by individual members of the organizing group, the extensive debriefing shared by the group and subsequent discussions among ourselves and with participants.

Individual learning from the workshop in general
We concluded that in Australian culture we are better at sharing experiences and values, rather than the principles and assumptions that underlie that

Figure 13.3 *Social learning experiences interpreted through a Johari window*

experience and determine their constructions of reality. Since the latter is fundamentally important to social learning in environmental management, tools to facilitate this type of sharing are essential for anyone organizing such a process. For instance, the facilitation process will have to accommodate the contributions of different learning styles, both within the organizing group and among other participants. Moreover, it is not possible to assume that each individual or group is aware of the important ways in which learning styles affect one's own and others' learning.

Tensions between learning styles associated with knowledge transfer and collaborative processes can undermine social learning processes if not explicitly addressed. One of the issues in resolving these tensions in social learning is that there will always be great diversity in learning preferences when people are drawn from the social sciences, the biophysical sciences, members of the general community or government and practitioner groups. What is needed is general agreement among the whole group on applying the basic rules of collaborative engagement, as outlined by Bohm (1996). However, putting these rules into practice in our own actions and planning in the organizing group and in the workshops proved more challenging than anticipated. Social learning processes can benefit from strong facilitation that ensures individuals abide by agreed rules of dialogue, and that learning processes are consistent with the desired learning outcomes.

Learning from working with our own organizing group

The organizing group had originally approached the task of developing and implementing a new and innovative learning process with cautious engagement and expectations of warm collaboration. Much of our planning was based on previous experience. We all tended to retreat to our comfort zones of familiar processes, modes of communication and theories or practices when conditions were difficult. This makes it all the more important when developing new processes for social learning to ensure that they are carefully constructed on shared adult learning principles, are well explained and transparent and led with mutual understanding.

Conflict and interpersonal tensions may not be comfortable, but they are part of a process of deep learning and can be a catalyst for social change processes. When experimenting with new learning processes, especially among familiar colleagues, you can expect only partial collaboration due to pre-existing agendas, differing personal experiences and competing demands. Where, as is inevitable, a learning experience is not completed to expectations, it needs processes to allow the event to be fully embraced and explored so as to learn from shared successes and failures. This requires that reflective times be explicitly worked into the learning process.

Learning from working with or observing other groups

Some caution with the social learning process from some participants appeared to us to lie on a continuum: the closer the subject of social learning was to being a participant's specialist area, the more critical and guarded the interaction became. If knowledge and power are equivalent, as Foucault (cited in Morris and Patton, 1979) would hold, then challenging the knowledge on which individual or group power is based can be threatening and adversely affect the learning process. Finding ways to focus on the learning process rather than the learning content is particularly challenging in academic forums.

When learning forums mix academic and field-based practitioners in one learning process, it must be accepted that the process will be assessed differently depending on the learning objectives, past experiences and personal filters among the participants. This disjuncture can impede or energize the learning, depending on the process provided. Negotiation and conflict management methods can be of value here. In our own case, the workshop was separately assessed as a good process done very well, a good process not done very well and a poor process done better than could be expected. It's hard to believe we were all part of the same process!

Learning from the experience of the whole group

Collaborative learning for a large group requires a commitment of time. This type of social learning needs to be iterative and occur over a longer timeframe than any one workshop can permit. Pre-existing social groups and knowledge boundaries are extremely strong. We found that pre-workshop processes, such as sharing abstracts and joining in email discussion groups, can help reveal these boundaries and move beyond them, as could a more general use of the Johari window and Kelly's personal construct theory. These techniques, drawn from psychology, sociology and management, can be most successful in providing frameworks that sanction and encourage lateral thinking and pluralism. They can facilitate new alliances for transdisciplinary and collaborative learning, on which to build long-term change. Time is needed to establish these alliances because of the number of complex variables that need to be negotiated, such as learning approaches, communication techniques, network connections, assumptions and values, and synthesis processes.

The debriefing process had sharpened our understanding of what we were all looking for in this book, and provided a stronger platform on which to move to the next stage of the process. The follow-on workshop was designed for the larger group to:

- collaboratively write chapters for a book on social learning
- advance the collective understanding through critical reflections and insights of others on their writings and work
- share their individual experience and learning with a wider audience
- take action in the community to advance social learning for sustainability.

The subsequent writing workshop for all the chapter authors and some other supportive individuals contributed to each of these goals. In this workshop we changed the format to start with a focus on a predetermined and agreed task (participants' collaborative chapter reviews), followed by a session generating an open learning agenda to consider future learning and collaboration possibilities. This reversed the original workshop process of placing the open agenda setting ahead of the task structure – and it is the order we would recommend.

Several innovative projects and collaborations emerged from the second workshop process, partly due to the increasing trust between members of the organizing group and workshop participants, and the greater clarity and sharing of the organizing group's individual goals. For instance, one member's primary goal was a good publication, one the opportunity to refine their own chapter, and another to revisit the social learning process of the group. All goals could be met by recognizing them in the planning process.

Reflections on the threads of social learning

Chapter 1 set some general criteria for exploring and interpreting the process of social learning in environmental management. These include five threads that weave throughout such a process, making up its texture and its continuation as an important social change process. The threads are reflection, systems orientation, integration, negotiation and participation. They therefore make a valuable foundation from which to re-examine our own experiences and share our learning, both among ourselves and with others.

Reflection/reflexivity

Several instances during the process of developing the book illustrated the importance of reflexivity (reflection on the learning and change arising from reflections of events) for our central theme. We attribute the mixed experience and reception of the first workshop at least partly to lack of reflexivity in the early stages of the planning, and to not building reflexivity into the workshop. We needed to allow participants to reflect not only on their research/experience, but also on the learning process. Lack of time, distance between organizers and lack of familiarity with reflective processes were important factors in this initial neglect. In retrospect, we have learned that reflexivity is integral to social learning processes. The reflective exercises were needed to fully tap our own learning, and incorporate that learning coherently into the overall process. In the later stages of the process, we were able to build on our mutual learning, and subsequently design a mutually rewarding writing workshop.

Systems orientation

Throughout the planning process we referred to Kolb's (1983) experiential learning cycle as the foundation of the social learning system within which we were working. Such a systems perspective suggests that Kolb's learning cycle should not be seen as a continual cumulative process, where knowledge or understanding improves with each iteration. In the model of adaptive systems advanced by Gunderson and Holling (2002), processes of growth and accumulation are also associated with destructive phases of undoing and reorganization (see Chapter 3). Again, it was suggested that at times an unwillingness to let go of cherished beliefs and positions partly prevented groups from moving towards the new understandings. At other times, the tensions and seeming failures of learning processes may just be the inevitable outcome of one way of knowing and learning collapsing before another can emerge.

Integration

The discussion on integration in Chapter 1 noted that it was necessary to be clear about just what is being integrated. In social learning, people, skills, knowledge and social roles are being connected in new ways. In environmental management, environment and people are being related to one another in new ways. Whether they are being integrated (that is, becoming one) or are forming new networks or relationships is one of the contested questions of the social learning process.

One of our principal interests in developing this book was the ability to go beyond the boundaries, whether they are between places, people, governments and/or knowledge sectors. In our reflections on the process mentioned earlier, we identified a considerable number of boundaries operating within the process. Boundaries based on age, academic level, social ideologies or environmental values will often be important, but were not apparent in this particular process. However, we did observe boundaries operating between different learning styles, separate affinity groups, workshop organizers and participants, and theorists and practitioners. The evaluation report in Box 13.3 reveals that the pre-workshop social dinner, the free discussion themes and the overall workshop social climate appeared to have worked best in opening up the boundaries.

Negotiation

The principal avenues of negotiation employed in our process were the rules of dialogue (Box 13.1) and the facilitation process linking the events (Box 13.2). The twin issues needing considerable negotiation proved to be (a) the choices between the elements of traditional conference design and the open learning experience (Table 13.1); and (b) the different expectations of the process between practitioners and researchers, both within the organizing group and among the participants. We noted earlier that Bohm's rules of dialogue as the mode of communication were not always followed. The first workshop participants were reminded of the rules, but there was no follow-through guidance within the workshop. In other words, we needed to be better at practising what we were preaching.

Participation/partnership

Since social learning is based on human relationships, partnerships within the organizing group, and between members of the organizing group and the participants were key to generating social learning. Partnerships are negotiated, not born. Most of us in the organizing group had pre-existing partnerships with each other, and with many of the participants. Most of the workshop participants were not strangers to each other. The pattern of our partnerships with the participants varied widely, based on being professional colleagues, friends, workmates, mentors, and collaborators on other projects. We are too close to the issue to conclude definitely, but can surmise that this pattern was in some senses an issue, because it strengthens some subgroups and leads to differing sets of expectations that can go either way: fragment the process or provide the foundations for greater synthesis. Affirmative action to re-balance existing associations and loyalties may be a necessary tool in designing the processes of social learning.

Conclusions

Standing out from the experience of organizing group members is the need to acknowledge and plan for the distinctive differences between standard practice in organizing workshops and conferences and the special demands of the social learning process. The experience described here uncovers both inhibiting and enhancing factors for fostering social learning. Chief among the inhibiting factors were the difficulty of creating trust in a learning process that differs from the familiar model; the need to transfer the standard practices of team building, facilitation and conflict management into a new open learning environment; and the tension between the need for structure and the need for remaining open to innovation.

One particular lesson came from adapting the open space technique to an outcome-based programme. It became clear that beginning the first workshop with an open process led to expectations that this freedom would continue, and to tensions when recalled to previously established goals. Our conclusion is that the reverse would have been more productive, that is, starting with clarifying and defining the task and then moving to an open learning process to explore the potential for new ways of fulfilling the task. This approach worked much better in a later writers' workshop.

The boundaries created by professional expertise, personal learning styles and attitudes to innovation were firmly established and intermittently erupted, swamping the learning process. The two theoretical tools the organizing group used to interpret programme planning and group learning as part of their debriefing process opened up fresh avenues for mutual learning and understanding. It was a salutary lesson on the need to find pathways for shared reflection as a key process in the social learning process. Such pathways did, in this case, help us learn to practise what we were preaching, and incorporate reflexivity, negotiation and partnership into own small group social learning.

References

Bambridge, P. (2002) 'Open space educational technology', workshop briefing notes

Bannister, D. and FranSella, F. (1986) *Inquiring Man: The Psychology of Personal Constructs*, 3rd edn, Routledge, London

Bohm, D. (1996) *On Dialogue*, Routledge, London

Bordieu, P. and Wacquant, L. (1992) *An Invitation to Reflexive Sociology*, Ruthven, New York

Bruner, J. (1999) *Acts of Meaning*, Harvard University Press, Cambridge, MA

Creswell, J. (1997) *Qualitative Inquiry and Research Design. Choosing among Five Traditions*, Sage, San Francisco

Flyvbjerg, B. (2001) *Making Social Science Matter: Why Social Inquiry Fails and How it Can Succeed*, Cambridge University Press, Cambridge

Gang, P. and Morgan, M. (2002) 'Curriculum notes', The Institute for Integrated Studies, Endicott College, Beverly, MA, www.ties-edu.org/ accessed 10 January 2005

Glaser, B. G. and Strauss, A. L. (1967) *The Discovery of Grounded Theory*, Aldine, Chicago

Gunderson, L. and Holling, C. (eds) (2002) *Panarchy: Understanding Transformations in Human and Natural Systems*, Island Press, Washington, DC

Kelly, G. (1955) *The Psychology of Personal Constructs*, WW Norton, New York

Knowles, M. (1980) *From Pedagogy to Androgogy*, Cambridge, New York

Knowles, M. S., Holton, E. F. and Swanson, R. A. (1998) *The Adult Learner: The Definitive Classic in Adult Education and Human Resource Development,* 5th edn, Butterworth-Heinemann, Woburn, MA

Kolb, D. (1983) *Experiential Learning: Experience as the Source of Learning and Development*, Prentice Hall, Englewood Cliffs, NJ

Kolb, D., Osland, J. and Rubin, I. (1995) *Organisational Behaviour: An Experiential Approach*, Prentice Hall, Englewood Cliffs, NJ

Luft, J. and Ingham, H. (1955) *The Johari Window*, Western Training Laboratory, Lansing, MI

Morris, M. and Patton, P. (eds) (1979) *Michel Foucault: Power, Truth, Strategy*, Feral Publications, Sydney

Parkes, M. and Panelli, R. (2001) 'Integrating catchment ecosystems and community health: The value of participatory action research', *Ecosystem Health*, vol 7, no 2, pp85–106

Schön, D. (1983) *The Reflective Practitioner: How Professionals Think in Action*, Basic Books, New York

van Manen, M. (1990) *Researching Lived Experience. Human Science for an Action Sensitive Pedagogy*, Althouse Press, London, Ontario

Wenger, E. (1998) *Communities of Practice: Learning, Meaning and Identity*, Cambridge University Press, Cambridge

Whyte, W. F. (ed) (1991) *Participatory Action Research*, Sage Publications, London

Section 5

Learning for the Future

14

Lessons from the Past, Learning for the Future

Valerie A. Brown, Meg Keen and Rob Dyball

At a glance

- The case studies in this book reveal the extent to which environmental managers require skills in change management, which calls for social learning between the diverse interests of the groups involved
- Overall, the chapters offer an environmental manager the basis for designing and delivering a social learning process that applies the five social learning strands: reflectivity, systems orientation, integration, negotiation and partnership
- A social learning approach to environmental management involves a combination of personal learning, community engagement, collaboration with relevant professional and interest groups, and partnerships with the organizations providing resources
- How the five learning strands are linked at each stage of social learning depends on the context and the management objectives of the programme concerned
- Reflections on mutual learning at each stage facilitate an ongoing process of social learning and adaptive environmental management.

Five strands of learning

Social learning for improved environmental management hinges on our abilities to work together collectively and constructively. This can be achieved only if we cross the jurisdictional, disciplinary and social boundaries that divide us. The chapters of this book have explored how linkages between learning individuals, communities, experts and governments can be forged and strengthened in environmental management. The five strands of social learning that were introduced at the beginning of the book have been found to weave together the diverse knowledges necessary to achieve progress towards a more sustainable future.

It is hoped that through the book's broad coverage the reader can find some useful parallels to their own experience. By reflecting on the chapters of the book as a whole, they can derive general guidelines relevant to anyone involved in environmental management. These guidelines are useful to those who need to design, implement or evaluate a programme for improved environmental management.

We begin by reviewing some core propositions raised in the first chapter (pp5–7):

- Locally and globally, environmental management takes place in a context of serious concerns about how human activities are affecting global ecological integrity and so threatening a healthy and humane future
- Any lasting change of a sustainable future will depend on establishing social learning processes that aim to improve the management of human and environmental interactions, through an ongoing process of experiential learning and reflection
- Social learning can address the complexity of these interactions and bring about long-term benefits, provided there is the capacity to apply all five of the interwoven strands of social learning.

The five essential social learning strands of reflection, systems orientation, integration, negotiation and participation provide a sound foundation for social learning in environmental management. Using these strands, the environmental manager can enter into a social learning spiral that involves 'diagnosing' the present condition of people and place; 'designing' a programme that can help achieve their potential for a sustainable future; 'doing' appropriate steps to deliver the programme, and 'developing' the next round of programmes based on learning from experience and reflection (see Figure 1.3).

Each of these stages is a learning process in itself, and each builds on the one before in a spiral that develops over time. The five strands are present in various forms throughout this process, but play differing roles at each stage. This is described throughout the book and illustrated in Figure 14.1.

At each stage of the learning spiral, the environmental manager collaborates with a range of principal actors whose knowledge and values reflect different traditions of understanding – and this raises additional challenges. By traditions we are referring to the personal experiences that underpin a particular way of knowing. These traditions can be related to a discipline, professional training or cultural norms of a locality. As noted by Ison (Chapter 2), they can serve as a network of prejudices or pre-understandings that provide possible answers and strategies for action. Traditions are not only ways to see and act, but also ways to conceal. When traditions of understanding differ, dialogues are needed to understand each person's perspective and negotiate a way forward (see Box 13.1).

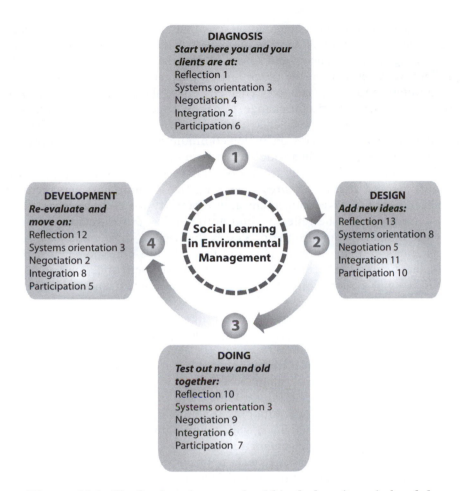

DIAGNOSIS
Start where you and your clients are at:
Reflection 1
Systems orientation 3
Negotiation 4
Integration 2
Participation 6

DESIGN
Add new ideas:
Reflection 13
Systems orientation 8
Negotiation 5
Integration 11
Participation 10

DOING
Test out new and old together:
Reflection 10
Systems orientation 3
Negotiation 9
Integration 6
Participation 7

DEVELOPMENT
Re-evaluate and move on:
Reflection 12
Systems orientation 3
Negotiation 2
Integration 8
Participation 5

Social Learning in Environmental Management

Figure 14.1 *The five learning strands within the learning spiral and the chapters in which they are discussed*

These dialogues across traditions of understanding are a time for learning and development – a process in which the environmental manager may take various roles, but often the principal ones are facilitator or change agent. Other possibilities include playing the part of team leader, administrator, planner, educator or expert adviser. Depending on the size and complexity of the project, the manager may take on some or all of these parts, or may be required to change roles as the project evolves. An example of the latter is the changing roles of the manager in the project that reduced feral animals in rangelands (see Chapter 4).

As the manager and their team progress through each stage of the learning cycle, the team members will need to bring together a portfolio of skills. Diagnosis of the situation needs keen and accurate observation, coupled with some experience of the people and place. Design of a change programme based on that diagnosis requires imagination, creativity and the capacity to engage with other actors and look outside the expectations of the existing traditions of knowing, decision making and acting. Doing, that is putting the design into practice, requires skill on the practitioner's part, since even a well-designed programme can fail if it is poorly enacted. These skills include the ability to create a suitable platform for change, to negotiate across interest groups, and to nurture a dialogue between stakeholders that encourages critical reflection and development. Chapter 8, on linking community and government, presents examples of this process in a wide range of communities.

Developing a programme from a one off-event into an ongoing process of learning and change requires evaluating the learning and management experience, which takes judgement and a capacity for clear interpretation. Evaluations need to be reflective and appreciative, critically assessing not only the outcomes, but also the processes that lead to those outcomes, as in the chapters on living to learn (11) and the reflective practitioner (13). The assessment should reflect on the effects of management style, personal and organizational assumptions and values, cultural context and the complex dynamic interaction between ecological and social systems. The consistent thread binding the stages together is the need to apply the five strands of social learning. Reflection, systems orientation, integration, negotiation and participation are required at every stage.

To sum up, the social learning process in environmental management follows four essential stages, calling on the capacity for accuracy (diagnosis), creativity (design), practical skills (doing) and judgement (developing) in turn. Each stage will be successful only if all key interest groups are actively engaged in management activities, while taking into account that each group comes from a different management tradition. The glue that allows the learning process to continue and the staged tasks to be completed is made up of the five strands of the social learning process. This is shown in Figure 14.2.

The practice of environmental management is never as neat as Figure 14.2 suggests, and in real life the stages of social learning overlap, circumstances change and managing partners may disagree. Because of this reality, the social learning strands become ever more crucial in the continuity and delivery of any successful programme. As a guide to operating in this uncertainty and complexity, we will summarize how the learning strands operate from within communities, government agencies, and personal and professional arenas, respectively.

Learning partnerships with communities

The patterns of interactions involving communities are variously interpreted through Chapters 4–7, in the community section of this book. The reflections themselves come from people based in action research, community learning, geography of place and community development, respectively. They are working in a range of environments: a river catchment trying to combine industrial

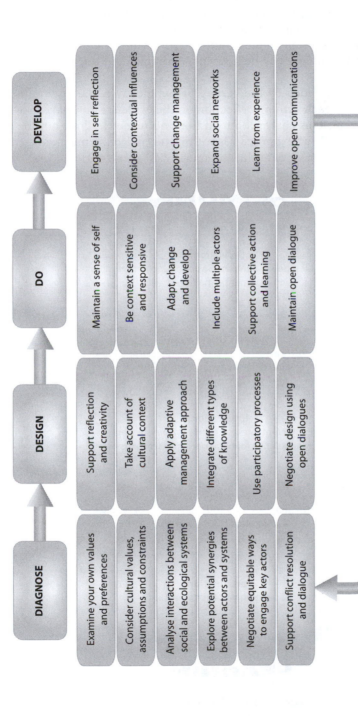

Figure 14.2 *Practical example of applying the five learning strands to environmental management*

and rural uses; a sparsely populated semi-arid grazing region; a richly fertile and very beautiful tropical plateau; and a new industrializing traditional society. Furthermore, while there is a range of expertise and knowledge within every community, specialist contributions from natural and social science, engineering and planning may be needed to complement this existing knowledge.

The richness provided by the variety of perspectives and environmental contexts allows for each author's reflection on the evidence they have provided (that is, *reflexivity*). This enables both author and reader to draw out the core aspects of the social learning processes within the environmental management system, from the perspective of the community (Figure 14.3).

COMMUNITY

Reflection:
Revealing power relationships affecting community environmental management

Systems Orientation:
Recognizing associations between people and place
Valuing different types of knowledge

Integration:
Involving different interest groups within the context of collaborative management and learning

Negotiation:
Strengthening bonding and bridging social capital
Forging trusting relationships

Participation:
Engaging whole community

LEARNING

Figure 14.3 *Social learning strands of a community-based environmental management system*

Permeating each community are power relationships that affect environmental management and social learning processes. These power relationships can shift over time and according to the issues of interest (Foucault, 1980). A *systems orientation* addresses this challenge by recognizing that all systems are really systems of interest to some person or group. Addressing power relationships early in a project enables learning processes that create the space for the full range of issues and concerns to be presented, moving people beyond entrenched positions and narrow conceptualizations of the problem or issue (Chapter 2). Getting a fuller understanding of the issues of concern from different perspectives within a defined system is a crucial first step to integration. As immediate agreement is unlikely, the completion of this integration step will require negotiation.

The *negotiation* process can be easier in situations where there are strong social capital and high levels of trust. This assumes that social capital creates constructive bonds between community members and thus facilitates social learning and collective action. However, a community with strong bonds and tight social networks can also be conservative and thus resist processes that introduce new ideas or extend learning networks. Similarly, bridging social capital can provide the means for a community to access the knowledge and resources of external players, and thus stimulate reflection on internal community power relationships and conservative ideas (Chapter 5). Conversely, the same bridging capital can result in local communities being dominated by powerful external interests (Chapter 4). Environmental managers need to be able to appreciate the dual nature of social capital, its relationship to power and the implications of this for environmental management.

Engagement of the whole of community in social learning processes aimed at improving environmental management will inevitably involve tensions, given the heterogeneous nature of communities, diverse traditions of understanding and embedded power relationships. Various chapters of this book suggest mechanisms by which these tensions can be handled, including soft systems methodology (Figure 2.1), participatory action learning (Figure 4.1), collaborative learning (Figure 7.1) and felt knowing methodology (Chapter 10). The iterative learning cycle allows us to trial and develop these and other methods over time, adapting them to the context and community needs.

Learning partnerships with government

Government or other sponsoring or resourcing organizations often take a leading role in initiating and implementing social learning in environmental management. In the post-industrial era, resourcing organizations can be major corporations, but in the cases considered in Section 3 of this book, the sponsoring organization for the social learning programmes is some level of government. However, many of the principles and issues discussed have wider applicability across all forms of organization.

When government manages the social learning system, it can support constructive social learning processes and drive system change (Figure 14.4). The relationships and functions of government organizations are strategic, that is, driven by the need to achieve an outcome. In a partnership with government, other management traditions are obliged to orient their participation to that goal. The case study chapters describe the partnership with government from the perspectives of the government agency, the environmental management specialist and a local council manager, respectively. The complex interactions between these actors often give rise to tensions between cultures, values and behavioural patterns.

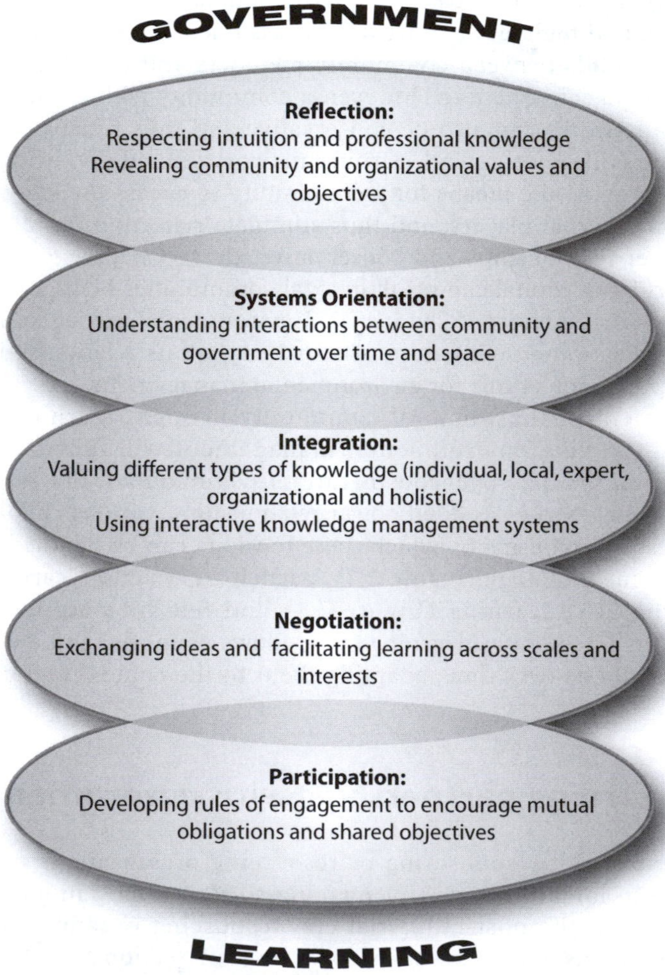

GOVERNMENT

Reflection:
Respecting intuition and professional knowledge
Revealing community and organizational values and objectives

Systems Orientation:
Understanding interactions between community and government over time and space

Integration:
Valuing different types of knowledge (individual, local, expert, organizational and holistic)
Using interactive knowledge management systems

Negotiation:
Exchanging ideas and facilitating learning across scales and interests

Participation:
Developing rules of engagement to encourage mutual obligations and shared objectives

LEARNING

Figure 14.4 *Social learning strands of a government-initiated environmental management system*

The power relations that exist in any cooperative venture are present in both formal and informal ways when one of the parties carries the additional authority of an agent of government. Different branches of government may have differing degrees of influence with each other, for example those from an environmental versus a treasury department. Within the same department, both formal and informal degrees of influence might also be at play, as was clearly demonstrated by Critchley and Scott (Chapter 9). They showed that the influence of field staff officers at the coal face of environmental management needs to be partnered with those bodies closer to the central decision making areas.

Furthermore, a government body will typically bring a particular kind of expert knowledge to the project, and this may conflict with the local and community knowledge held by other parties. Even if both kinds of knowledge agree about the process and issues, they may disagree about the values each places on different aspects of those same processes and their outcomes, as was demonstrated in Chapters 3 and 5. It is essential that when an environmental manager acts as an agent of government, they reflect on their part in these different networks of power. They will need to consider what strategies might be deployed to bring the differently situated and empowered agents together for a common objective.

Taking a systems orientation is a valuable step towards clearly reflecting upon these community values and where they accord or disagree with the goals that the government perceived as important. Mapping each party's understanding of the environmental system that needs to be managed better is a crucial part of this process. Often different agents will identify very different objectives and processes as being a part of the system to be managed and set very different spatial and temporal boundaries against which the goals of the management project are to be set. Clearly, no common and enduring agenda can be pursued while these differences remain.

In pursuing *integration*, the power relations of the different parties again come to the fore. No genuine agreement will have been achieved if one party uses its authority to coerce an agenda that the others do not acknowledge. The challenge to integration includes gaining an appreciation of the different kinds of knowledges of the parties involved, and collaboratively developing strategies to meet these challenges. Processes to achieve this integration are exemplified by Brown and Pitcher in their discussion of the Cool Communities Programme (Chapter 8). It must not be assumed that power differentials always involve the powerful party forcing the others to pursue their particular agenda, although this can happen (see Chapter 7). However, often the engagement of external players allows a community to access both expert knowledge and the means to enable an outcome that it is powerless to achieve by itself. In this case, properly negotiated and handled, power can be strategically deployed for good environmental management outcomes.

Facilitating the open exchange of ideas and enabling mutual learning is not without its difficulties, for both expert and lay agents alike, as Chapters 2 and 12 demonstrate. However, the reward is in the outcome, as parties come together to achieve outcomes that neither could alone. But in the case of environmental management, with its inherent dynamic, outcomes are seldom fixed goals or finishing points. The success of any project is always an invitation to reflect and re-commence the learning cycle.

Essentially, a collaborative, enduring institution of learning is formed around the environmental management process. This is to use Dovers' (2001, p5) definition of 'institution', which extends the notion of a formal institution to include local enduring custom that 'allows organised and collective efforts toward common concerns and the achievement of social goals'. He acknowledges that 'although by definition persistent, institutions constantly evolve'. The challenge for a government body, as a highly formal institution, is to allow itself to become a genuine partner in this more adaptive arrangement in which social learning in environmental management can evolve.

Learning partnerships, personal and professional

Social learning is affected by our professional training, our life experiences, and the social and personal values that guide our decisions. When we analyse environmental management, there is often an implicit assumption that decisions are objectively based on facts and the careful weighing up of costs and benefits. In fact, all our decisions have a subjective element. The concept of sustainable development, which is the goal of so many of our environmental management programmes, explicitly recognizes the importance of openly addressing the norms, values and ethics that underlie our decision making processes. This has been recently highlighted by the efforts of the international community to establish an Earth Charter that challenges us to examine our values and choose a better way. It calls for us to search for common ground in the midst of our diversity and to embrace a new ethical vision (you can view the Earth Charter at www.earthcharter.org).

The chapters in the fourth section of this book (11–13) examine the ethics and values behind our environmental education, professional training and actions and provide yet another way in which the five strands of learning can be integrated into the practices of environmental managers (Figure 14.5). These chapters argue that we need to create spaces in which normative – that is value-based – issues can be openly discussed and debated. However, it is clear from a number of the preceding chapters that, to establish such a deeply reflective dialogue, we must be aware of the impediments to learning, as well as to our achievements.

The core principles on which we base our actions, the places with which we identify and the practices with which we are familiar all shape our learning preferences and our approaches to environmental management. It is these, taken together, that can constrain our learning systems or create potential learning outcomes that exceed those we could achieve individually. A paradox that emerges from systems thinking is that interactions between system components both constrain and enable system behaviour.

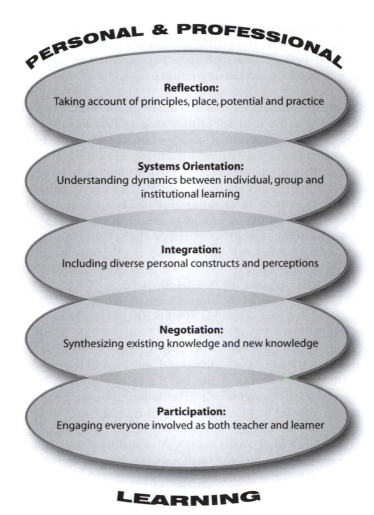

Figure 14.5 *Social learning strands of educational programmes for environmental managers*

Part of understanding a dynamic learning process is gaining an appreciation of how the values, assumptions and experiences of individuals, groups and organizations affect collective action. Professional training can encourage reflection on our relationship with nature and the implications of our actions. When reflecting on values, assumptions and actions, the learning process must go beyond words and dialogue, and into the affective domain of emotions, experiences and 'felt knowing' (see Chapters 10 and 11). It is at this deeper level of affective domains, mental constructs and cultural norms that the rationale for our actions often lies.

Social learning in environmental management can include processes to ensure that both the normative and rational dimensions of management are woven together in our analytical processes. Some innovative methods to help reveal personal constructs and mental models are described in this book (see Figures 10.1 and 13.2). Other tools have been created to help practitioners reflect on actions and the underlying rationales. Some of these tools are outlined in Table 14.1.

A commitment to integration and synthesis both within and outside our peer groups was important in conceptualizing and writing this book. There are many challenges in structuring processes by which people from different professional, disciplinary and cultural backgrounds can come together in a meaningful way. People can often feel that their identity and social status are threatened when their concepts, behaviour patterns or norms are critically examined. Ison (Chapter 2) explores this issue, arguing that learning is significantly affected by personal and organizational concepts of identity and meaning. To overcome some of these challenges, the environmental manager can adopt Bohm's rules of dialogue or other means to clarify rules of engagement; but it is our experience that these rules can be challenging to implement in practice (Bohm, 1996; Chapter 13).

Embedded within many of the tools presented in this book is a strong commitment to negotiated outcomes that synthesize existing knowledge and new knowledge across interest groups, and in some cases extend this knowledge to a wider community. Inevitably this approach to social learning will give rise to conflict and tensions. Conflicts and tensions between social groups and individuals can be uncomfortable, but they also represent an opportunity for new insights, learning and social development to emerge. As made clear in almost every case study, for negotiations and integration to be successful, we don't have to share the same interests but we do have to understand each other's interests. Once understood, we have to consider whether these interests can be integrated into a wider process of decision making and social action, or whether further dialogue is needed to create greater common ground.

In Chapter 12, Stocklmayer and colleagues describe encountering significant resistance to workshop techniques designed to allow scientists to communicate their science to a wider audience, particularly those decision makers who need to translate scientific findings into policy and programmes. By establishing a reflective process that involved supportive peer groups, Stocklmayer and colleagues enable scientists and other professionals to better assess their professional culture and how their own practices and the culture need to change. This resonates with the broader finding that it is through engaging, communicating and integrating that we reveal our own ignorance and gain new insights. To commence this process of critical reflection, we often need a supportive environment that includes our peers and others significant to us.

Throughout the book a strong theme of learning partnerships emerges. Like the presence of conflict, diversity adds a challenge to learning – there is so much more to synthesize and integrate – but it also provides the necessary ingredient for success in social learning. It is through diversity of knowledge, experience and beliefs that a more complete understanding of the complex interactions of social and ecological systems can emerge.

Table 14.1 *Social learning process and tools for environmental management*

Process	Description	Tool
Developing policy and principles: Creating awareness and ownership	To sustain learning across scales and sectors, people have to own the problem. This may require joint definition of the problem and the learning agenda	Negotiated learning (Chapters 5, 7, 8, 13) Learning agreements (Chapter 7)
Describing people and place: Developing knowledge	Knowledge can be developed through many pathways that integrate different ways of knowing at the personal and interpersonal levels	Internal reflection (Chapters 2, 10, 11) Open learning (Chapter 13) Soft systems methods (Chapter 2) Systems analysis (Chapters 2, 3)
Designing potential: Facilitating learning and change	Learning across social and personal divides can give rise to conflict. There is often a need for an 'honest broker' who is committed to process – rather than outcomes – or clear rules of engagement	External facilitation (Chapters 8, 11) Bohm's rules of dialogue (Chapter 13) Principled negotiation (Chapter 13)
Doing in practice: Connecting to place	All learning is contextual – the place and the people matter. Spending time in place, or listening to those who have, can enrich policy and practice. Rich learning occurs when it is grounded and varied	Place-based learning (Chapter 6) Field trips (Chapter 11) Participatory and collaborative management (Chapters 4, 5, 6, 7, 8)
Developing the principles: Evaluating processes and practices	Processes are as important as outcomes, and both need to have success criteria agreed on by all stakeholders engaged in the learning process. Evaluation and reflection are essential elements of social learning and should be included in the design at the earliest stage possible	Participatory monitoring and evaluation (Chapters 5, 7) Adaptive management (Chapters 3, 6, 7) Collaborative learning (Chapters 4, 5, 6, 7, 8)
Decisions into practice: Resourcing our learning	Learning takes a variety of resources, including financial, human, organizational and societal. Learning activities should be linked to needed resources	Mentoring and professional training (Chapters 11, 12) Strategic planning (Chapters 2, 4, 8, 9) Organizational learning (Chapters 2, 7, 9)

So what have we learned?

At the beginning of this book we posed five questions for the reader to consider as they read and reflected on the chapters. In these final pages we don't
intend to provide 'the answers', as they are many and varied, and we hope
there was ample material in the book to provide a range of ideas relevant to
these questions. But here we briefly reflect on each question and the issues it
raises for us, now that we have come this far in our learning journey.

> *What are the social learning processes embedded in current environmental
> management policies and programmes, and how do they relate to different ways
> of knowing and engaging?*

All environmental policies and programmes have implicit or explicit learning
processes. To date, too little reflection and attention has been given to social
learning processes needed to improve environmental management. The result
has been an ad hoc mix of policies, programmes and learning that has not taken
into account the context in which the learning is to occur, nor the attributes
of the potential learners. For social learning in environmental management to
be effective, it must be purposeful. The stages of learning should be carefully
crafted to build on each other over time. To get the approach right, it needs to
be negotiated so that different ways of knowing and engaging can be woven
into a process of social learning. Creating the space for such negotiations may
require skilled facilitation and new institutions to mediate power relations.

> *How can environmental management approaches facilitate the creation of
> learning opportunities that bridge different disciplines, subgroups within society
> and levels of governance?*

Approaches to constructive social learning in environmental management are
open, adaptive and collaborative. They are created through actively engaging
the key actors, not by merely replicating 'successes' in any available context.
Bridging social divides inevitably involves conflict management and creative
thinking; thus we need rules of engagement and time for reflection. When the
learning processes challenge personal identity, social beliefs or cultural norms,
time for reflection is crucial – even when time is highly constrained. Reflection
can occur in different forums depending on the purpose. In groups of mixed
and diverse social actors, our mental and affective frameworks are exposed –
we are challenged and must critically reflect on why we do what we do. But the
exposure also can result in defensiveness. Both these processes were evident in
the multidisciplinary workshops used to design this book (see Chapter 13).

In supportive and relatively homogeneous groups, we can be complacent
and narrow in our reflections. But if something has happened to disturb that
complacency, then mutual reflection on what it will take to share a common
purpose can create a setting that is conducive to further collective learning.
Learning is partly a process of letting go of the familiar – to do this we need a

safe environment to retreat to and reconsider. The value of such an approach was exemplified by the science communication workshops described in Chapter 12. Like the figure of eight used in adaptive management (see Figure 3.1), reflective processes need to engage in cycles of creation, consolidation, critical evaluation and change.

Do our present dialogues, negotiations and participation processes enable a wide variety of social learning opportunities in environmental management?

If we agree that all social interactions and all decision making processes are social learning opportunities, there is no shortage of variety in environmental management or elsewhere! Perhaps the question needs re-framing. Do we appreciate the wide variety of social learning opportunities available to us and enhance each opportunity through fully implementing the five strands of learning? As environmental managers, we need to maximize learning and work with others to re-frame environmental management from a perspective that sees that there are problems to manage to one that embraces the possibility of creating something better through collaborative learning processes (Daniels and Walker, 1996). Learning from each other does not require that we understand or accept each other's knowledge, but it does require that we try and appreciate the range of knowledge available and creatively work towards a synoptic or holistic perspective.

How is our ability to act and adapt environmental management approaches affected by social structures and relationships?

Social structures and relationship are part of environmental management systems. Our learning and our development are both enabled and constrained by them. A systems perspective enables us to view social structures and relationships as if they were coupled to a biophysical ecological system, although in reality they are but parts of a dynamic complex whole. This view allows us to think about how the social domain of interests, values, knowledge and power changes the energy and material flows in the ecological domain and how, in turn, the effects of these modified flows are fed back to influence change in the social domain. The behaviour of the complex whole is inherently unpredictable and we must always be aware that even well-intentioned strategies to manage these change processes might lead to surprising outcomes. Furthermore, we must always be aware that these outcomes are felt differently by differently situated actors, some of whom might welcome certain changes while those same changes might harm the interests of others. So, while we have discussed means of adaptively managing for good environmental outcomes throughout this book, we must always ask the additional question of 'good for whom?'

Are our processes of reflection and learning in environmental management fragmented and unable to discern the more subtle patterns of change over time and space?

Our environmental management efforts have been fragmented by social boundaries that artificially divide disciplines, ways of knowing, resource management regimes, geographic regions and nations. Our formal social learning processes are to some extent constrained by these divides – and indeed some of the divides have enabled us to make great advances by simplifying problems and issues. However, social learning in environmental management is a framework designed to bridge divides.

The case studies in this book provide examples of how this can be successfully done, whether the learning needs to occur across government jurisdictions, social groups, professional disciplines or through a combination of these. The five strands of learning, with their explicit emphasis on reflection, systems orientation, integration, negotiation and participation, are boundary spanning processes. Recognizing subtle patterns of change over time and space requires long-term critical and pluralistic engagement. Practically, we need many eyes that can see differently. Our vision is enhanced if we can share those insights through strong social networks and resolve our differences through structured dialogues that manage conflict but don't deny it. Diversity, dialogue and development are fundamental to social learning.

Conclusions

Social learning in environmental management is essentially about managing change. Every environmental management practitioner is involved in larger questions such as: What is the purpose and direction of the change? How do we as a society create more equitable processes to share knowledge and engage in decision making that leads to a more sustainable environment, locally and globally? In this sense, everyone is an environmental manager, since we are all influencing and being affected by the answers. Changing social and organizational structures lead to the need to reflect critically on the cultures and values on which our decision making processes are based. Part of this critical reflection is accepting that there is not only *one* sustainability solution based on a single knowledge set.

Each environmental context will encompass different relationships between people and place. There is thus an array of possible sustainability pathways. These pathways will be affected by knowledge 'matrices', that is, the mix of understandings that are a product of the diverse experiences, values and principles of those in a particular place. Social learning processes allow us to better share our understandings and to negotiate social change in a way that takes account of a diverse range of worldviews. The more we build up our knowledge matrix through shared understandings, the greater the insights we can gain. Fourteen chapters offer fourteen different parts of the matrix, a fraction of the possible sets of relationships. But within these chapters we hope there are approaches and principles that can be used to build a vision relevant to your context.

The management of issues for sustainability requires the integration of our thinking across disciplines, sectors and knowledge groups. It is not about one way of knowing or one way of doing. Sustainability is about relationships, dependencies and networks that can facilitate such integration in environmental management. Ultimately this systems orientation is intended to lead to greater equality between social groups, as well as a holistic approach to decision making that affects social and ecological systems. Core principles of a social learning approach that have emerged from our work are described in Box 14.1.

Box 14.1 Principles of social learning for environmental management

1 Reflexive processes that critically consider actions, assumptions and values are integral to all social learning processes in environmental management
2 A systemic learning approach takes account of the interrelationships and interdependencies between social and ecological systems and is essential to achieving progress towards sustainability
3 Social learning in environmental management is a commitment to integrating ideas and actions across social boundaries, including those that divide professions, communities, cultures and ecosystems
4 The negotiation of learning agendas and indicators of success across the whole community is essential
5 Conflict and tensions arising from synthesizing different types of knowledge should not be avoided, but do require facilitated negotiations
6 Social learning is participatory and adaptive, and fundamentally about a commitment to equitable decision making on social and environmental issues
7 Social learning in environmental management takes into account social and environmental relationships and structures, particularly those pertaining to power relations
8 Social learning is about supporting social change processes by transforming organizations, institutions, and individual and group identities in a way that increases sustainable environmental management
9 Social learning promotes a culture that respects and values diversity, transparency and accountability in working towards a sustainable future.

Social learning is about development, but it must also allow a collective 'letting go' of ideas, practices and values that no longer contribute to a sustainable future. The learning process is essentially social, because sound environmental management requires us to link our personal and local behaviours to outcomes at broader scales. This vertical and horizontal integration of ideas and practices helps us to gain a deeper understanding of different traditions of knowing. This, in turn, can help shift our focus from constraints and artificial

Figure 14.6 *The web of social learning*

jurisdictional and disciplinary boundaries to the opportunities for creative new approaches to action and learning that support sustainability. Environmental managers are leaders, not followers, of change.

This book is a beginning, not a final end point. It is a beginning – perhaps even a catalyst – for social learning processes that advance sustainability as core to environmental management. Social learning is rather like a spider web, with many different components all interacting and affecting movements towards social action and change. While it is impossible to untangle and dissect a web and still maintain its essential character, we can embark on an experiential and adaptive process of learning that strengthens rather than weakens the web. Each time we find a new web of social learning, we need to work with it gently, probing to see how the parts are connected and the strands are related. Figure 14.6 illustrates the web of social learning that has begun to emerge from this book. We encourage you to build on it and learn from it. Most importantly, we hope you'll join us in our efforts to establish social learning processes that support sustainability in environmental management.

References

Bohm, D. (1996) *On Dialogue*, Routledge, London

Daniels, S. E. and Walker, G. B. (1996) 'Collaborative learning: Improving public deliberation in ecosystem-based management', *Environmental Impact Assessment Review*, vol 16, pp71–102

Dovers, S. (2001) *Institutions for Sustainability*, Australian Conservation Foundation, Canberra

Foucault, M. (1980) 'Power and strategies', in Gordon, C. (ed) *Power/Knowledge: Selected Interviews and Other Writings*, Harvester, New York

Index